MAKING INDIA WORK

Making India Work

William Nanda Bissell

PENGUIN
VIKING

VIKING

Published by the Penguin Group

Penguin Books India Pvt. Ltd, 11 Community Centre, Panchsheel Park, New Delhi 110 017, India

Penguin Group (USA) Inc., 375 Hudson Street, New York, New York 10014, USA

Penguin Group (Canada), 90 Eglinton Avenue East, Suite 700, Toronto, Ontario, M4P 2Y3, Canada (a division of Pearson Penguin Canada Inc.)

Penguin Books Ltd, 80 Strand, London WC2R 0RL, England

Penguin Ireland, 25 St Stephen's Green, Dublin 2, Ireland (a division of Penguin Books Ltd)

Penguin Group (Australia), 250 Camberwell Road, Camberwell, Victoria 3124, Australia (a division of Pearson Australia Group Pty Ltd)

Penguin Group (NZ), 67 Apollo Drive, Rosedale, North Shore 0632, New Zealand (a division of Pearson New Zealand Ltd)

Penguin Group (South Africa) (Pty) Ltd, 24 Sturdee Avenue, Rosebank, Johannesburg 2196, South Africa

Penguin Books Ltd, Registered Offices: 80 Strand, London WC2R 0RL, England

First published in Viking by Penguin Books India 2009

Copyright © William Nanda Bissell 2009

All rights reserved

10 9 8 7 6 5 4 3 2 1

The views and opinions expressed in this book are the authors' own and the facts are as reported by him/her which have been verified to the extent possible, and the publishers are not in any way liable for the same.

ISBN 9780670083213

Not for sale in the United Kingdom

Typeset in Sabon by Eleven Arts, New Delhi

Printed at Chaman Offset Printers, Delhi

In memory of my beloved father,
John Latane Bissell

Contents

Acknowledgements

I have had the good fortune of family and friends who have all contributed to the ideas in this book and I thank them for all they have done.

To my parents, John and Bim Bissell, who gave my sister and me a universe full of love, ideas, curiosity, and gave me the values which have made my life so rich.

To my maternal grandfather, Rai Bahadur Pran Nath Nanda, a great man who I was fortunate to live with for the first fourteen years of my life.

To my tutors, Mridula Gupta, Ranjan Pal and Aditya Bhattcharjee, who by helping me pass my exams made it possible for me to miss lots of school, and still get educated as I travelled with my father through India.

I owe much of my political awakening to Larry Lifschultz, who came into my life at an age when its direction could have been different; to Richard Celeste who made sure I had a front-row seat at the great spectacle of American politics; and to Sir Mark Tully who offered me an internship at the BBC in India and took me under his wing.

To Sunita Narain and the late Anil Agarwal who founded the Centre for Science and Environment and who have inspired and taught me most of what I know of India's environmental challenges.

To Saurabh Mehta and Rahul Gupta whose friendship and guidance helped me get started in business.

To my mentor, Sunil Chainani, whose rigour and strategic thinking is behind much of Fabindia's success and without whom the experiment in community-owned companies would not have got off the drawing board.

To Monsoon Bissell, my sister, and David Rohde for their enduring faith in the ideas in this book and who got me to start writing them down.

To my sister-in-law, Mini Kapoor, who reads more than anyone else I know and who found me all the perfect books that lit my path, just when I was grappling with ideas and needed a solution.

To my friends Pritam Singh and Ravi Kaimal. Pritam and I have shared hundreds of ideas on business and he always has a unique take on the world. Ravi Kaimal's thoughtful insights into technologies and the changes they will bring into our lives helped with many of the ideas on the cashless economy.

To Nandan Nilekani, Arvind Singhal, Mukti Khaire, Madhukar Khera and Prakash Tripathi who have supported the vision of community-owned companies.

To my aunt and uncle, Marie and Tim Prentice, who gave me a home in Cornwall, Connecticut, and whose knowledge of their community and generosity of spirit helped me understand the strengths of communities. To my friends in the community, Gordon Ridgeway, David Rich and David Colbert who gave me great insight into the way communities can manage themselves.

To Hari Kapoor and Amit Judge, who, in running the Resident Welfare Association of Panchsheel, taught me a lot about the issues in Delhi's urban enclaves.

To the late Nirmal Wadhwani, who as the Sub-divisional Magistrate of Bali helped me understand the administrative challenges confronting the region, and to the people of Bali who have welcomed me into their lives for seventeen years.

To Steve Alter, whose memories, love and knowledge of the hills of Mussoorie made it possible for me to write the section on the 'Community of Mussoorie'.

To my father-in-law, Vijai Kapoor, whose encyclopaedic

knowledge of India, her Constitution and the challenges of administration helped shape most of the major ideas in my book.

To James Cox-Chapman, who worked on the original version with great enthusiasm and energy and, in many ways, got the project started.

To Ella Saltmarshe, who rewrote most of the original manuscript and in the process shortened it greatly.

To Ashok Matthews, who worked on much of the statistical data.

To Atul Mishra, who tracked down each fact, checked it and helped me with developing many of the models that underlie the central themes of the book.

To Jane Lynch who edited the final version of the manuscript.

To my readers, K.C. Pant, A.K. Shiva Kumar, Donald and Lucy Peck, and Lois Hager whose thoughtful comments helped greatly.

To Sandeep Dutt, who took the manuscript to Penguin.

To my support group at Penguin India—Ravi Singh, whose enthusiasm for this book was a vote of confidence when I needed it most; Ranjana Sengupta, who is a joy to work with; and Aakash Chakrabarty, who worked with great sincerity on all the details and took my manuscript to publication.

To my mother-in-law, Manju Kapoor, who looked after our children on my trips away.

And, to my wife Anjali—the wind in my sails.

Preface

An overheard conversation in a small bookshop in Dehra Dun galvanized me to write this book. A group of young army cadets joked that they were going into battle for a large corporate house in the country. One of them exhorted his colleague to replace the 'motherland' in the traditional Indian battle cry, 'Hail to the motherland',* with the name of this corporation. The same week this corporation announced that they were looking into the privatization of water.

Their joke hit home. Increasingly, the government is withdrawing from even basic activities, leaving these to entrenched corporations who are able to manipulate policy to suit the interests of a tiny corporate elite. This is being done in the name of free market policies which in much of the developing world have moved formerly socialist economies to become states characterized by nepotistic crony capitalism. India is at risk of moving in this direction.

The army cadets were joking, but many business leaders speak, rather hopefully, of a future in which India is ruled by a CEO. It is now so easy to buy your way into government. A senior bureaucrat remarked that the Rajya Sabha is beginning to look like an extension of the Confederation of Indian Industry.† As you will

*'Jai Hind' and 'Bharat Mata ki Jai'.
†The Confederation of Indian Industry (CII) is India's premier and most influential business association, with a direct membership of over 7000 organizations from private as well as public sectors. Founded over 112 years ago, it works to create and sustain an environment conducive to the growth of industry in India.

see in this book, I am a firm believer in the power of markets, but what is occurring in India today is not 'free market' capitalism.*,1 If nothing changes, this vision of one of the country's business leaders could easily become a reality: 'From the moment every Indian wakes up to the time they go to sleep they will use one of our products. Their water, their cellular networks, their vehicles and the oil that fuels them, will all be provided by us.'

The elite in India gain too much from the status quo to provide the answers or facilitate genuine change. And politics is increasingly becoming a hereditary right. Almost every major political party is controlled by children of former or current leaders. Of the fifty-one members of the Lok Sabha born on or after 1 January 1967, twenty-five come from political families.† One of our hereditary leaders even suggested converting his parents' government house into a museum to give the family a permanent residence on a valuable piece of land in the centre of Delhi. Many in the business world, civil society and media enjoy cozy relationships with the political establishment. And they are unlikely to bite the hand that feeds them.

The antipathy of the public towards corrupt politicians is deep-rooted. Recently, when speaking to a group of Indian university students, I asked them about their solutions to the country's problems. One of them answered that the army should line up all politicians and gun them down. When I asked if anyone else supported this view, almost the whole class seconded the idea.

One of my greatest fears is that our current state of government dysfunction, combined with a growing public frustration, might produce an authoritarian political leader whose simple solutions

---

*India may be heading towards perversions of capitalism we witness around the world. One of these perversions is crony capitalism, where business is run in such a close alliance between the government and business elites that the government creates favourable conditions for business. Another perversion is phoney capitalism, as evidenced in Russia and oil-rich states of the Persian Gulf where there is really no concept of a return on capital as huge windfall profits lead to massive investments.

†The fourteenth Lok Sabha.

could capture the imagination of the masses who are waiting for a messiah. In times of great confusion such leaders are more able to seduce the masses with their clarity of purpose, which is often nothing more than an oversimplified world view.[2] In India we experienced this when the then Prime Minister Indira Gandhi dissolved the Parliament and declared a state of Emergency in 1975.* The Emergency was a period when India's notoriously late railway trains ran on time, slum areas were arbitrarily bulldozed and fundamental rights guaranteed by the Constitution were suspended for the first time in the republic's history.

Searching for The Answer

The enormity of the challenge of India has created a culture of short-sighted optimism, both at home and abroad. From the glowing references in Tom Friedman's bestseller *The World is Flat* to the *new* India to the gushing adulation heaped on its businesses by the Western media, India is constantly fed by an establishment drunk on visions of grandeur. Expressions like 'the world's next superpower', 'the Indian Century', 'the future is India' have entered popular phraseology, quickly displacing the old myths of a land of 'endless red tape' and 'gurus and snake charmers'. A senior journalist at one of the country's leading English dailies recently announced in conversation: 'We are out of the business of printing bad news.' *The Times of India* inaugurated the year 2007 with its new slogan, 'India Poised: Our Time is Now',† portraying a country

*When the Allahabad High Court found her guilty of corruption and electoral malpractices to win a Parliament seat, the opposition pressurized her to resign as prime minister. She sought refuge in the Emergency provisions of the Constitution and declared a state of internal Emergency with remarkable swiftness.

†From its own front-page advertisement to billboards across cities, *The Times of India*'s idea of 'India vs India' was forcefully impressed. The campaign argued there are two Indias—the optimistic leader and the sceptic follower—and that the two must be united. Indian celebrities punctuated the campaign with a new 'anthem' for this new, poised, united India.

ready to demand its rightful place alongside the world's wealthy and powerful nations. But business, media and political leaders are in danger of inflating their rhetoric or worse, using it as a form of denial. India may be growing at breakneck speed, but it is still desperately poor.

This book is the result of my search for a solution to the problems India faces. I have a unique advantage. I belong to the super elite in India with access to government, business, political and media leaders; and yet, I have the perspective of an outsider. My father was one of the few foreigners who made his home in India in the late 1950s. He started a business that I run today, working with artisans in rural India. I owe a great deal to the hundreds of people who have spoken to me about their dreams, their stories, and I have tried to reproduce some of these in the book without naming specific incidents which in any way could reveal the identity of my narrators. The confidence that I have enjoyed has given me an insight into many aspects of governance, corruption and courage. Late one night, on a train coming down from the mountains where I had been writing this book, I found myself sharing a carriage with a senior member of a government-controlled oil company. He openly explained the whole edifice of corruption in the bidding process for oil exploration blocks. At the end of our conversation I asked him why he told me all this. 'You obviously love this country,' he replied, 'and I do too.' That feeling was shared by many people who spoke to me about the challenges they faced.

The central assumption of this book is that poverty in India is a result of the government's criminally inept management. It is not inevitable. It is not fated. It is not incurable. Its perpetuation is not an accident of fate or karma. It is a tragedy that is simply due to a failure of leadership.

I believe that there are solutions and that there is a dire need for new vision and vigorous debate. I have offered the ideas in this book in the hope that they will help our leaders and the public look at the challenge of India in a new light.

In this book I ask you to re-imagine India. At times, I will ask you take such huge leaps of faith that you may be incredulous. But with political will and a mandate from the people, another India is possible. I want you to look at our future with fresh eyes and see a country experiencing rapid growth, a thriving environment and virtually no poverty. My key effort here is to make the invisible visible, to make the abstract concrete. As Indians we all possess abstract rights in name, but we have no tangible claim on these vague and lofty ideals. In this book, I ask people to see India as a place where people's rights translate into real benefits. Every 'right' will be measurable and therefore achievable. Every asset will be accounted for and therefore tradable.

The future of India poses a great challenge to current paradigms of international development, governance and social organization. The world cannot afford to let India fail. And yet it cannot afford to let it succeed either, at least not in the way success is currently measured. If India as well as China were to catch up, world consumption rates would triple.[3] For our country to achieve wealth in a world of limited resources requires a fundamental shift in our ways of thinking. If we do not change our mindset, we risk losing our planet in our attempt to gain material prosperity for and in the name of the poor. This book is a proposal for rapid, environmentally sustainable and democratic growth.

Notes

1. Countries like Mexico, which gave away a 'monopoly' phone licence to Carlos Slim Helu making him one of the world's richest people overnight, present examples of crony capitalism. See Brian Winter, 'How Slim Got Huge', *Foreign Policy*, November–December 2007. The Russian economist Grigory Yavlinsky was one of the earliest to have foreseen phoney capitalism in post-communist Russia; see 'Russia's Phony Capitalism', *Foreign Affairs*, May–June 1998.

2. If only to highlight how fragile political freedoms are, I recommend Naomi Wolf's latest book, *The End of America* (Vermont: Chelsea Green, 2007). This immensely thoughtful and timely intervention

Introduction

*No problem can be solved by the same level of consciousness
that created it.*

Albert Einstein

India is not a poor country. It is a poorly managed country. The
dark side of India is the poverty of her people. The country
accounts for 36 per cent of the world's poor—more than in the
whole of Africa—living on less than a dollar a day.[1] Nearly 40 per
cent of the malnourished children in the world live in India,[2] and
over 40 per cent of the children under the age of three are
malnourished (that is, underweight).[3] That a nation so rich in
human and natural resources could have over 77 per cent of the
population classified as 'poor and vulnerable' (with per capita
daily consumption of up to Rs 20 in 2004–05)[4] points to
catastrophic administration, not to any inherent flaws of the
land or the people.[5] All other issues including India's chronic
caste and religious tensions pale in significance to, and are often
the result of, poverty. This book outlines a new development
path for India and the world. The following ideas, if applied,
will drastically reduce poverty, stimulate rapid economic growth,
regenerate the environment and create high-quality essential
services. This growth would not be urban-led, resource-intensive
or consumption-fuelled. All this would occur in the context of
efficient government, reinvigorated democracy and reduced

bureaucracy. In short, these ideas, if applied, will accomplish the impossible.

At the same time, this is no pie-in-the-sky book. It combines an unabashedly idealistic vision with a clear route of how to get there. As such, this is an audacious book. We no longer have time for timidity or hesitation. The development challenge facing India is colossal. The environmental crisis facing the world is enormous. We cannot continue blindly muddling on, hoping that it will all work out. This is a call to action.

Any attempt at economic reform, or better governance and equality, cannot succeed without addressing the needs of the poor. The great nationalist, Mohandas Karamchand Gandhi, had this advice for policy makers: 'Recall the face of the poorest and the weakest man whom you may have seen, and ask yourself if the step you contemplate is going to be of any use to him. Will he gain anything by it?'[6]

India thinks it has the solution to poverty: consumption, consumption, and even more consumption. But as Gandhi also said, 'The earth provides enough to satisfy every man's need, but not every man's greed.'[7] The world cannot support the large and growing populations of India and China consuming at Western levels.[8] We cannot consume our way out of poverty. It is simply not a road open to us, the late arrivals. If current patterns of consumption are the only way to keep the global economic engine running, we are doomed to failure. Yet, we have to generate opportunity and growth if we are to take billions of people out of poverty. This book offers a way to do this.

The Ideas

The first step is to end the denial. We cannot be a superpower with 60 per cent of the population living in miserable conditions and we cannot be a superpower unless we create our own development path, stopping the national trend of adopting economic policies just as they are reaching their sell-by date. First was the Nehruvian* period of Fabian socialism,† which was already twenty years out of date when initiated, quickly followed by nationalization, a few years before the idea of state-controlled business was thoroughly discredited.[9] Today we have jumped aboard the consumption-driven development bandwagon just as the headlines are proclaiming it will lead to a global environmental catastrophe. It is time for India to create its own development path.

This book is about a series of transformative ideas that have the potential to make India a nation in which each citizen can be guaranteed a basic quality of life. Through the course of the book I describe a symbiotic system. It is a system built around the goal of maximizing self-interest over common good. Here, sustainable economic growth, environmental regeneration and the alleviation of poverty work together. Instead of waiting for prosperity to trickle down, wealth is generated from the bottom. Each chapter describes a different aspect of this new system. The ideas in this book defy generalization. You may classify one concept as socialist and the following as capitalist. I ask you to suspend judgement until the last page when I hope it becomes clear how these ideas can work together to address the real challenges of India.

No one understood the real challenges of India better than Gandhi. And no one offered better solutions to those problems than Gandhi. The 'official' legacy of Gandhi as the leader of the freedom struggle tends to downplay his ideas about governance and sustainable development. Of course, he played a vital role in

*The vision of politics, society, economics and foreign policy of India's first prime minister, Jawaharlal Nehru.
†The founders of Fabian Society in London in 1884 sought to attain a socialist society not through revolutions (as orthodox Marxism would have it) but through gradual reforms. The British Labour Party has its lineage in Fabianism. Given Nehru's world view Fabian socialism was an attractive option. An India emerging from the violence of Partition could not afford a revolution, but strong measures were needed to guarantee social and economic equality alongside civic and political ones.

India's struggle for Independence. But I believe his greatness lay in anticipating the problems that India (and the world) would face in the twenty-first century and in the solutions he proposed. There is no monopoly on interpreting Gandhi. He himself famously refused to lend finality to his thoughts. The Gandhi I have understood, however, offers three guiding principles of organizing society, politics and economics.

The first is sustainable living. Need, and not greed, has to be the basis of all consumption. He was against mindless procurement of goods and services that served little actual purpose. His life personified this Spartan sensibility.

The second principle is of appropriately scaled institutions. Gandhi's plan for economic development and political empowerment was rooted in a profound scepticism of the centralized state, an institution too distant from the lives of most Indians. He conducted his most successful politics in protest of the colonial state. Though the immediate objective was the defeat of British rule, the core purpose of Gandhian mass politics was to make people powerful through direct actions. It has been fashionable to talk of Gandhian 'village republics' and the Panchayati Raj institutions. When we follow Gandhi closely, we find in his writings and speeches a constant effort to make people realize the importance of decentralized, local, scaled institutions that are accessible to people. This creates a democracy driven by real and constant participation of people and is hence more responsive to their needs.

The third principle was a caution: do not mindlessly ape the West. In December 1928, Gandhi wrote in *Young India*: 'God forbid that India should ever take to industrialism after the manner of the West. The economic imperialism of a single tiny island kingdom (England) is today keeping the world in chains. If an entire nation of 300 million took to similar economic exploitation, it would strip the world bare like locusts.' In the twenty-first century, the world's environment is increasingly stressed by the addition of millions of new consumers aspiring to ape Western levels of consumption. Many see Gandhi as a dated, parochial leader who espoused a kind of medieval idea of economic organization. Though some of his specific solutions were rooted in the technology and prevailing economic situation of his times, I have tried to look at these solutions using the benefits of present-day technology and modern management practices.

In the proposals offered in the following pages, I have adapted these three core guiding principles of Gandhian philosophy of action to modern situation. My effort is to show that these underlying principles are sufficient to build a new, sustainable, accessible and realistic framework for the governance of India. To the three Gandhian principles, I have added three related aspects. All the solutions proposed in this book are based on these:

1. People are inherently good. Any political system should be developed to give each individual a sense of personal responsibility for and authority over his actions. Individual responsibility and accountability are the basis for a society that enjoys widespread legitimacy.

2. Modern capitalism, while it trumpets the virtues of costs and pricing, does not have a mechanism to capture the value of that which matters most: our environment. Bringing hidden costs and assets into the working economy will not only cause growth to soar, but also regenerate the environment. This is not *green* capitalism but *real* capitalism.

3. Self-regulation should be the guiding principle of all of our systems. Nature shows us many examples of complex systems that successfully self-regulate without the need for a command structure that requires constant interventions. Traditional building techniques highlight the value of following nature's lead. I built my Delhi home with modern materials of brick and concrete with reinforced steel. Several years later, I constructed a small house in Rajasthan using local masons and traditional building techniques which have evolved over hundreds of years. Inside this desert house the temperature was incredibly constant, despite the extremes in temperature

between day and night, summer and winter. The temperature of the Delhi house varied by two to three degrees from the outside temperature throughout the year. In summer, when it was 40°C outside it was 37°C indoors, whereas the house in Rajasthan had was cooler by 10°C. This means that it is possible to live without air conditioning in summer and heating in winter in Rajasthan, but not in Delhi. So, much of what the modern world has given us only works because of external interventions. It would save so many resources if we just let nature do much of the work for us.

The ideas contained in this book are very much a product of my experiences. My father was an American who came to India with a Ford Foundation grant in 1958. He stayed and went on to found a company to promote village-based arts and crafts, which at that time were predominantly hidden from the world. He came from New England Protestant stock with its austerity and emphasis on community participation. My mother is from an exuberant Punjabi tradition of enormous social networks. Her family emigrated from what is now Pakistan at the time of Partition in 1947. I grew up in a joint family in Delhi: my devout aunt recounting the Hindu myths; my grandmother telling me the stories of growing up in a small village in Balochistan; and my grandfather, who worked for the colonial Indian government, narrating first-hand accounts of empires and great battles. My parents themselves were at the centre of much of what happened in India in the 1970s and 1980s and I travelled extensively across the country with my father. When at home in Delhi, I would sit in on the frequent dinner parties, where an extraordinary array of politicians, artists, scientists, architects and journalists would debate new ideas. In my father's words, anyone was welcome to dinner 'as long as they had something interesting to say'.

Many of the ideas I was exposed to in India over this period came from some of the foremost left-wing thinkers of the time. However, while in boarding school and later at college in the US,

I had the opportunity to visit the former USSR and former Yugoslavia and observed first hand the human cost of communism. At the same time, my liberal education in the US exposed me to the early American writers, most notably Henry David Thoreau and James Madison, whose writings on governance influenced me deeply. During the years between college and writing this book, there have been a few books, in particular, that have left a lasting impression on me: Bruce F. Johnston and Peter Kilby's *Agricultural and Structural Transformation*, James Scott's *The Moral Economy of the Peasant*, Hernando de Soto's *The Mystery of Capital,* and *Saving Capitalism from the Capitalists* by Raghuram Rajan and Luigi Zingales. The ideas of these authors and their books are part of the brick and mortar of my book.

After graduating from Wesleyan University in 1988, I returned to India to start an artisan's cooperative. My desire to start such a cooperative came from an ideological bent that favoured mixing market ideals and what I used to think of as the best of the socialist experiments. I began working with leather workers and tanners, part of the former untouchable castes, in a remote village about 100 kilometres from Jodhpur in western Rajasthan. After three years it became clear that the collective decision-making structure of the cooperative made it virtually impossible to function as a viable business.[10]

I lost my ideological bearings and entered a period of uncertainty. This ended abruptly on the evening of 21 May 1993 when my father suffered a massive cerebral stroke, which left him incapacitated. I immediately joined Fabindia, the craft-based retail business he founded in 1960 and had run until that point. My first five years coincided with a turbulent phase in the business, as we made the transition from exports to domestic retail. My father died in 1998 when we were emerging from this period and I took over as managing director soon after. Over the last seven years the business has grown twenty-five fold. My proudest achievement is that the commercial success of Fabindia has been accomplished while staying true to the company's original mission of providing a market for goods produced by artisans.

Building a business in India is an ongoing lesson in the challenges faced by entrepreneurs. Mindless government regulation creates endless and enormous distortions. I run an ethical business and am law-abiding, which has often meant spending huge amounts of time and energy navigating through an unnecessary bureaucratic maze. Once, when trying to secure a building permit, a bureaucrat told me, 'If I clear your file immediately, I might face a vigilance inquiry as it will be perceived that I have acted in undue haste.' The soon-to-retire bureaucrat decided that the best option was to pass the buck, by delaying the application until it became someone else's responsibility. If I had paid off the right person, I would have had a permit the same week.

This situation will be familiar to most Indians, as it defines their relationship with a monopoly extractor called the Government of India. Whenever I am in New York, Indian workers resident in this city come by to petition me to see if I can use my influence to help them renew their passports. It turns out that the Indian embassy in the US sends the passport renewal details to the local police who in turn, realizing that the applicant is abroad, demand absurd sums of money from the family in India to verify that the person came from that particular village or town without which a passport renewal is not possible. I suggest that their families beg for relief and settle. How can a government treat its citizens like this? The poor with their lack of 'connections' suffer the most.

Every time I hear lofty words spoken from the pulpits of power these images keep coming back.

The basis for India's policies lies in the period immediately after the country gained Independence when policy making was majorly based on an assumption that the behaviour of the new citizens—no longer subjects of a former regime—would be directed towards the common good of the nation rather than towards individual self-interests. When these initial policies failed, the government created a second set of laws and initiatives in which citizens are conceived of—to the other extreme—as inherently criminals and dissidents. The result has been a body of law that is massive, complex and often contradictory. Such a legal system ends up benefiting the lawbreaker and penalizing the law-abiding citizen who is tied down in debilitating regulation.* Reading the *Federalist Papers*† I realized that the founders of the United States had a profound distrust of governments, anchored in the political philosophy of John Stuart Mill and Thomas Hobbes.‡ They saw government as a necessary evil and sought to limit its powers and the control it would exert over the citizenry. Such caution is absent from the Indian view of government in which it is seen as an undisputed good. As Madison wrote in 'The Federalist No. 10':

*The rapid growth of the IT industry highlights the possibilities for progress when government does not intervene. By the time the government woke up to its success and attempted to regulate the industry, it was already too big.

†Between October 1787 and August 1788, eighty-five articles were published in New York newspapers under the pseudonym 'Publius'. The authors—Alexander Hamilton, James Madison and John Jay—dealt with issues that were critical to the new nation, including: federalism, checks and balances, the separation of powers, and pluralism and representation. The remarkable foresight of the *Federalist Papers* has made them a benchmark for interpretations of the US Constitution and matters of the role of government and individual rights and privileges. 'Federalist' nos. 10, 51, 78, and 84 are considered especially important for their contribution to the distinction between a democracy and a republic (10), federalism (51), judicial review (78) and bill of rights (84).

‡Thomas Hobbes's *Leviathan* (1651) was strongly influenced by the experience of the English Civil War—identified with the state of nature—and argues for a strong and effective sovereign who could provide security to people. However, central to Hobbes' argument was that the social contract made to institute the state would become void if the government no longer protected its citizens. John Stuart Mill, in *On Liberty* (1859), classically defined liberalism in the defence of individual sovereignty—economic and moral freedom—from state. My ideas about government and freedom have evolved in interlocution with these two works and their central theses.

The two great points of difference between a Democracy and a Republic are, first, the delegation of the Government, in the latter, to a small number of citizens elected by the rest: secondly, the greater number of citizens, and the greater sphere of country, over which the latter may be extended. The effect of the first difference is, on the one hand to refine and enlarge the public views, by passing them through the medium of a chosen body of citizens, whose wisdom may best discern the true justice of their country, and whose patriotism and love of justice, will be least likely to sacrifice it to temporary or partial considerations.[11]

India's first leaders bequeathed to the nation an extraordinary constitution. However, the government structure itself was a cocktail of inherited British imperialism, the socialism of its new leaders and pre-colonial feudalism. In an effort to maintain the unity of the republic, the authors of the Indian Constitution created a strong Central government.[12] This concentration of powers added yet another ingredient to the cocktail by depriving people of the opportunity to build robust local government.* This danger of such deprivation recalls the writing of Alexis de Tocqueville, an early observer of the American form of federalism, in which he so brilliantly argues the strength of the republic was flowing from the union of hundreds of independent town communities.[13] Granville Austin, who wrote a comprehensive account of the debates, struggles and issues faced by the members of India's constituent assembly, explores why the road of federalism was not taken. According to Austin, the framers of the Indian Constitution were well aware of the American experiment in federalism but they also realized that India, unlike America, was not starting from a

*Although the Constitution does allow for a form of local government in the Panchayati Raj system, in practice these institutions have been largely neglected and under-resourced. Today panchayats are plagued by a lack of power, the absence of people's involvement, weak democratic practices and a shortage of funds.

clean slate. The idea of a republic called 'India' had to triumph over narrow sectarian boundaries of caste, religion and provincial attachments if the country was to survive its infancy. In their wisdom, they chose a path of strong central authority vested with the Union government with limited powers given to the states and little or no powers delegated to community governments.* The resulting over-centralized system did not address the needs of the majority of Indians, scattered across this vast country.† As Romesh Thapar wrote of the subverted objectives of the Congress Party in his 1977 classic, *The Indian Dimension: Politics of Continental Development*:

> The 'public sector' has been reduced to a vast employment racket for the elite and its hangers-on, managed by careerist bureaucrats who have little management skill and no commitment to the objectives of the party. Urban and rural 'administration' is a kind of overlordship vitiated by the worst aspects of a hierarchical system. An antiquated system of

*Part XI of India's Constitution (Articles 245–63) covers the relations between the Union and the states. Of particular import is Article 246 which mandates a division of power between the two, itemized through Lists. The Union List consists of ninety-seven areas, including defence, currency, banking, and foreign affairs, in which the Union has sole jurisdiction. The State List comprises sixty-six areas, such as public order and policing, state taxes and duties, agriculture, sanitation, local governments and public health, which fall under state jurisdiction. There is also a Concurrent List comprising forty-seven items, including economic and social planning, criminal law and procedure, marriage, education, welfare, labour and contracts, over which both the Union and states can legislate. The centrist bias of this division of power is evident from that fact that any residuary powers—those not covered by the three lists—are vested in the Union. In case of conflict of interest over a subject in the Concurrent List, the Union's writ prevails. Finally, during constitutional emergency, the Union takes over all subjects of legislation. My proposals for 'right scaling' are a response to this centralization of power and authority.

†Interestingly, Gandhi was opposed to this highly centralized administration, envisioning instead, a nation that drew its strength as a republic of village communities.

rules and regulations, of theoretical accountability, the result of the mechanical accretions from planned or free enterprises, blocks performance at all levels into lazy action only by the nudgings of corruption. These aspects of the national scene suffocate the massive achievements of the Indian people.[14]

The time has come for a new system of government in India: one that is both highly localized and based on a coherent framework. India's policy makers need a set of core principles that are widely understood and provide a rationale, language and context for the actions of its citizens. Like all well-conceived frameworks this would guide decision makers, provide a shared frame of reference and have high levels of legitimacy amongst its members.

Throughout history, effective frameworks have been used to carry out both great good and great evil. But one thing is clear: they enable their members to collectively reach unprecedented levels of achievement.* A good case is the overall unity of the British imperial system, which in its heyday allowed a tiny nation to rule much of the world.† I am no supporter of colonialism, but I use this example to show the effectiveness of frameworks. In this case, the framework encompassed the legal, military, police and civil service right down to the imperial system of measurement. Its resilience came from a high degree of standardization ranging from compiling land revenue records to imposing a system of district level administration.‡ My grandfather who worked within the colonial system would often tell me stories of how when a territory was annexed, the British administration would rapidly consolidate their hold over the local

---

*In this context I define success as collective endeavours that achieve the goals of their leaders.

†I want to make it very clear that I do not subscribe to the goals or values of the example given.

‡Romesh Dutt, an Indian economist, wrote *The Economic History of India* in 1902, which is a meticulous account of how the British empire established itself in India.

population. They compiled records of land, population, topography and brought in colonial officers from a civil service cadre of trained administrators. The local rulers were no match for the imperial juggernaut. The imperial framework was brilliantly designed to efficiently annex and hold vast territory. Unfortunately, when the Indian Republic came into existence in 1947, its leaders, instead of constructing a new framework, simply tinkered with the existing colonial one. The resulting administrative system did not 'fit' the context and challenges faced by the new nation and this has contributed to many problems confronting India today.

The framework I am proposing in this book is built around three principles:

1. Fair markets

The market structure is the best system to effectively allocate resources and signal supply and demand through prices, provided certain core preconditions are met.

   i) Removal of all distortions: Distortions* severely impact the efficiency of markets and have a cascading effect, creating a need for increased intervention that in turn leads to further distortions. Once these are removed, the resulting system will be largely self-regulating.

  ii) Standards: These codify quality into measurable and therefore tradable quantities. The resulting uniformity is the prerequisite for allowing something to be traded.

 iii) Exchanges: These provide the marketplace for trading to occur and, via price, determine the relative value of what is being traded.

  iv) Regulator: An institution that functions like an umpire to both ensure the transparent, smooth running of standards and exchanges, and to prevent formation of monopolies.

*A distortion refers to conditions that create economic inefficiency, such as: unregulated monopolies, tariffs, import quotas, unfactored costs and externalities, or certain kinds of taxation.

2. Appropriate scale

Today we face a huge 'democratic deficit' and do not have a say in the issues that immediately affect our lives. For example, I feel very strongly about the management of the park near my house in Delhi, but have no mechanism of communicating these views to the people in charge of it because there is no appropriate forum, only the enormous Municipal Corporation of Delhi* or civic associations that have no power. I propose the 'rightsizing' of representative forums to allow for meaningful democratic participation.

3. Transparency

The first two principles depend on a high degree of operational transparency. Harnessing technology is the key to achieve this.

The basis of true capitalism is the correct pricing of goods and labour. By goods I mean anything that is used and can be quantified, including all natural resources. Many social and environmental problems we face today are a result of a skewed model that obscures the real costs. In reality a polluting factory reduces the value of the product it manufactures, but because the company does not pay for the pollution it generates, the cost of manufacturing the product is unaffected. Real costing would demonstrate that preserving the environment and eradicating poverty are not mutually exclusive. The resulting system would allow for rapid economic growth that is not consumption-driven, and is both equitable and environmentally sustainable.

A system of real costing would enable wealth to be allocated in new ways. From my experience of working with impoverished communities across India, I have realized that poverty is partly a result of the assets of the poor not being valued, combined with limited or non-existent opportunities for trading these assets. In contrast, the rich are wealthy because their assets are valued and easily tradable. Furthermore, because much of what the rich consume is not correctly factored in costs, they have a surfeit of

*It is the world's second-largest municipal corporation.

liquidity that leads to excessive consumption.* Real costing would correct these imbalances.

Imagine that assets resemble a spectrum only a small part of which is visible. Now let us say that the assets of the rich lie in the 'visible' spectrum while those of the poor lie in the 'invisible' part. What is needed is the policy equivalent of UV filters to enable us to see the invisible. What is needed is a mechanism to assign value (for ownership and trade) to the assets which are already owned by the poor or are theirs by right.

I will illustrate this point with two examples from my own life. I am one of the major shareholders of Fabindia. My assets in the form of shares get easier to value and trade as the company grows in size. The value of the shares is easily calculated because a number of institutions such as investment banks, private equity funds, stock exchanges and leveraged buy-out funds provide instruments to assign value to companies over a certain size. These different instruments allow 'the capitalist' to choose the one that gives the highest price. However, as is described below, the specialized instruments of these institutions can only capture the value of a very small percentage of the wide variety of human enterprises that exist.

I am also part of a group that runs a school, built on a small piece of 'wasteland'† in Rajasthan. When the school trust bought the land in 1992, it was a barren, dry, hard piece of earth. On the rare occasions that it rained, I would watch the water fall, collect into tiny rivulets and then flow off the land, leaving it bone dry

*Conspicuous consumption refers to the lavish spending on goods and services that are acquired mainly for the purpose of displaying income or wealth rather than utility. The term was coined by the Norwegian American economist and sociologist Thorstein Veblen in his 1899 book *The Theory of the Leisure Class: An Economic Study in the Evolution of Institutions*. He used it to describe the behaviour of the nouveau riche, which had emerged as a result of the accumulation of wealth during the Second Industrial Revolution.
†In 2000, India's land use ministry classified approximately one-fifth of its entire territory (nearly 63 million hectares) as un-irrigable 'wasteland'. This figure is increasing rapidly.

after just a few hours. There was no other external source of water. I began to work with an architect friend to convert every inch of the central portion of the land into a giant water collector by mapping the contours and using the natural slope of the land to draw the water into a large rectangular reservoir that we dug out. For the following six years we managed to trap the water that fell, with increasing amounts of success, raising the capacity of the reservoir. The water it contained was sweet, which is a rare commodity in India.* As time went by, a jungle grew up around the reservoir as a result of the water seeping into the soil. It was the densest vegetation I had seen in that arid part of Rajasthan. Following this success, I decided it would be a good idea to create more of these reservoirs, sell the surplus water and get the government to pay for reforesting the land, especially because at this time the government was spending vast sums on reforestation and generally getting nothing in the way of forest cover.[15] However, because there was no existing infrastructure for assessing the quality of water produced or the diversity of the forest, nor an instrument for pricing these natural commodities, my idea could not be translated into a valuable business. My new jungle had no value. An activity vital to environmental regeneration was 'worthless', while the market for treated water sold in disposable non-biodegradable plastic continues to be highly valued.

As the authors of *Natural Capitalism: Creating the Next Industrial Revolution* describe:

It is not the supplies of oil or copper that are beginning to limit our development but life itself. Today, our continuing progress is restricted not by the number of fishing boats

*In India, much of the fresh water that comes from rivers or underground sources is unpalatable and 'hard' due to its high mineral content and therefore must be heavily treated before drinking. What is referred to colloquially as 'sweet' water, because of its taste, has a potable level of mineral content and, in particularly arid areas of the country, is available only as harvested rainwater.

but by the decreasing numbers of fish; not by the power of
pumps but by the depletion of aquifers; not by the number
of chainsaws but by the disappearance of primary forests.
While living systems are the source of such desired materials
as wood, fish, or food, of utmost importance are the *services*
that they offer, services that are far more critical to human
prosperity than are non-renewable resources . . . A healthy
environment automatically supplies not only clean air and
water, rainfall, ocean productivity, fertile soil, and watershed
resilience but also such less-appreciated functions as waste
processing (both natural and industrial), buffering against
the extremes of weather, and regeneration of the atmosphere.
Humankind has inherited a 3.8-billion-year store of natural
capital. At present rates of use and degradation, there will
be little left by the end of the next century . . . The stock of
natural capital is plummeting and the vital life-giving services
that flow from it are critical to our prosperity.[16]

The price of products must be based on both their production
costs and their environmental costs. Until then, consumers will
be underpaying, creating artificial surpluses which they will use
to consume more. Plane flights, nuclear power, synthetic clothes
and disposable gadgets are just a few examples of what we
consume while only paying a fraction of their true costs. I once
asked a waste management specialist what it would cost to
biodegrade my new running shoes; his answer was several hundred
to a thousand dollars. That meant that when I bought the shoes I
was receiving what amounted to a 90 per cent subsidy, the selling
price only represented the costs of manufacturing and transport,
and not responsible disposal.

This book is both idealistic and pragmatic. Its blue sky thinking
is firmly rooted in the specifics of governance strategy, taxation,
finance and law, outlining a detailed blueprint for a new role for
government within the Indian Constitution. The first part of the

book focuses on the economy, the second on government and social organization, and the third on the transition itself. Throughout the book I use examples from my country, India, home to one-sixth of humanity. While the political solutions are India-specific, the economic framework I have created is applicable to any country.

In chapter 1, I discuss the nature of the problem, explaining why pressing poverty and a looming environmental disaster mean that we urgently need a paradigm shift. I also introduce three case studies that reoccur throughout the book to illustrate the impact of my arguments in rural, small-town and urban settings; India lives in these three divisions. Chapter 2 is about the foundations of a 'true' market economy, while chapter 3 deals with the nuts and bolts of public expenditure and taxation. Chapter 4 discusses political reform of the executive and legislative branches of the government, outlining a richer, localized version of democracy. Justice for all is the focus of chapter 5, while the structure of social organizations is the concern of chapter 6. Chapter 7 looks at habitat planning. In chapter 8, I describe the practical steps needed to implement this framework. The final chapter draws all of the work together to describe in detail what India could look like after my reforms have been implemented.

I have written this book because I am deeply worried about the future of democracy. Globally, democracy faces threats on many levels. In India, the younger generation's frustration with the current political system is translating into impatience with democracy itself. I frequently hear young, intelligent people saying how much easier it would be to have a more authoritarian system of government, such as in Singapore. To defend democracy against totalitarianism, we must overhaul our political system.

Cynicism towards democracy is caused by the democratic paralysis we experience in India. Political vacillation, red tape and pork barrel politics mean that the government does not keep pace with our fast-moving world. Take the defence ministry's decision to purchase 197 helicopters in the year 2000. In December 2007, when the purchase still had yet to be completed, the procurement process was cancelled due to bureaucratic risk aversion, political influence, and tortuous procedures. As a result, soldiers working in high-altitude areas will needlessly lose their lives to illness, accidents and cases of altitude sickness because the military's 1960s vintage helicopters are unable to reach them.

The challenges we face today are too big, our current models of government and economics too ineffective and our time too short to continue with a piecemeal approach to reform. This book provides an integrated framework covering key areas of society and economy in order to address these challenges now. While each idea stands alone, only the proposal in its entirety will achieve maximum impact because each of these policies is designed to reinforce and support the others.

The ideas contained in this book are genuinely revolutionary. Yet the words used to describe them—inclusive growth, environmental sustainability, poverty eradication—are rendered meaningless by overuse. Every oil company now claims to be environmentally sustainable and every multinational corporation to be in favour of inclusive growth. I ask the reader to put aside any cynicism he or she might have towards these terms and to read what follows with an open mind.

Indians love to hate their politicians. In this large, 'argumentative' nation, it is the one thing we agree on. A whole vocabulary has evolved to describe their misdeeds, and it is used by vegetable sellers and millionaires alike. But, I do not blame India's politicians for the current state of the nation. Having met hundreds of them, it is clear that whatever their intentions might be, the task of governing India is so enormous, so complex and so unresponsive to piecemeal approaches and they have an impossible job. The ship is simply too unwieldy to steer. The system itself locks them into failure. The framework in this book will make governing India a far easier task. It is for India's policy makers, current and future, that I have written this book.

Notes

1. World Bank, *India: Country Assistance Strategy* (World Bank Group, 2001).
2. UNICEF India, *Children's Issues: Nutrition.* Available at http://www.unicef.org/india/children_2356.htm.
3. International Institute for Population Sciences (IIPS) and Macro International, *National Family Health Survey (NFHS-3), 2005–06: India* (Mumbai: IIPS, 2007), vol. 1.
4. National Commission for Enterprises in the Unorganised Sector, *Report on Conditions of Work and Promotion of Livelihoods in the Unorganised Sector* (New Delhi: National Commission for Enterprises in the Unorganised Sector, 2007). Available at http://nceus.gov.in/Condition_of_workers_sep_2007.pdf.
5. Estimates of poverty vary even within the government. According to the Planning Commission, the percentage of population in poverty had declined from 36 per cent in 1993–94 to 26 per cent in 1999–2000. More recent estimates for 2004–05 place the percentage of population below the poverty line at 27.8 per cent. The Planning Commission attributes this increase to a change in methodology for the computation of poverty estimates. Although this poverty estimate is higher than the earlier official estimate for 1999–2000, this should not be, according to the Panning Commission, interpreted to mean that poverty has increased between 1999–2000 and 2004–2005. It only means that the 1999–2000 official estimates had underestimated comparable poverty. See Planning Commission, 'Towards Faster and More Inclusive Growth—An Approach to the 11th Five-Year Plan' (New Delhi: Government of India). Needless to add, there is more human poverty than mere income deprivation that such measures attempt to capture. If we adopt the human development framework, and define poverty as multidimensional deprivation, the magnitude of poverty in India increases manifold to include those deprived of basic education, health care, water, sanitation, access to law, nutrition and so on.
6. See http://www.mkgandhi.org/gquots1.htm.
7. See www.mkgandhi.org.

8. Jared Diamond, 'What's Your Consumption Factor?' *The New York Times*, 2 January 2008.

9. An incisive analyst of Indian politics, writing in 1977, had this to say about the effects of the marriage of one-party dominance with a series of outdated ideas: '[T]he 'commanding heights' are now in control of men accustomed to serving the objectives of powerful vested interests. The 'public sector' has been reduced to a vast employment racket for the elite and its hangers-on, managed by careerist bureaucrats who have little management skill and no commitment . . . These aspects of national scene suffocate the massive achievements of the Indian people.' Romesh Thapar, *The Indian Dimension: Politics of Continental Development* (New Delhi: Vikas, 1977), pp. 45–46.

10. A book I read at the time by Mancur Olson, *The Logic of Collective Action* (Harvard University Press: Cambridge,1965), p. 2, articulated many of my frustrations with collective organization. He argues that groups generally do not act to advance their common interest, stating that if 'members of a large group rationally seek to maximise their personal welfare, they will not act to advance their common or group objectives unless there is coercion . . . or . . . some separate incentive' This, however, doesn't apply to small groups, as I will go on to evidence.

11. See James Madison, 'The Federalist No. 10', *The Fedaralist Papers* (New York: Bantam Classic, 2003), p. 55.

12. See Granville Austin, *The Indian Constitution: Cornerstone of a Nation* (New Delhi: Oxford University Press, 2002) for an argument of why a centralized state was necessary to ensure the unity of the new nation immediately after Independence.

13. See Alexis de Tocqueville, 'The need to study what happens in the states before discussing the government of the Union', in *Democracy in America*, trans. George Lawrence (New York: Anchor Books, 1969), pp. 61–98.

14. Romesh Thapar, *The Indian Dimension: Politics of Continental Development* (New Delhi: Vikas, 1977), pp. 45–46.

15. For example, in 2007, the Punjab Forest Department set a target for increasing its tree cover that was exactly the same as the one it had set ten years earlier, even though Rs 400 crore (US$100 million)

had been spent on 'reforestation' in the meantime. See Aditi Tandon, 'Old is New, Punjab's Forest Policy Uncovered', *The Tribune*, 8 August 2007.

16. See Paul Hawkin, Amory Lovins, and L. Hunter Lovins, *Natural Capitalism: Creating the Next Industrial Revolution* (New York and Boston: Little, Brown and Company, 1999), p. 3.

The Case for Change

The most salient fact about India is that it is very poor and very backward. There are so many other things to be said about it but this must remain the basis of all of them. We may praise Indian democracy, go into raptures over Indian music, admire Indian intellectuals—but whatever we say, not for one moment should we lose sight of the fact that a very great number of Indians never get enough to eat.

Ruth Prawer Jhabvala, *Out of India*

Failed Ideas

Sunita* is a member of my domestic staff. She lives with her husband, a rickshaw puller in New Delhi and their five children, one of whom is retarded because he was deprived of oxygen at birth. Driving a rickshaw through the polluted streets of New Delhi, her husband developed severe respiratory problems. He could not afford adequate health care and so began to spend most of his time at home. This forced Sunita to work longer hours, leaving her disabled son unattended. One afternoon a local gang attacked her son, took him to a local park and raped him. Sunita and her husband did not report the crime to the police as they

Epigraph: Ruth Prawer Jhabvala, *Out of India* (New York: William Morrow and Company, 1986), p. 14.
*Name changed to protect privacy.

1

were afraid the police would pick them up instead. This horrifying story illustrates how a number of factors—poor education, poor health care, a polluted environment and the inability to assert legal rights—combine to produce devastating results. When you are poor and living on the edge of subsistence, a small misfortune can push you quickly down into a tailspin. With nearly four out of five Indians living in poverty, millions of Indians are caught in a lethal web.

We are told that the 'way out' is to let the economy grow, so that millions will be rescued from poverty as their income grows, and as they buy more goods and services, jobs and opportunities will be created that will translate into further growth, and so on. The problem with this image of a consumption-driven economy is that the supply of most of what we need is finite. Even air and water are limited. When the First World nations were developing, they used this model to create economic growth for half a billion people; and it is the consumption of the First World that has caused most of the environmental damage that we see today. What is happening now is that the rest of the world's six-and-a-half billion people want to embark on the same journey. But there are not enough resources to support seven billion people travelling down the same road.

Our current economic model is failing. It is failing the common Indian and the majority in our planet. We are facing a global crisis. Though we are consuming about 25 per cent more natural resources than the planet can replace,[1] some 2.7 billion people, live below the US$2-a-day poverty line.[2]

If China and India adopt the Western road to development, it is likely to lead to an environmental breakdown. Overpopulation is often cited as the crux of the problem. However, the real issue is consumption. It is not about numbers of people but how much they consume.* For everyone on earth to live at the current average level of consumption in the US we would need the equivalent of

*An example of this is the launch of the world's cheapest car, the Tata Nano, costing Rs 100,000 (US$2383, according to early 2008 conversion rates). This

four planet Earths to sustain us.[3] If the entire developing world were to suddenly consume at US levels it would be as if the global population had ballooned to 72 billion. Yet, the world can barely support the one billion already consuming at these levels.[4] We are living on precarious ecological credit, rapidly depleting the reserve of natural capital. All the signs show that the earth's systems are unable to cope with the consequences of human activities with climate change as the ultimate consequence of human demands on the environment.[†] Forests are shrinking dramatically; over-pumping of freshwater supplies is causing catastrophic results.[5] In many countries, rivers are running dry.[6] Fishery collapses have become pandemic. Grasslands are deteriorating in every continent and we are facing such high levels of species loss[7] that scientists are labelling this period, a great extinction.[8] In short, the world is in an 'overshoot and collapse' mode.[9]

The Consumption Myth

Time is running out. But, governments across the world are still convinced that resource-intensive consumption-driven growth is the Holy Grail of development. It has become a policy addiction. Governments are increasingly becoming aware of the fact that they cannot keep administering the drug of growth. Yet, they are

---

will dramatically increase the number of cars driven in India, resulting in grave pollution and increased congestion. Currently, there are approximately ten million cars on India's roads; the Tatas expect an annual demand of one million for their low-priced car Nano.

[†]The planet is warming and it is happening as a result of human activity. Most scientists agree that a temperature rise of at least 2°C by the year 2050 is inevitable. They also agree that any rise beyond this limit will have devastating consequences. The Himalayan glaciers—the vital dry season source of fresh water for over a billion people in South Asia—will disappear. The melting of the Greenland ice sheet will become irreversible, and will accelerate the rise in sea level that will affect millions of people in coastal cities worldwide. Scientists have repeatedly warned that to stay below 2°C of global warming, the world's emissions of greenhouse gases will need to decline within the next ten or fifteen years.

fearful of the withdrawal symptoms that will follow the 'coming off' and so keep on going. However, even by its own standards, this style of growth is not working, as wealth is not reaching the poor. Take the example of the US where wealth generated from 2001 to 2006 has flowed almost exclusively to the rich. The only households in 2006 which exceeded their earnings in 2000 were the top 5 per cent; everyone else's earnings had dropped.[10]

Consumption-driven growth is an inefficient way of achieving reduction in poverty. Between 1990 and 2001, for every growth of US$100 in the world's per capita income, just US$0.60 made its way into the hands of the people who needed it and contributed to raise the poverty level to above US$1-a-day. With this ratio, to achieve poverty reduction by one dollar, an extra US$166 worth needs to be produced and consumed globally.[11] Such an approach is both economically and ecologically inefficient.

The final nail in the coffin of the consumption-driven model is that it often does not equate to higher living standards.* Take the example of 'forced' consumption. In Delhi today, the air is so polluted that 68 per cent of Delhites suffer from some form of respiratory illness.[12] As we buy more medicines and visit the doctor more frequently, our consumption levels increase. Our poor physical health shows up as economic good health on the consumption balance sheet. My biggest financial outlay this year has been the purchase of three expensive air purification systems and two water filtration systems. Again, pollution and poor water quality actually increase my consumption levels, but are indicators

---

*In a recent editorial, geographer Jared Diamond speaks of numerous cases where high consumption rates contribute nothing to quality of life. For example, the US per capita oil consumption is double that of western Europe, yet the US standard of living is lower by most indicators, including life expectancy, health, infant mortality, access to medical care, financial security after retirement, vacation time, quality of public schools and support for the arts. See Jared Diamond, 'What's Your Consumption Factor', *New York Times*, 2 January 2008.

of poor quality of life. These situations of 'forced' consumption exacerbate the division between the rich and the poor, as the latter often cannot afford to take either preventive or palliative measures. The existing system is failing because it is founded on a narrow view of what constitutes an asset. It is blind to the limits of natural resources, blind to the non-financial elements of well-being and the value of unpaid work. It is, ultimately, an inefficient way of maximizing that ultimate good of human society: happiness. It is time to take off the blinkers and broaden our definition of wealth. Across the world, there is increasing recognition of the dire trouble the planet is in and the tiny window of opportunity we have to save it. It is time for India to lead the way and create a development path to take us through these troubled times.

India

The mismanagement of our nation generates needless suffering. When I was growing up in Delhi, I used to go for a walk every evening with my grandfather. We would go around the colony where we lived and he would often talk about the follies of Third World leaders. One of his favourite comments had to do with what he called 'the three models of development': communism, capitalism and 'tokenism'. My grandfather explained that when leaders substitute rhetoric for sound economic and political policies it amounts to tokenism.* He would often speak at length about what bad leadership does and the structural violence it imposes on those who are unlucky enough to live in countries with bad leadership. Structural violence is not the dramatic violence unleashed on Hitler's Germany or Stalin's Russia or

---

*An example of First World 'tokenism' would be American President George W. Bush's 'Mission Accomplished' speech and performance—landing a fighter jet on USS *Abraham Lincoln* in a flight suit—on 1 May 2003. This was a carefully orchestrated public relations manoeuvre to draw attention away from the core issues of the Iraq war and larger foreign policy concerns.

Mao's China, but the omnipresent tragedy of what happens when societies do not work. Our driver at home pined for a son and he eventually had one. One hot summer in Delhi when the public water supply—erratic as it is—collapsed, his infant son contracted typhoid. He was misdiagnosed by a quack, given adulterated medication and died of dehydration. As Stalin is supposed to have once said, 'The death of an individual is a tragedy; the death of a million is a statistic.' Our driver's baby boy was a statistic, killed because he was born in a Third World country to poor, uneducated parents. Poor management condemns people by locking them into a life in which their opportunities are limited in every way. A majority of Indians lead wretched lives because of a system that perpetuates, rather than alleviates, their poverty. Poverty breeds extremism that threatens to tear the country apart. The Naxalites, armed left-wing extremists, now affect over 170 of India's 602 districts—a 'red corridor' stretching through central India from the country's border with Nepal in the north to Karnataka in the south and covering more than a quarter of India's land mass.[13] The armed revolutionaries and militia will continue to expand their reach as long as such epic poverty persists.

Meanwhile, chronic mismanagement and corruption ensures that access to basic resources is in peril. The crisis is not far off. Carrying on with business as usual will have catastrophic consequences. Take the example of water. In March 2008, which is not exactly summer, a water crisis had already hit Delhi. At times, water production was down by 30 per cent in three of the main water plants, and many areas of the city were cut off. Summer water demand exceeded the amount Delhi could provide by over 25 per cent.[14] Simultaneously, the government watchdog had released a report detailing how the government's flagship rural drinking water scheme was plagued with corruption and incompetence.[15] This includes vast amounts of money spent on laying pipes in West Bengal connected to an unsustainable water source; a sum of Rs 23.5 million (US$589,000) was spent on uninhabited or non-existent villages in Arunachal Pradesh and another Rs 38.5 million (US$965,000) on 705 wells in an area of Madhya Pradesh that was already fully covered for drinking water. The Comptroller and Auditor General* routinely produces such scathing indictments of government policy, which are, in turn, routinely ignored by government officials.

Poor management is another term for inefficiency. When resources are wasted in a rich country, it is a pity. When resources are wasted in a poor country, it is tragedy on a grand scale.

The other quarter of India, though economically better off, bears testimony to another kind of inefficiency: that of highly resource- and capital-intensive growth. In simpler language, it is growth that consumes a disproportionate share of resources while the total cost is either disguised or not taken into account. It is like a 1960s jet engine that delivers the desired thrust but consumes a huge amount of fuel to do so.

A Lost Opportunity

Sixty years ago, an independent India took the high road of visionary change under the leadership of an extraordinary group of individuals who brought the ideas of human rights and the principle of governance by the people to a nation emerging from the dark ages of feudalism and caste beliefs. Indians trusted their leaders who were driving this change, often with little idea where the high road would lead to. The year 1947 was a turning point and a moment of victory after a great struggle. But even with the best of intentions, the map we were following was already out of date. India has a sorry history of embracing ideas that are past their sell-by date. It adopted Fabian socialism after it had been discarded by other countries; it pursued the 'nationalization of

*The Comptroller and Auditor General of India (CAG) is a constitutional authority responsible for auditing the receipts and expenditures of the Union, state governments and bodies that are substantially financed by the government.

Figure 1.1: Gross domestic product (GDP) growth comparison

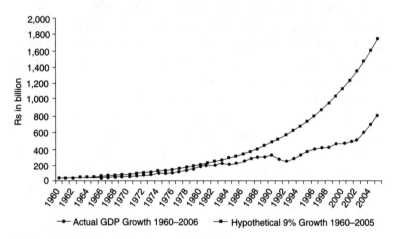

—•— Actual GDP Growth 1960–2006   —•— Hypothetical 9% Growth 1960–2005

Source: World Bank Development Initiative.

the commanding heights' of the economy even though this approach was clearly failing in other nations.* And now, India embraces consumption-driven economic growth, just when the world is realizing that such a path is unsustainable. Outdated ideas have wasted the lives of two generations, as Figure 1.1 indicates. If, from 1960, the economy had grown at a consistent 9 per cent, compounded yearly, the current GDP would be greater than twice its present value.

The Indian government's tendency to adopt outdated policies has wasted productive lives, squandered opportunities, and weakened democracy to the point that it increasingly functions through patronage of various kinds. The arrival of the corporate

*The term 'nationalization of the commanding heights' epitomized the character of the Nehruvian course to India's modernization. 'Commanding heights' were sectors of crucial importance—steel, railways, aviation, communication, banking, physical infrastructure including dams and canals, etc.—which the central planners kept under stifling state control.

member of Parliament, in the Rajya Sabha, takes the patron–client relationship to a new level, creating monumental conflicts of interest. The owner of one of India's biggest airlines, Vijay Mallya, is a permanent invitee to the consultative committee on civil aviation and a member of the standing committee on industries, whilst the media magnate, Vijay Darda, is on the standing committee of communications. Later in this book, I will recount the story of an industrialist who wanted a Lutyens's bungalow in Delhi, so he decided to simply buy his way into the Rajya Sabha.* The public grows increasingly cynical as they view the machinations of the political class.† A Rajasthani farmer I recently met summed it up rather well in a comment made during a discussion on local irrigation policy: 'Policy? What policy?' he asked. 'All of them are for "sale".'

Seizing the Moment

In the words of Jawaharlal Nehru, as he ushered in India's Independence at the stroke of midnight on 15 August 1947, 'A moment comes which comes but rarely in history, when we step out from the old to the new, when an age ends, and when the soul of a nation, long suppressed, finds utterance.'[16]

Today, the moment is a little different and the crossroads less visible. No war or calamity has preceded this turning point. Yet the decadence is there for all to see—generated by a confluence of demography, technology, and a discrediting of ideas that have shackled our minds. We have an opportunity to introduce a model of development that is in harmony with our future rather than a

---

*Located in the heart of New Delhi, Lutyens's bungalows (which are named after the British architect who designed New Delhi in early twentieth century, Sir Edwin L. Lutyens) are reserved for government use and residence, including the residential use of: the President, the prime minster, senior members of the judiciary, armed forces, civil services, and other political offices.
†In India, there is literally a hereditary political class with hundreds of 'democratic dynasties'.

copy of a worn idea from the past. Almost 60 per cent of Indians are under the age of thirty.[17] The country's staggering demographics means that this figure (630 million) is more than double the entire population of the US. One of the largest workforces in the world is about to enter the market. This is India's greatest resource. How this human capital is utilized will define the future of the nation, and the world. Today, the majority of India's youth are not destined to be doctors, software professionals or workers in outsourcing firms. Most cannot move up the economic ladder and are often treated as little more than a pair of human hands, uneducated even if they complete school. We have a responsibility to better the lives of this new generation and allow them to flourish.

The Goal

The goal of this book is to reduce poverty. I define poverty as the absence of: adequate nutrition, clean water, basic sanitation, education, enforced constitutional rights, basic health care.[18]

Each of these elements is closely related to the other. Clean water and basic sanitation reduce the odds of contracting most diseases,[19] as is basic primary education necessary for creating the required awareness.[20] Enabling the poor to assert their constitutional rights would lead to subsequent benefits like improved health to better education, as they would be able to lobby against polluting industries and demand better services.

Wealth and poverty are part of an interlinked spiral. You are moving either up or down, but are rarely stationary. Movement gathers momentum, and so at either end you accelerate. At the top, many billionaires comment that making the first million is the hardest. After this, they begin to experience the accelerative effects of prosperity and their wealth rockets upwards. It is very difficult for the super-rich to become poor. Take the example of Lawrence J. Ellison, the founder of Oracle. Ellison would have to spend US$30 million a week—US$183,000 an hour—on things that cannot be resold, like parties or meals, just to avoid *increasing* his wealth.[21] At the bottom end, conditions rapidly deteriorate into a 'tailspin', resulting in destitution or death, as illustrated by the horrendous example of Sunita at the beginning of the chapter.

Yet, although the majority in the country are caught in this deadly tailspin, India's government continually fails to take measures against poverty, though a substantial portion of the state and Union budgets are allocated for this cause. This is because most development schemes of the government are ineffective. The Indian government stymies economic growth through a tax system that stifles enterprise and then consistently misspends the resulting tax revenue. In this book, I have proposed tax reforms that will stimulate enterprise and development reforms that will reduce poverty. Water and nutrition are vital for life. The ability to defend rights is vital for liberty. Good health and education are vital for the pursuit of happiness. This must be the birthright of each Indian. That they have been denied this for sixty years is an unparalleled tragedy.

The Case Studies

I use three communities to illustrate my ideas: one rural, one small-town, and one urban. India lives in these three areas: 600 million people live in rural India, 300 million in small towns, and 200 million in cities.[22] I live in each of these areas at different times of the year. If the proposals in my book are implemented, each community would look very different.

The city: Panchsheel

My first case study is the area of Panchsheel, my home. It is a south Delhi neighbourhood, which includes an affluent space and an urban slum, making it a good illustration of the issues facing urban India, home to 200 million Indians. Panchsheel Park is a gated colony, split in two by a large, eight-lane ring road. For the most part, the leafy streets are home to large, expensive houses, guarded by watchmen. The area is surrounded by the red stone ruins that are evidence of the area's former incarnation as the ancient city of Siri, built in the fourteenth century.*

A common Delhi phenomenon, the ancient village of Shahpur Jat, is now a poor, slum-like collection of tenements, while what was farmland until the 1960s is the site of plush houses that sell for a fortune. A few minutes' walk from my house, the tenements of Shahpur Jat belong to a different world. The noisy, narrow streets are crammed with stalls, music blares out and shoppers haggle with the fishmonger. Explore one of the tiny walkways leading off the street and you will find families living under tarpaulins in the shadow of the ancient Siri walls. The area is not uniformly poor; some locate businesses or artisan workshops there to take advantage of the low rent. Shahpur Jat constitutes a very small area of the Panchsheel community, which is for the most part one of the most desirable areas of Delhi.

At the end of the book, I will describe another Panchsheel. One where the streets of Shahpur Jat are paved, every household has hot water, and a state-of-the-art sewage system runs through the neighbourhood. While the large parks remain, the rest of Panchsheel will look very different.

The town: Mussoorie

The second case is of a small town, Mussoorie, with 26,000 inhabitants in the district of Dehra Dun, in the foothills of the Himalayas, where I spend time in the summer.[23] Nestled in forested slopes, at an altitude of 2000 metres above sea level, the town looks out to snow ranges in the north-east, and the Doon Valley and the Shivalik Ranges in the south. These spectacular views, the mild summer climate and its location as a gateway to the

---

*Siri was built by Alauddin Khilji of the Khilji dynasty (AD 1296–1316) within the period of the Delhi Sultanate (AD 1191–1526).

Yamunotri and Gangotri shrines, make Mussoorie a popular hill station. Alongside tourism, education is the other mainstay of the local economy as the town is home to a number of prestigious private schools.

In the town, monkeys leap off rooftops whilst honeymooners walk arm in arm down the wide Mall, with its elegant wrought-iron lamps, horse rides, and stalls selling trinkets. Mussoorie combines the modern hallmarks of any Indian town—Barista coffee, Bata shoes, Dominos pizza—with crumbling antique shops, men deeply involved in their carom games along the roadside and young boys roaring up the main street on motorcycles.

The resort's popularity places a heavy demand on local resources. Rubbish runs in rivulets down the forested hills. The available water supply is not sufficient to meet even half of the summer demand.[24] Raw sewage is disposed of in storm drains, and in high summer the stench is overwhelming.

Later in the book, I will describe a clean Mussoorie, free from rubbish and traffic, where the local community itself will be wealthy and able to profit from its forested hills, without chopping down a single tree.

The village: Sewari

My third case study is rural India, where 600 million Indians live. I have focused on a small rural community where I spend time in winter. Sewari is a community in the district of Pali in western Rajasthan. Small, dusty villages lead on to fields of wheat, which in turn merge into the dry, scrubby desert that stretches out to the Aravalli Mountain range.

In the village of Sewari, men with large moustaches, gold earrings and bright fuchsia turbans wander the narrow streets. Women with thick white shoulder bangles carry terracotta pots on their heads and queue by one of the village taps. Children play with home-made kites. The majority of the local population is involved in subsistence agriculture. Travel out of the village and you may drive over straw left to dry on the road, past a goat herder and his flock, or a garlanded tractor.

Lest this paints too idyllic a picture, I would add that the inhabitants of Sewari are very poor. Drinking water is contaminated. There is no sewage system, little electricity, no waste disposal and little access to health care. In spite of this, the people of Sewari are great entrepreneurs, with every family sending at least one member to Mumbai or the Gulf. Their remittances run the local economy.[25]

My proposals would reverse Sewari's fortunes by identifying and valuing their 'invisible' assets. The ability to cost and trade their environmental assets would dramatically enrich the community. Its poverty-stricken inhabitants would find themselves sitting on a proverbial oil well.

In the following chapters, each idea will be referenced with the effect it will have on the lives of the people who live in these three communities.

Notes

1. World Wildlife Fund, *One Planet Mobility: A Journey Towards a Sustainable Future* (Surrey: WWF-UK, 2007).
2. Shaohua Chen and Martin Ravallion, 'How Have the World's Poorest Fared Since the Early 1980s?' Policy Research Working Paper No. 3341 (Washington DC: World Bank, 2004). Available online at http://econ.worldbank.org/files/36297_wps3341.pdf.
3. Craig Simmons, 'Can the Earth keep up with human consumption?', *The Guardian*, 22 February 2001.
4. Jared Diamond, 'What's Your Consumption Factor?' *The New York Times*, 2 January 2008.
5. For example, in the Indian state of Tamil Nadu falling water tables have dried up 95 per cent of the wells owned by small farmers, reducing the irrigated area of the state by half over the last decade. See F. Pearce, 'Asian Farmers Sucking the Continent Dry', *New Scientist*, 25 August 2004.

6. Take the example of China's Yellow River that crosses five provinces in its 4,000 km long journey to the Yellow Sea. It first ran dry in 1972, and since 1985, has often failed to reach the sea. See L. Brown, and B. Halweil, 'China's Water Shortages Could Shake World Food Security', *World Watch*, July–August 1998.

7. One in four mammals, one in eight birds, one-third of all amphibians and 70 per cent of the world's assessed plants on the 2007 International Union for Conservation of Nature Red List are in jeopardy of extinction. Species Survival Commission, *IUCN Red List of Threatened Species*, 2007.

8. According to archeological records, there have been five great extinctions since life began. The last happened 65 million years ago when a sudden environmental change led to the obliteration of the dinosaurs. Whilst all previous extinction events have had natural causes, this sixth great extinction has human origins. See, Richard Leakey and Roger Lewin, *The Sixth Extinction: Patterns of Life and the Future of Humankind* (New York: Doubleday, 1995).

9. L. Brown, *Plan B 2.0: Rescuing a Planet under Stress and a Civilization in Trouble* (New York: Earth Policy Institute, 2006).

10. Leader, 'A sobering census report', *The International Herald Tribune*, 30 August 2007.

11. Andrew Simms and David Woodward, *Growth Isn't Working: The Unbalanced Distribution of Benefits and Costs from Economic Growth* (London: New Economics Foundation, 2006). Available at, www.neweconomics.org/gen/uploads/hrfu5w555mzd3f55m2 vqwty502022006112929.pdf.

12. According to the Delhi government's annual report on economics and statistics, issued by the office of chief registrar (births and deaths), respiratory diseases are the biggest killers in Delhi. In the year 2006 alone, 9,164 Delhites died of respiratory diseases, primarily caused by air pollution and environmental factors. In 2005, respiratory illnesses caused 6,014 deaths in the capital. Esha Roy, 'Bad Air: City's Biggest Killer', *Indian Express*, 9 December 2007.

13. 'A spectre haunting India', *Economist*, 17 August 2006. Print edition, available at http://www.economist.com/world/asia/displaystory. cfm?story_id=7799247.

14. Moushumi Das Gupta, 'Not Yet Summer, But Water Crisis Is Here', *Hindustan Times*, 3 March 2008.

15. Ganesh Pandey and Ravish Tiwari, 'UPA Mega Drinking Water Scheme is also Going Down the Corruption Drain', *The Indian Express*, 4 March 2008.

16. Jawaharlal Nehru, 'Tryst with Destiny', *Constituent Assembly Debates*, 15 August 1947.

17. *Census of India*, 2001. See http://www.censusindia.gov.in/.

18. There is a vigorous debate on definitions of poverty. For examples, see 'What is Poverty?' *Poverty in Focus December 2006*, International Poverty Centre (Brasilia: United Nations Development Programme). Whilst quantitative measures, such as those setting a threshold of one or two dollars a day are often used, poverty is multifaceted and cannot just be reduced to income. There are geographical, cultural and political factors that amplify or reduce the impact of income on each individual. The economist and Nobel laureate Amartya Sen highlights the fundamental link between development and freedom, stating that poverty must be seen as the deprivation of basic capabilities rather than merely as lowness of income. Amartya Sen, *Development as Freedom* (Oxford: Oxford University Press, 2001).

19. Unclean water and inadequate sanitation, taken together, are the world's second largest killers of children, with 4900 dying every day as a result of diarrhoea. But when clean water and sanitation are readily available, infant and child mortality rates are reduced by nearly 50 per cent. United Nations Development Programme, *Human Development Report 2006: Beyond Scarcity, Power, Poverty and the Global Water Crisis* (New York: United Nations Development Programme).

20. For example, in Africa, children of mothers who receive five years of primary education are 40 per cent less likely to die before the age of five than children of uneducated mothers. Lawrence H. Summers, *Investing in All the People: Educating Women in Developing Countries* (Washington DC: World Bank, 1994).

21. Goolsbee, Austan, 'For the Super-Rich, Too Much is Never Enough', *The New York Times*, 1 February 2007.

22. According to the 2001 census, 742,490,639 people or 72.2 per cent of the population lives in rural areas and 286,119,689 people or 27.8 per cent of the population in urban areas. The census does not

account for the in-between category of towns. The figures provided here are standard working estimates.

23. *Census 2001*. See http://www.censusindia.gov.in/.

24. Rakesh Kumar, district magistrate of Dehra Dun, who is responsible for the administration in Mussoorie, in 'Mussoorie is Fast Losing its Charm', *Hindustan Times*, 8 June 2007.

25. Remittances are money sent home by migrants working in another country. They play a crucial role in economies of developing countries. About 10 per cent of the total population of the planet benefits directly from remittances. In 2006, more than US$300 billion were sent by 150 million migrants to their families in developing countries. This is more than twice the size of total international aid flows. India and China were the largest recipients of remittances in Asia in 2006 at US$24.5 billion (2.7 per cent of GDP) and US$21.07 billion (0.79 per cent of GDP) respectively. See Remittance Forum, 'Sending Money Home: Worldwide Remittance Flows to Developing Countries'. See also http://www.ifad.org/events/remittances/maps/index.htm.

2

Markets for All

*The behavior of government is determined, in part, by public
mood. But to a greater extent, it is also determined by the special
interests being regulated. This is why the free market system is
fragile. Not economically (as Marx theorized), but politically.
While everyone benefits from competitive markets, no one in
particular makes huge profits from keeping the system
competitive and the playing field level. Thus, nobody has a strong
vested interest in promoting and defending free markets.*

Raghuram Rajan and Luigi Zingales,
Saving Capitalism from the Capitalists

True Markets and Their Importance

An economy based on a 'true' market—that is, one that reveals
hidden costs and assets—will allow India to create a system
that will facilitate rapid, inclusive and environmentally sustainable
growth. It will also help in introducing a new vision of exchange—
an economy where cash is dematerialized and replaced by a smart
card—and a new, revolutionary policy tool, the Targeted Catalyst
(TC). The TC system would build quality public services in the
process of alleviating poverty. I shall elucidate more on this in the
next chapter.

Epigraph: Raghuram Rajan and Luigi Zingales, *Saving Capitalism from the
Capitalists* (Princeton: Princeton University Press, 2004), p. x.

Markets, at their best, price and self-regulate with extraordinary accuracy, better than any other method known to us. Complex societies are built when human creativity increases the 'supply' of goods by boosting the productivity of the resources employed, which leads to high return on capital. This surplus is what has made each great era in history possible, by allowing increased specialization and providing a market for the surplus to be spent. Michelangelo, Shakespeare and Einstein are all products of societies in which a great number of citizens did not have to worry about their basic needs and could therefore pursue more 'value-added' activities.

Left to themselves markets would ensure that huge profits are the exception and never the norm. Markets relentlessly force entrepreneurs to reinvest a large part of their earnings if they are to continue to be competitive. For this to happen, markets must be allowed to both create and destroy businesses. Today, however, the world suffers from skewed markets. These distortions can be categorized into two areas:

1. A limited definition of what constitutes an asset

As I have discussed in the Introduction and chapter 1, we have a very limited definition of what constitutes wealth. When one thinks of a 'resource' one probably thinks of oil, gold, coal, phosphate—the classic resources valued by global prices. I would extend that definition to encompass water and air, and further still to biodiversity, forest cover, and solid and toxic wastes. Valuing these resources is a theme in this chapter.

Markets work according to the information they receive or have access to. The more information they have, the better they work. Excluding environmental and social assets from the market system is destroying our world and leaving billions in poverty. I have outlined a series of policies that work to create true, undistorted markets which can reverse the spiral of poverty.

2. Government overregulation

Overregulation by government has a negative effect on the economy. The Indian government is regulating its businesses into the ground. It argues that regulation is necessary for the public good, but, in reality, it stymies growth through heavy taxation.[*,1] The proceeds are then frittered away on inefficient expenditure. Classic interventionist tools such as subsidies, grants and heavy-handed regulation distort markets and impose a heavy cost on society, often hurting the very individuals they are meant to help. All regulations should be subjected to a cost–benefit analysis. I would argue against any form of intervention that creates distortions and prevents markets from working.

I am not suggesting a libertarian framework.[†] Governments are necessary and state intervention to end poverty is vital. However, I argue that interventions that strengthen markets are much more effective policy tools for poverty alleviation than current welfare

---

*India's tax regime is a cumbersome three-tier system regulated by the Central government, state governments and rural and urban local bodies. The Central government levies taxes on income, customs, Central excise, sales and service etc. State governments levy value added tax, alcohol excise duty, stamp duty on asset transfer, agricultural income tax, etc. Utility and octroi taxes, among others, are levied by local bodies. The range of direct taxes—income tax and capital gains tax for example—has steadily risen over time. Indirect taxes levied on goods or services rather than on persons or organizations include excise duty, customs duty, service tax and securities transaction tax.

†The foundation of libertarianism is the principle of individual liberty, on the basis of which, libertarians argue that constraints imposed by the state on persons or their property are a violation of liberty. The philosopher Robert Nozick most comprehensively argued the libertarian view in his work *Anarchy, State and Utopia* (New York: Basic Books, 1974).

‡P. Sainath, in *Everybody Loves a Good Drought*, narrates the following example of what becomes of welfare expenditure from one of central India's most backward areas: 'The official mockingly calculates the possible uses of all the funds now spent in the name of the Pahadi Korwas. If the money were simply put into bank fixed deposits, none of these families would ever have to work again. The interest alone would make them very well off by Surjuga's [name of

expenditures.‡ Governments generally justify regulation by citing public good, but rarely acknowledge its side effects.

Real Costs

A central tenet of the model I am about to outline is a vastly expanded definition of wealth. In India, the poor are actually rich in natural assets such as mineral resources, forests, watersheds and biodiversity zones. Poverty is partly a result of these assets not being valued, as well as the non-existent or limited opportunities for trading these assets.

Just examine the geography of 'poverty' in India for a moment. The maps in Appendix 2 show that many of India's poorest citizens live in its richest ecosystems.

A system that values all environmental assets will show that the poor are not so impoverished after all and the resources of the rich are overvalued. We live in a topsy-turvy world where we rarely pay the true price of anything. Costs are either externalized or subsidized. Take the example of suburbia, a subsidized community in the US. The United States government pays for the construction of most roads, thus removing a major cost hurdle to the development of suburban sprawl. By its spread and low density, suburbia makes effective public transport difficult and expensive, so private automobiles become the only way for suburban populations to remain mobile. Every public service—from sewage lines to mail routes—becomes more inefficient because the lack

---

the area] standards. Meanwhile the rip-offs continue. While we are in Rachketha, a local advocate tells the NGO activist: "In this year's drought, all I did was sub-contract one small dam. I bought a scooter [two wheeler]. If there is drought next year, I shall buy a jeep." *Nobody thought of asking Ramdas what he really needed, what his problems were, or involving him in the solution. Instead, in his name, they built a road he does not use, at a cost of Rs 17.44 lakhs.* "Please do something about my water problem, sir," says Ramdas Korwa as we set off across the plain, journeying two kilometers to his road to nowhere', pp. 13–14 (emphasis added).

of density imposes a cost. Governments obscure this cost by paying for these services rather than passing the costs on to those who benefit from this subsidy—suburban residents.[2]

Ignoring hidden costs reduces incentives for efficiency. Just as I would not spend hours searching for a product online if it were only a few cents cheaper, why would my business spend time and money pioneering a new, greener product, if I will make a small saving? Today, it is simply not worth investing in efficiency, as the two following examples illustrate:

(a) Fuel is heavily subsidized and we only pay a fraction of its real cost.[3] A system of real costing would result in greater energy efficiency. Skyrocketing fuel prices following the oil shock of the 1970s suddenly produced huge efficiency incentives for manufacturers. Japanese automakers revolutionized car manufacturing. The large vehicles of the 1950s and 1960s were replaced by far more compact and energy-efficient models. However, once oil prices stabilized and fell, the efficiency incentive evaporated, and efficiency dropped in the 1990s.[4]

(b) Large subsidies mean that airlines do not have to pay the entire cost of the fuel they consume. Thus they have had limited incentives to make their engines more efficient. Take the example of Boeing. Over a period of forty years, the company produced new models of large planes with small increases in fuel efficiency of roughly 10 or 15 per cent each time.* However, there is evidence that they had the technology to facilitate the equivalent total increase in efficiency in fifteen years.[5] They did not use the technology because the economic benefit of efficiency was not accurately priced.

A system of real costing will result in real benefits by creating huge efficiency incentives. This system requires local control over local resources in order to tap into the expertise local residents

*Namely, models 707, 747, 777 and 787.

have about their environment. Take the example of a group of leather tanners I worked with. They belonged to the lowest rung of the caste system and had received no formal education.* Yet, they had detailed knowledge about using local vegetables and minerals (as opposed to toxic chemicals) to tan and dye leather without damaging the environment. A system of real costing would value this form of localized knowledge, which can be found across the world and use it before it is lost forever.

If we remove the invisible subsidies and reveal hidden assets, our assumptions about the wealth of communities will change dramatically. Sewari, the poor rural village, can now trade its huge surplus of drinking water, biodiversity and potential for forest cover, whereas the wealthy urban colony of Panchsheel would be forced to buy basic services.

The Regulation Addiction

The Government of India regulates business to debilitating levels.[†] Having run a retail business, Fabindia, in India for the last ten years, I have had an intimate window into the effects of constant regulatory interventions. While the government's intentions are almost always laudable, the distortions that these interventions create have consequences that the regulators fail to imagine. They ensure that people like me spend 80 per cent of our time trying to operate lawfully within the regulatory environment, which the regulators make more complex every year. The thicket of legal and statutory compliances required of a business like Fabindia is as follows:

- Central Excise/Customs
- Central Sales Tax Act

*Dalits, or those in the 'untouchable' castes, are divided into separate subgroups with tanners as the lowest of the low due to the perceived 'impurity' of their occupation, which requires them to work with cow hides.
[†]As evidence, those sectors left relatively untouched by government, such as IT, show rapid growth rates.

- Companies Act, 1956
- Competition Act
- Contract Labour Regulation Act
- Copyright Act
- Currency Withdrawal Tax Act
- Design Act
- Drugs and Cosmetics Act
- Employees State Insurance Act
- Fringe Benefit Tax
- Food Laws
- Income Tax Act, 1961
- Minimum Wages Act
- Packaged Commodities Order
- Payment of Bonus Act
- Payment of Gratuity Act
- Payment of Wages Act
- Provident Fund/ Miscellaneous Provision
- Rent Control Act
- Service Tax Act
- Stamp Duty Act
- Standards of Weights and Measure
- Trade and Merchandise Act
- Trade Tax Act
- Value Added Tax (VAT) Act
- Works Act

Every line in this list can result in an enormous headache for anyone trying to do business in India. The Indian Companies Act, with 651 sections, is one of the largest and most complex laws of its kind in the world.[6] This complexity imposes enormous costs for the businesses and entrepreneurs who drive prosperity.*

*India's tax policy and compliance requirements were criticized by none other than the former governor of the Reserve Bank, finance secretary and economic advisor to the prime minister, Bimal Jalan, in his book *India's Economic Policy: Preparing for the Twenty-First Century* (New Delhi: Penguin Viking, 1997), pp. 46–67.

Businesses often have to choose between survival and compliance. If the legal burden is too great, citizens begin breaking laws and new legislation only exacerbates the problem. Honesty in business is punished. The World Bank ranks India 134th out of 175 economies on a variety of indicators that index the ease of operating a private business.[7] It is no surprise then that activities get driven underground into the informal economy.[8] And, no wonder, the government has little legitimacy and citizens have little respect for their laws.

To make matters worse, regulations are often exploited by the affluent to increase their wealth further. An extreme example of this is what I call 'manipulated asset classes', referring to assets that increase substantially in value with a small change in regulations. Take the example of land use classification. A decade ago, some friends bought agricultural land on the outskirts of Delhi for about US$7500 an acre as an investment. Today the land is worth US$75,000 an acre. There are certain developers, however, who have the 'ability' to dramatically increase the land's value, by changing its classification from 'agricultural' to 'urban'. With that manipulation the land is suddenly worth US$2 million an acre. Then there are the 'super-developers' who can also change the classification of Floor Area Ratios so they can get another massive premium on the same asset.* The government says that this regulation is meant to help the general population, but it results in filling up the coffers of the elite. Many among the richest in India owe their spectacular wealth to their ability to own or develop these 'manipulated assets'.

Such asset manipulation flourishes in areas under communist rule in India. Many Indian communist leaders espouse, with good

*Floor Area Ratio (FAR) represents the ratio of total floor area of a given building to the size of the land on which it is built. Municipal authorities impose limits or ceilings on FARs to ensure that developers do not build floor space beyond permitted level. However, the biggest players in the development sector continually lobby for relaxation of FAR limits. For example, the Confederation of Real Estate Developer's Associations of India proposed that the government increase the limits in January 2008 in order to enable greater profits for private developers.

intention, policies that have severely limited the market's ability to respond to growing demand. Here governments often create shortages by limiting the possibilities of ownership. Those who already own assets benefit hugely as there is little competition. Everyone else loses out; quality is low, prices are high and there is no opportunity for anyone other than the elite, who already own assets, to enter the marketplace. The communist leadership then makes this an election issue by railing against the wealthy, a group that benefits greatly from their policies.

The New Economic System

A new economic system needs to replace the present system to ensure rapid and environmentally sustainable growth. The first step would be to bring many assets that are currently invisible into the fold of the market. These assets would then be categorized by a Standards Authority and traded through a system of exchanges, with a regulator to oversee the process. The National Exchanges would provide the marketplace for everything from water to wheat to education, while the Standards Authorities would inform the public about the quality of goods or services being provided.

In short, the prerequisites for a 'true' market are:
a. Oversight by government
b. Standards Authority
c. System of exchanges
d. The regulator

a. Oversight by government

For the proposed model to work, the government must change its activities from regulation to oversight. Today, the Indian government is both umpire and batsman. No sport would allow a referee to be a player, so why should we allow our government to get away with this? It is one of the worst legacies of socialist

India that the government is able to distort markets by constantly creating new rules, often to benefit its own interests. Take the example of the civil aviation ministry intervening to protect the state-owned airline, Air India. In 1994, it broke the public sector monopoly on overseas carriers, allowing private airlines into the market. But crucially, it kept the highly profitable Gulf routes for itself, denying lower fares to the thousands of ordinary Indians who travel to the Gulf countries.[9] This intervention, which benefited a couple of carriers, has been bad for customers, bad for the airline industry and bad for the economy.

b. Standards Authority

Information is the key to an individual's ability to successfully participate in a market. Each Standards Authority would ensure that all market players have close to 'perfect' information. Standards would codify assets such as air quality, water purity and biodiversity into measurable, and therefore tradable, quantities. Standards ensure uniformity in quality assessment, a prerequisite for the tradability of a commodity. Take the example of water. The Standards Authority would measure and rate the quality of drinking water. With this information it would become possible to trade the potability of drinking water on the Exchanges. The same logic would apply to all goods and services from health care and legal services to wheat and rice.

The Standards Authorities would create classification systems for assets that signal price. Imagine yourself to be a buyer who seriously questions the quality of the service you are buying. Uncertainty about quality indicates that it is unlikely that you will agree on a price with the seller. A system of standards will eliminate much of this uncertainty and encourage exchange.

A separate Standards Authority will be necessary for each major sector. The staffing, management and efficiency as well as oversight and public safeguards for the Standards Authority and its subdivisions will be laid down in chapter 6. Without effective standards it is not possible to know about the quality of water a community is trading on the Exchange, or the quality of education a particular school is providing. The same logic applies to health care, sanitation, forest cover and legal services.

The example of the Apgar Score, which rates the conditions of babies at birth on a scale of one to ten, is illustrative of my point.[10] It was invented by Dr Virginia Apgar, one of the first women to be admitted to the surgical residency at Columbia University's College of Physicians and Surgeons. She was appalled at the care that many newborns received. But as a woman in a man's world, and one who was not an obstetrician, she did not have the authority to challenge conventions. Instead, she developed a rating system. An infant got two points for crying, two for moving all four limbs, two if it was pink all over, and so on. This caused a revolution in neo-natal care. An intangible and vague entity—the condition of newborns—was converted into numbers that people could collect and compare. Virtually every child born in a hospital came to have an Apgar Score recorded at one and five minutes after birth. Competitive doctors wanted to produce better scores, and it soon became apparent that a baby with a low Apgar at one minute could be resuscitated to have an excellent score at five minutes. This meant that neonatal intensive care units developed in addition to changing how childbirth itself was managed. The results have been dramatic. From 1915 to 1997, the infant mortality rate declined by more than 90 per cent and maternal mortality rate by almost 99 per cent.[11] There is no better example of the positive effects of standards.*

c. System of exchanges

The establishment of credible standards ensures smooth and easy trade. An exchange is a marketplace where goods and services are

*This positive trend is clearly not attributable to the Apgar test alone. Increased hygiene, use of antibiotics, availability of medication and immunization have all had an important role to play.

bought and sold. Each sector would have its own exchange, similar to current stock exchanges, complete with brokers in front of television screens. Information is the currency of exchange, and, provided it is backed by great volumes of transactions, it enjoys a legitimacy that no other mechanism can provide. EBay is a type of an electronic exchange, as are the carbon credit trading systems and all stock markets. Similarly, a Railway Exchange, a Water Exchange, a Power Exchange and even a Hazardous Waste Exchange can be set up.

Technology has provided us with all the tools necessary to ensure that the work of the exchange can be widely communicated so that 'pockets of distortions' are eliminated. I have learnt a lot from my investment banker friends about the 'price discovery mechanism': the more public a transaction is, the more accurately it gauges price and the more widely accepted that price is. Open public exchanges create widespread demand, due to the confidence felt by prospective buyers about the price. The reason global stock markets have become the principal sources of capital is that they bring together millions of potential investors, thereby creating both a depth of demand and a high degree of liquidity. The more the number of buyers, the more accurate the price is. No other method produces prices that have the same degree of legitimacy. Any restriction on buyers or information, such as lack of transparency or communication, will ultimately limit the accuracy of prices.

For instance, when I was setting up a leather workers and weavers cooperative in Rajasthan in the late 1980s, I realized that the traders were making a huge profit by buying low from the artisans in their guilds and selling high to retail consumers. I tried to enter the market by offering a much higher price for the leather goods in one village, expecting the best leather workers to come and join us. This did not happen though. The traders hid this information from their guild members. A visiting economist and friend suggested I advertise my rate on a billboard on the main road, thus communicating this information widely.

The exchanges I have envisaged deal with two types of goods:

1. Apportionable entities such as water, electricity, solid waste, bandwidth, that can be measured (in litres, kilowatts, cubic metres and megahertz and so on) and physically transferred from buyer to seller.

2. Entities such as clean air, forest cover and biodiversity cover, which are calculated as aggregates and therefore better traded on the basis of per capita amounts rather than priced as discrete units. These per capita amounts would be 'bought' for each citizen by his or her community, an idea that I shall explain in detail in chapter 4.

d. The regulator

Though the well-managed Standards and Exchanges would function as autonomous bodies, there would be a need for a vigilance mechanism. The regulator would be an organization with its own division in the National Exchanges and would be critical to their smooth and fair operation. Mostly invisible, it would act as a watchdog, monitoring the ownership of goods and service providers. The regulator would only become active if competition reduced the number of independent operators below a defined threshold, or there appeared to be some form of collusion between bidders either during the auction or while operating services. The actions of the regulator could lead to severe distortions, which is why it would only act in instances of a violation that materially prevented the market from functioning in an 'uninfluenced' manner. Any evidence of price fixing or monopoly* will prompt the regulator to serve notice to the firms concerned to either disband or sell stakes or companies, to reduce or eliminate the concentration of ownership in a particular area.

*While it may vary in certain cases, no one entity of ownership should control either directly or indirectly more than 50 per cent of the goods and services provided in a particular field.

In chapter 6, I shall outline a system of reforms that would result in the transparent ownership of organizations. With the transparency provided by the exchanges it would be much easier for the regulator to monitor prices and measure the effects of alliances on the price of services offered.

The Indian government already has regulators in some areas such as insurance, electricity generation and telecommunications. But the absence of adequate standards and public exchanges means that the regulator cannot function effectively. Take the instance of the telecommunications regulator in a recent case where the defence forces made an extra spectrum for mobile communications available to the government. The regulator, instead of acting as a referee, became an active player and a power broker.[12] This could result in an oligopoly in what is currently an extraordinarily competitive sector.[13] As I write about this, a court judgement is pending on this issue as a group of providers has challenged the grounds on which the spectrum was allocated. This situation highlights the vital importance of an impartial regulator.

Environmental Protection

The introduction of an all-encompassing market will force the issue of the hidden cost of environmental degradation out of the closet and exert its true cost on the economy. Organizations would no longer be able to externalize environmental and social costs. The system of Standards Authorities and Exchanges would make it much easier to trade natural assets such as clean air and water. In all cases, the Standards Authorities would firstly create a rating system for all assets. For example, with forest cover this could be in terms of density, type of trees or amount of coverage, and so on. These assets could then be exchanged.

Water is another such instance. The community of Sewari has a big reservoir that provides a large surplus of water for its small population. The reservoir is poorly maintained and thousands of litres of water are lost annually due to leakages and siltation. Under this new system, water will suddenly become an asset. The growing cities will become increasingly thirsty and will need to buy water on the National Water Exchange. Sewari will have an incentive to manage its water more efficiently in order to have more to sell on the Exchange. The community of Panchsheel in Delhi will suddenly find that it has to pay a lot more for its water. This could lead to a reduction in consumption. Panchsheel may decide it wants to take advantage of the monsoon rains to reduce water costs and so build an efficient water harvesting system or a grey water processing system.*

Biodiversity and Forests

Left to itself the new free market will not include all natural assets within its apparatus.

Though biodiversity and forest cover are not part of our daily lives—in the sense that they are not user assets—they are vital to our survival as a species.† We need a specific financial instrument to include them in the market: the Environmental Per Capita Quota (EPCQ).

---

*Grey water is waste water generated from activities like dishwashing, laundry and bathing. It is low on nitrogen, pathogens and easy to decompose. One way of recycling grey water is through reed beds or a planted filter where waste water is passed through a sand bed containing plant species such as bamboo, canna and reeds. The roots of these plants utilize the nutrients present in waste water, reducing its biological oxygen demand (BOD) and chemical oxygen demand (COD). The sand bed further purifies the water which could be reused in toilets and for gardening.

†Protecting biospheres is not just an ethical and economic imperative; it may also decide our fate as living beings. Losses of insects, spiders, fungi, annelids—each unique in its own way—spell tragedies for ecologists. But for humanity at large losing a species that may contain genetic information useful to us—an Amazon rainforest plant for a crucial medicine or an Asian leaf mould for a new antibiotic— can be a very big loss. As William W. Murdoch points out: 'Unfortunately, such genetic material, once lost, can never be reconstituted.' See Murdoch, The Poverty of Nations (Baltimore: Johns Hopkins University Press, 1980), p. 290.

The system would operate at the community level. Every citizen would be registered for the EPCQ at birth. Every community would be obliged to have sufficient EPC credits for all its members. Communities with surplus forestry or biodiversity credits would sell them to those who lack them. The Standards Authority would determine the price per unit and ratings system. The management of these assets at the community level is outlined in chapter 8.

For example, a rural community that includes forested land or a rich local biosphere would have sufficient per capita credits for its members and would be able to sell surplus units. However, an urban community may not have any EPC credits and so would have to buy these from others who do. Panchsheel is a community that would need to buy almost all its forest cover and biosphere credits from the Exchange. The Exchange would only trade surpluses of communities such as Mussoorie which would have more forest area per capita than it needs or Sewari which has more of both forest and biosphere area. EPCs would allow rural communities to benefit from their local resources without depleting them.

As the price for forest cover increases, due to deforestation, the Exchanges would signal to all that there are profits to be made. This would inevitably result in communities and businesses making investments in the following:

- Upgrading their forest cover or natural zones so that they qualify as biospheres;
- Increasing the area of existing biospheres;
- Starting the process of reviving biospheres such as India's extensive grasslands and wetlands, which are being rapidly destroyed.

Such a system would incentivize reforestation and biodiversity conservation, both in urban and rural areas. It would also change the balance of wealth, with rural communities able to profit from their abundant natural resources without depleting them. Today, because communities rarely benefit from protected biospheres, protecting the environment is often at odds with supporting the local economy. The Bharatpur Bird Sanctuary in Rajasthan was once famous all over the world, and housed species from as far afield as Afghanistan, Tibet and Central Asia. On trips to the sanctuary as a child, I would be amazed at the number of birds. I have vivid memories of colours and sounds of the thousands of species that made the sanctuary their home. On my last trip a few years ago, it was clear that the sanctuary was dying. Today, UNESCO is threatening to withdraw its recognition of the site due to shortage of birds.[14] In 2006, migratory birds were down to 100 compared to 10,000 the previous year.[15] While this is in part due to drought, local farmers are also known to divert water from the sanctuary for irrigating their crops. As long as environmental assets are not accounted for and managed by local communities, such stories will continue to be common.

Waste

With consumption as the sine qua non to economic health in the developing world, we risk drowning in our own garbage.[16] As I outlined in chapter 1, our globe cannot support a situation where India and China follow the West's path to affluence. A consumption-driven model of growth within the current economic system is simply not an option. Instead, I suggest that by accurately calculating disposal costs, consumption can be reduced and rapid economic growth stimulated through the creation of a large new area of economic activities—disposal industries.

In the current system, the disposal cost of a product is not built into its price. If I buy a pair of shoes, I am not paying for the cost of biodegrading them. Excluding disposal costs from the market has produced a world where we are creating dangerous quantities of waste and encouraging excessive consumption through artificially low prices. In the following model the producer would pay for the disposal.[17] This system would have a raft of environmental benefits. Industries would rapidly invest in making more biodegradable products, once they have to bear the disposal costs. Higher prices would also mean that consumers would buy the cheaper, environment-friendly products, buy less and use products for longer durations. Furthermore, a huge recycling industry would be generated, as any company that can reuse waste products would make large profits.

In this new model, the disposal cost of every product would be assessed and graded by the Standards Authority. The resulting rating would be marked on the product.[18] The manufacturer would include this cost in the price of the commodity. While the price of a notebook with a plastic cover and PVC* ring binder would shoot up, a paper and cardboard one would only be slightly more expensive. When I am done with my notebook, I would contact an authorized disposal company. Recycling incentives, such as the ones currently in place in some states in the US, where glass bottles and aluminium cans have a return value, would encourage the consumer to return the product.

The disposal company would, in turn, return the Radio Frequency Identification (RFID) disposal voucher to the manufacturer who would reimburse them with the disposal credit. The company would then use this money to dispose the product. If the disposal company developed efficient degrading methods, it would be able to use the savings as profit. Let us take the example of an US$80 pair of sneakers for which the disposal cost has been rated as US$200. The consumer now pays US$300 for the shoes. When they are worn out, the consumer contacts the disposal company who collects the sneakers, returning US$20 to the consumer for doing so. The disposal company then presents the RFID voucher to the sneaker company, who are obliged to pay US$200. The disposal company in turn pays a recycling company US$180 to

---

*Attempts to dispose of polyvinyl chloride (PVC) release dioxin, one of the most toxic compounds ever developed, into the atmosphere. As a persistent organic pollutant, dioxin endures a long time in the body due to its chemical stability and ability to be absorbed by fat tissues. Exposure to it in minute quantities can cause cancer, brain haemorrhage and serious health problems.

take the waste. Thus it makes US$20 on each pair of sneakers. However, the profit does not end there. This particular recycling company specializes in reusing some of the material creating new products, and so is a double winner. In addition to being paid for the raw materials (the old sneakers), it makes a new product to sell. Such a system would generate large dismantling, recycling and disposal industries. Any waste that cannot be decomposed or reused would be sold on the Waste Exchange.*

Traceability is the key to this process so that manufacturers can be linked to the product in order for it to be able to travel along its return pathway. Take the example of the computer I use.†
When it needs replacing, it would either be shipped back to its manufacturer in China, or disposed of locally using the disposal voucher. The non-recyclable elements of the computer would be the producer's responsibility. The producer would either have to pay for them or sell them as waste on the Exchange.

India's poor would be the greatest beneficiaries of my proposals. In many ways these people are the richest in the country in terms of natural resources and biodiversity, but they are the poorest of the poor in terms of income. The mechanisms of Standards, Exchanges and correct apportioning of the costs, and pricing of benefits would suddenly create large new areas of wealth where previously none existed. In the next chapter, I suggest a way of increasing wealth while simultaneously improving the quality of basic services and enriching the environment that will end the misery of the poor in India.

---

*As technologies change, there would need to be a system for adjusting the disposal cost rating.

†Laptops and desktop computers contain toxic elements like lead, chromium, mercury, cadmium and polybrominated flame retardants. These are persistent bioaccumulative toxins (PBTs), which linger in the environment and settle in living tissue, posing severe health risks like cancer, nerve damage, and reproductive disorders. PBTs, like dioxin, increase in concentration as they move up the food chain and reach dangerous levels in living creatures, even when released in minute quantities.

Notes

1. Recent predictions indicate that the total tax burden on companies is likely to exceed 40 per cent in India, compared with a global average corporate tax rate of 27 per cent. See Gaurav Taneja, 'What Constitute the Essential Ingredients of a Good Tax Regime?' *Mint*, 23 February 2008.

2. The suburbia model, however, is being replicated across the world and this has got global urban planners worried. Haya El Nasser, 'Modern Suburbia Not Just in America Anymore', *USA Today*, 15 April 2008. Available online at http://www.usatoday.com/news/world/2008–04–15-suburbia_N.htm.

3. The true cost of oil includes the huge costs associated with climate change, which could rise to at least 5 per cent of global GDP each year, and if more dramatic predictions come to pass, the cost could be more than 20 per cent of GDP; geopolitical costs of securing access to oil, including military expenditure, loss of human life and all the other costs associated with war. (To give an idea of the cost of war, the US is spending US$16bn a month on running costs alone in Iraq and Afghanistan. That is the entire annual budget of the UN.) There are health costs in the form of diseases such as asthma and cancer that result from the petroleum industry. The costs of extraction and transportation on the environment is huge, and include the impact of oil spills (in addition to large and high profile spills such as the Exxon Valdez disaster, small spills are a normal part of shipping oil). Between 1984 and 1990, over 6 per cent of petrol transported by sea was spilled. See Nicholas Stern, *The Economics of Climate Change* (Cambridge: Cambridge University Press, 2006); Joseph Stiglitz and Linda J. Bilmes, *The Three Trillion Dollar War* (London: Allen Lane, 2008) and Terri Tamminen, *Lives Per Gallon: The True Cost of Our Oil Addiction* (Washington DC: Island Press, 2006).

4. Robert J. Samuelson, 'Cheap Gas is a Bad Habit', *The Washington Post*, 14 September 2005.

5. See John Newhouse, *Boeing versus Airbus: The Inside Story of the Greatest International Competition in Business* (New York: Vintage Books, 2007).

6. See http://www.companylawinfo.com/colawinfosite/statutes/ comp_act56_amendments/index.shtml for full text of the Act.

7. The World Bank Group, *Doing Business Report 2007*, p. 70.

8. The Peruvian economist Hernando De Soto, giving a vivid example of what he calls 'the obstacles to legality', attempted to open a tiny garment factory in Lima, Peru—a byzantine procedure that ultimately required thirty-one times the average Peruvian monthly wage and 289 days. Hernando De Soto, *The Mystery of Capital* (London: Bantam Press, 2000), p. 15.

9. See the article 'Fly in their ointment', *The Indian Express*, 30 August 2007.

10. This example is taken from Atul Gawande, *Better: A Surgeon's Notes on Performance* (New Delhi: Penguin India, 2007), pp. 146–48.

11. This maternal mortality rate is for the period 1990 to 1997. D.L. Hoyert, K.D. Kochanek, S.L. Murphy. *Deaths: Final Data for 1997* (Hyattsville, Maryland: US Department of Health and Human Services, CDC, National Centre for Health Statistics, 1999). See also, *National Vital Statistics Report*, vol. 47, no. 20.

12. Commenting upon the trap that the regulators of liberal democracies find themselves in, the economist Swaminathan S. Anklesaria Aiyar writes, 'Thousands of years ago Plato argued for the appointment of noble guardians to uphold laws and norms. But the question, who will guard the guardians remains unanswered till today.' See 'Regulate the Regulators to Ensure Higher Standards', *The Economic Times*, 13 February 2008.

13. India is currently home to the world's lowest mobile phone rates as a result of such competition. See A.S. Prashar, 'Mobile Telephony Price War Hots Up', *The Tribune*, 1 January, 2003.

14. 'Bharatpur Bird Sanctuary May Lose UNESCO Recognition', *The Times of India*, 13 March 2008.

15. Narayan Bareth, 'Drought hits India Bird Reserve', *BBC News Online*, 4 January 2007.

16. The well-known US 'garbologist' Dr William Rathje, claims that our current waste disposal system of well-designed and managed landfills actually 'preserve their contents for posterity [rather] than . . . transform them into humus or mulch . . . The garbage stays where it has been dumped, tightly compacted, but largely

intact.' See Rathje, *Rubbish! The Archaeology of Garbage* (New York: HarperCollins, 2001), pp. 112, 117.

17. This concept is expressed in the notion of Extended Producer Responsibility (EPR), which promotes the integration of environmental costs associated with products throughout their life cycles into their market price. For more details see OECD, *Extended Producer Responsibility: A Guidance Manual for Governments* (Paris: OECD, 2001).

18. This will be done with Radio Frequency Identification (RFID) tags. These can be applied to or incorporated into a product for the purpose of identification using radio waves. They have numerous functions; of interest here is their role in tracking products, ranging from cattle to clothing. For example, the Canadian Cattle Identification Agency uses RFID tags as a replacement for barcode tags. The tags are required to identify a bovine's herd of origin and this is used for tracing when a packing plant condemns a carcass. For more information, see http://www.canadaid.ca/.

3

Ending Poverty

People do not strive, generation after generation, century after century, against circumstances that are so constituted as to defeat them. They accept. Nor is such acceptance a sign of weakness of character. Rather, it is a profoundly rational response. Given the formidable hold of the equilibrium of poverty within which they live, accommodation is the optimal solution. Poverty is cruel. A continuing struggle to escape that is continuously frustrated is even more cruel. It is more civilized, more intelligent, as well as more plausible that people, out of the experience of centuries, should reconcile themselves to what has for so long been the inevitable.

John Kenneth Galbraith, *The Nature of Mass Poverty*

A lmost 80 per cent of Indians live on US$2 a day.[1] My sole purpose in writing this book is to reduce poverty. Today, rather than helping the poor, the Indian government has dealt a double whammy by hindering growth through heavy taxation and then squandering the resulting income through criminally inefficient expenditure. In the previous chapter, I discussed the importance of 'true' markets and the ways of building one. This by itself would transform the lives of the poor by recognizing their hidden assets. But this is not enough. In this chapter I shall introduce three key ideas:

Epigraph: John Kenneth Galbraith, *The Nature of Mass Poverty* (Cambridge, MA: Harvard University Press, 1979), pp. 62–63.

- A ground-breaking system of Targeted Catalysts (TCs) in which the very process of eradicating poverty will build quality public services;
- An economy where cash is dematerialized;
- Tax reforms designed to accelerate growth and reduce inequality without penalizing productive activity.

I use financial projections to show that these ideas are financially viable. The proposed tax reforms would actually *double* revenue from taxation, despite eliminating all taxes on productive activity and income. The proposed Targeted Catalyst scheme demonstrates that dramatically reducing poverty in India is within our reach. Another India is possible.

Expenditure

The problems with the current model

India's Union and state governments continually fail to alleviate poverty even though they allocate substantial portions of their budget to this cause. Most development schemes are poorly targeted; like using a hammer where a toothpick is needed, the chosen tool is not only too expensive, but also ineffective. On the basis of my reading in development studies, as well as my travels and discussions with local residents about projects in their communities, I have identified five main 'evaporators' of public money:

1. Scattergun approach: Aid is distributed widely as a temporary, stop-gap measure instead of targeting at those who need it. This is equivalent to growing a tree in an arid desert and pouring a bucket of water over it, thereby losing much of the water. A 'targeted' drip irrigation system would use the same amount of water much more efficiently, enabling the tree to thrive.
2. Overkill: Often, aid exceeds the local economy's ability to absorb it in accordance with the prescribed purposes and/or time frame.[2]
3. Planning blindness: The development project is conceived with little or no reference to the needs of the local community.

4. Outsider bias: Outsiders overspend on a project of questionable quality when the local community could accomplish the same task at a much lower cost.

5. Patronage: A project is mismanaged by groups that have mastered the patronage game and make a lucrative business through poor execution. The writer P. Sainath put it well when he titled his trenchant study of government aid to India's poor in *Everyone Loves a Good Drought*.[3]

India is littered with the skeletons of wasted government money. The efficiency ratio of government expenditure is abysmal. To get the effect of Re 1, government may have to spend thirty, fifty or even eighty rupees. Rahul Gandhi* recently stated that only 5 per cent of government spending reaches its intended recipients.[4] Because there is an efficiency ratio of 20:1, every Rs 20 spent, has the 'effect' of Re 1. In cases when government-sanctioned projects are paid for but never actualized, this figure is zero. The Fabindia School in Rajasthan partnered with the local government to split the cost of building its road. Both partners paid a contractor nominated by the local government. The contractor was well entrenched with local politicians and bureaucrats, and simply took the money and never did anything. Despite our protests, nothing happened. A local resident advised me that the only solution was to hire someone to physically threaten him. I refused. The road never got built and the school lost its money.†

As I write this, stories about disastrous development projects cry out from the front pages of Indian newspapers. Take the example of the government's flagship drinking water scheme, which

---

*Rahul Gandhi, member of Parliament, is the son of the late former prime minister Rajiv Gandhi and the current president of the Congress party, Sonia Gandhi.
†The road was finally built in March 2008 after local people, who had bought land speculatively along the proposed road, 'pressured' the absconding contractor into finishing the job. However, the resulting road is so shoddy that it probably will not last one monsoon.

has been panned by its own watchdog. It is fraught with diversion of funds, epic corruption and waste. In Punjab, Rs 10 million (US$250,094) was spent on fictitious works. In Madhya Pradesh, Rs 38.5 million (US$962,860) was spent on the construction of 705 tube wells in an area that already has sufficient drinking water when many other areas lack such infrastructure. In Arunachal Pradesh, Rs 23.5 million (US$587,720) was spent on projects in uninhabited or non-existent villages. The list goes on. Money is often spent at the behest of influential politicians involved in pork barrel politics, instead of responding to the villagers' needs. With over half of India's rural habitations without access to clean water, such corruption and inefficiency are quite literally, deadly.[5]

Take the following two examples, one from Rajasthan and one from the North-east. Just outside my farm in Rajasthan lie the ruins of a small dam. As part of a drought relief project, the government sanctioned funds for this dam on a river that only flows during the rainy season. While the dam would be useful, it was low on the villagers' list of priorities. The government built the dam anyway and poorly at that: at the wrong place and too short in length. It was useless. As a result of the contracting lobby, the government sanctioned another dam. This time, while the wall was the right length, substandard material was used. When I visited the project during construction and happened to lean against the foundation, it literally crumbled apart. The contractor's foreman, while helping me to my feet, pointed out that the shoddy foundation would be hidden from view once the earth had been put back in place. But not even the banks were adequately strengthened. They eroded soon after the first rains and the water just flowed around the dam. Today, after the expenditure of millions of rupees of public money, all that remains is a pile of rubble.

My friend, the late Sanjoy Ghose,[6] who worked with grass-roots organizations and was a crusader against corruption and an advocate of giving local communities a say in their governance, gave another example of how often money for the poor simply did not reach them:

One of the local boys said there was a method in [how the government went about] building embankments [for erosion control along the Brahmaputra River]. They would start long before the rainy season, but would be unable to finish in time. One flood would wash it all away, and the damage would mean a net profit for the engineers and the contractors involved in the project, because there would be nothing to show afterwards, and the money could be distributed around.[7]

The story of welfare in India is a story of abuse.* All this waste is paid for by taxes levied on productive activity. It is depressing to see hard-earned money literally evaporate, as it gets wasted on ill-planned projects, is siphoned off or simply used to fund the vast, cumbersome bureaucracy that is the Government of India. I believe that if local communities administered their own funds, they would increase efficiency tremendously.

This is not to say the state has no role in eliminating poverty. On the contrary, poverty reduction requires intervention by the state. It is the quality, cost and type of intervention that must change. In the following section, I introduce a new system of welfare that will eliminate the 'evaporators' listed above.

*For a poor country, it is important for India to remember the unintended consequences of aid. Graham Hancock warns in the context of international aid business: 'It [aid] is often profoundly dangerous to the poor and inimical to their interests: it has financed the creation of monstrous projects that, at vast expense, have devastated the environment and ruined lives; it has supported and legitimized brutal tyrannies; it has facilitated the emergence of fantastical and Byzantine bureaucracies staffed by legions of self-serving hypocrites; it has sapped the initiative, creativity and enterprise of ordinary people . . . it has sucked potential entrepreneurs and intellectuals in the developing countries into non-productive administrative activities; it has created a "moral tone" in international affairs that denies the hard task of wealth creation and substitutes easy handouts for the rigours of self-help; in addition, throughout the Third World, it has allowed the dead grip of imposed officialdom to suppress popular choice and individual freedom.' Lords of Poverty (New York: The Atlantic Monthly Press, 1989), p. 189.

The Solution: Targeted Catalysts

I believe that the process of alleviating poverty could itself build quality public services. Imagine a situation whereby when an individual's income falls below a certain level and he or she automatically receives credits to be used against six essential

Table 3.1: Components of a Targeted Catalyst

Voucher Type	Eligible to Purchase	Approximate Amount*
Nutrition	Fixed nutrition supplement	2000kcal/day per capita
Drinking water	Grade 1 drinking water	4.5 litres a day per capita[†]
Sewage disposal	Grade 2 potable water	130.5 litres per day in urban areas, and 35.5 litres a day in rural areas per household[‡]
Education	Median voucher for education	Full-time education from kindergarten through advanced degrees at the university level
Health care	Median voucher for health care services or insurance	To pay the premium on a basic insurance coverage for major medical with a small excess and a low deductible
Legal assistance	Median voucher for purchasing legal services	To pay for legal services provided by a registered member of the bar for preparing contracts and enforcing rights. They can be pooled in the case of class action suits[§]

*Standards taken from UN Millennium Development Goals.

[†] This is the World Health Organization-recommended daily amount for manual labour in high temperatures. See www.water.org.uk/home/water-for-health/medical-facts/adults.

[‡] Central Public Health Engineering Environment Organization, Government of India.

[§] This is when a lawsuit is brought by one party on behalf of a group of individuals all having the same grievance.

services: nutrition, drinking water, sewage disposal, education, health care and legal assistance (Table 3.1).* Then imagine that every service provider has a rating. The better the rating, the more the service provider will receive from the local government in return for the 'voucher' presented. This is the crux of the dual-pronged Targeted Catalyst concept: alleviating poverty by providing a booster shot of essential services to those in need, and building quality public services by ensuring that the better the service provider the more each TC is worth when they cash it in.

It is important to remember that TCs would be used in the context of the system of standards, exchanges and regulators described in the last chapter. The Standards Authorities would rate all service providers and make that information publicly available. Individuals would then be able to choose their service provider based on this rating. They could literally go online, look at all the schools in their area and pick the one with the highest rating. This allows every citizen to know the relative quality of what they are getting. For example, they can purchase drinking water over potable water, A-grade health care over B-grade health care and so on.

Someone with a TC could go to any service provider and get the same quantity of the service. The education voucher would give the recipient, say, one term at any school. However, the better their rating, the more money the school will receive from the community government† for that voucher. This signals to the provider that investment to improve the quality of their service will be rewarded. Rural schools will improve, good lawyers will set up practice in these communities and primary health centres would offer quality health care.

Table 3.2 illustrates this principle, showing the amount of money different grades of service providers would receive in exchange for a TC voucher. Remember that the holder of the TC will be able to purchase the *same quantity* of service from each

---

*This addresses the five components of poverty outlined in Chapter 1.
†The system of community government is outlined in the following chapter.

Table 3.2: Grades of payment to service providers

| | Level of Service (as certified by the Standards Authority) | | | | |
	Poor	Average	Median	Good	Outstanding
Value of Rs 100 voucher	Rs 70	Rs 85	Rs 100	Rs 200	Rs 300

provider. Naturally, they will use this with the highest level of service provider available, driving up standards.

This provides an enormous incentive for the service provider to improve their standards ranking as with each improvement their income grows substantially.

The scheme works a little like converting foreign exchange when you travel. So if you go to Europe your US$1 face value buys you a certain amount of Euros depending on the rate of exchange. The rating a service provider carries is similar to the exchange rate:

Voucher x Rating = Value encashed to service provider

The TC will function as a booster shot, a form of immunization. It is not an unrestricted welfare handout. Remember Sunita, from chapter 1, whose husband drove a rickshaw in Delhi's polluted streets and child suffered from severe learning difficulties because he did not get enough oxygen at birth? Ultimately, this example led to the horrific rape of a young boy. If TCs were introduced, firstly the child could have been born in a good hospital and so would never have been disabled. His sick father could have used his health care TC to get treatment and so the mother would not have been compelled to work long hours leaving her son unattended. Finally, even if the tragic crime had occurred, the family would have been able to use the legal TC vouchers to gain justice for their son.

Targeted Catalysts in action
Education

The remarkable neglect of elementary education in India is all the more striking given the widespread recognition, in the contemporary world, of the importance of basic education for economic development.[8]

Targeted Catalysts will drive up the quality of education. Take the example of a school I helped establish in Sewari, Rajasthan, that has been running for sixteen years and now has over 600 pupils. Because it provides a high-quality service it is more expensive; the teachers are qualified and are paid more, the buildings are well equipped and consequently the pupils do very well.* In 2008, the cost of educating each child was Rs 600 per month, compared to Rs 400 at a medium-quality neighbouring school and Rs 100 at a poor-quality one. At first it was an uphill struggle to persuade parents that it was worth paying more, as they had no way of judging the difference in quality. To many poor, illiterate parents, the fact that their child can read, write and speak English words is achievement enough. They are often unable to differentiate whether those English words are words learned by rote—for example, bat, cat, hat and so on—or coherent sentences. The new TC system would eliminate this problem in two ways:

1. Incentivizing quality: The better the performance of the school, the more money it would get from the local authority for each Targeted Catalyst it receives. The ratings system would ensure that, schools teaching with the 'bat, cat, hat' approach to English, for example, would receive less money than schools which enable their students of the same age to converse fluently. This would encourage schools to raise their standards.

2. Enabling parents to make informed choices: The Education Standards Authority would publish regular lists showing the quality rating of all the schools in the country, similar to the UK's League Table system.[9] This means that parents would be able to make better decisions about where to educate their children.[10]

---

*Native English speakers frequently teach there, the children go on educational trips both within Rajasthan and further afield, and some have even been involved in teaching adult literacy in a nearby village.

Health

Health care institutions, in a similar manner, would be rewarded for quality by a higher rating and therefore a higher return on the TCs presented. Similarly, regularly published 'league tables' rating for hospitals would enable patients to make informed choices. Currently, there is no way for a patient to judge the quality of health service. In the words of Vishal Bali, CEO of Wockhardt Hospitals, 'Even now, Indian hospitals are not required to provide information on the outcomes of treatments or procedures used. In such a scenario, there is a pressing need to have standardization norms to discipline the healthcare delivery process throughout the country.'[11]

The very act of implementing a ratings system pushes up standards, as demonstrated by the Indian private hospitals, which have upgraded their services as they vie for international accreditations.[12] The most prestigious of these is the one awarded by the US Joint Commission International. It has certified only seventy-one hospitals worldwide, including four private hospitals in India. Indian health care providers pushed up their services at these four hospitals in order to receive this valuable certification. My wife worked at one of these hospitals and was involved in the Herculean effort to raise their standards of patient care to the level required for accreditation. Once accredited, the US and other global insurance companies felt more comfortable about referring the hospital as an option for their patients coming to India.

Legal assistance

In the legal sphere, a range of criteria will rate lawyers according to experience and success ratio. Making this information available to the public will in itself transform access to justice in India. Currently, the wealthy have access to this information, whether through informal networks and recommendations, or through possessing the time, resources and expertise to seek out; whereas the poor and those not part of elite networks do not have this vital information when choosing a lawyer. I recently received a phone call from a UK firm, asking me to recommend lawyers in India for a database they are compiling. Companies that can afford it will be able to buy this valuable 'know-how'. Compiling a legal ratings system on a nationwide basis that makes this information available to all, rich and poor, is necessary.

Legal TCs will be equivalent to a unit of time. The holder will get the same quantity of time with his or her voucher regardless of the rating of the lawyer. The higher the rating of the lawyer, the more he or she will receive from the local government, when encashing the TC. This will allow the poor access to high-quality legal services, while incentivizing lawyers to provide better service to all.

None of what I have outlined here is science fiction: it is possible to implement these ideas now, provided a sense of purpose guides our leaders. I have made TCs the single instrument of intervention as I believe there to be no better way for the state to act on its moral responsibility to ensure the well-being of each citizen. It is a scheme that works both within the market system and allows highly targeted assistance. The delivery of welfare need not be the costly and clumsy affair that it is today.

Aggregate Economic Activity

The Citizens Database

The Targeted Catalyst system rests on a new way of managing exchange: an economy without physical cash, where every citizen has an electronic smart card that records his or her gross income and expenditure.[13] The information would be compiled into a *Citizens Database*, a digital record, allowing the government to link each citizen to his virtual cash account. In order to maintain the individual's right to privacy, the Citizens Database would not (unlike a credit card) retain any information about what, how or where the money is spent. All government interactions with the citizen like taxes, passport information could be conducted electronically. The Government of India is already rolling out pilot schemes for biometric identity cards, prior to issuing them to every citizen after the 2011 census.[14] The Multipurpose National Identity Cards will carry a National Identity Number and will be given to every citizen above eighteen years of age.

The Citizens Database is the foundation of the Targeted Catalyst system. It will record every citizen's total economic activity (measured by adding receipts and expenditures along with his cash reserves or savings). This total of a citizen's purchases and income would be tracked over time and recorded in the Aggregate Economic Activity (AEA) record. The information will reveal the total income and expenditure of an individual over a defined period of time (monthly or quarterly, for example). Each citizen's AEA will be compared to a 'poverty line' threshold. This was US$301 per year in the year 2007, defined as the total that an individual needed in order to be able to afford the six essential services (see Table 3.1). If a person's income falls below this line he or she would automatically receive the TC credits in his or her account. As soon as the individual's income reaches the threshold, the TC credits would stop. I have not picked an absolute number to define the poverty line as the cost of each of the components of the TC is what the poor need to survive. This is increasing as food prices and water scarcity increase the cost of the TC required to give the minimum amount of calories and water needed by an individual. The economic definition of the poverty line is a moving target, which will increase at the rate that each of its components does. For example, if the cost of education, food, water and sewage disposal grew rapidly, the TC total would grow pushing the line up which would increase the numbers who can qualify for assistance. This is particularly important today as rapid food price increases and water shortages are hitting the poor. As the entire economy would be dematerialized, the smart cards would capture all transactions; so money could not be 'hidden', and TCs could not be falsely claimed. This system of direct payments to the poor, would free the rest of the economy to function without constant government intervention in the name of poverty alleviation. The economy could grow rapidly while the TCs tackle poverty.

Using 'smart cards' to transfer money directly to the poor is already a popular concept. India's finance ministry and Planning Commission are researching the use of electronic smart cards to transform the distribution of money to the impoverished. In August 2007, the managing director of ICICI Bank* said, 'We already have the technology today to do this and it would be feasible to use it for putting money in the pockets of the rural poor within eighteen to twenty-four months.' ICICI is also introducing biometric smart cards that enable people to identify themselves by their thumbprints at ATM and other terminals. Lord Meghnad Desai, a professor at the London School of Economics, has suggested aid could be directly delivered via smart cards and N.K. Singh, a former top bureaucrat, has suggested that cards should be used for all government payments to the poor.[15]

A cashless economy will help the poor access India's banking sector. Millions of Indians borrow from private moneylenders at sky-high interest rates, because the banks would not lend money to them. Many years ago, I got lost hiking with a friend in the central Indian state of Madhya Pradesh. We came upon a farmer who generously offered to guide us back. As we walked, he told us his story. His life was destroyed after borrowing money from a local moneylender at exorbitant interest rates. First he sold his wife's jewellery. Then came the turn of his other non-essential possessions. Then, his land. When we met him he was reduced to praying for the rains in order to get a good crop to meet his payments. I still remember him—the human face behind the tragic statistics of the Indian poor, drowning in debt.† If someone wants

---

*Industrial Credit and Investment Corporation of India (ICICI) Bank is India's largest private sector bank with assets of US$100 billion and network in sixteen countries as of March 2008.

†Though microcredit is making a huge difference to the lives of the poor, the scale of the problem is vast.

a loan, he can simply show the banks his AEA records. With the proposals in this book, suddenly all of India will have accurate credit histories.

A Dematerialized Economy: The Practicalities

Paper money will cease to exist. Every transaction will be done electronically, on cheap (as little as US$0.75 each) card readers. The technology is already in place.* There are an increasing number of projects that are making money obsolete. In Japan, virtual payment is booming, Mobile Suica was introduced in January 2006 by NTT DoCoMo and East Japan Railway. It is a mobile phone-based smart card that can be used for buying rail tickets or for access to buildings. In France, Société Générale, in partnership with Visa Europe and Gemalto, piloted a project from July 2007, using a Visa Premier 'contactless' bank card to make small purchases; the whole transaction takes less than one second. In London, *The Evening Standard* newspaper is sold at specially equipped kiosks that require contact between a card and a scanner.[16] A cashless economy would have a profound, beneficial effect on the Indian economy by legitimizing all transactions and erasing the most common avenues for tax evasion.

India's wealth is grossly understated. A staggering amount of money travels to and from the country via countless invisible networks. This cash is neither recorded, taxed, or subject to any

---

*I recently saw a demonstration of this technology at work by a company that aims to decentralize banking through smart RFID cards and tiny, very inexpensive hand-held readers that could essentially function as a bank branch. The inventor, Anurag Gupta, of this technology sees it as a way to radically democratize financial services in rural areas, to bring banking to everyone. While I certainly support that idea, the peer-to-peer functioning of the system really grabbed my attention. It can read the amount of cash on a particular card account linked to their system. It also allowed two individuals to slide in their cards into opposite sides of the reader and complete a transaction. In the test, I 'paid' my friend Rs 10. When we checked a few seconds later, sure enough, I was Rs 10 poorer. This technology could easily be adapted into a national currency system.

exchange controls. On a recent visit to Dubai I met one of the top gold wholesalers on the famous Dubai Gold Souk.* The volume of his underground cash transactions—and the percentage that originated on the Indian subcontinent—was shocking. I heard the same story from a prominent family working in the diamond business in Belgium. Such fraud can allow money laundering and the financing of terror. One of these hidden cash routes—the ancient hawala network still operates on an honour code that dates back to the days of Arab Silk Road traders. Interpol states that hawala provides a scrutiny-free remittance channel.[17] Hawala networks are now reportedly the main way that Al-Qaeda transports funds.[18] A cashless economy would eliminate this.

Eliminating cash would also bring India's enormous informal economy into the open. Approximately, 92 per cent of our population works in the informal sector with its size estimated to be anywhere between 70 and 150 per cent of the current economy.[19] With my proposals, this would disappear. Everyone's transactions, from the paanwallahs' sales on Chandni Chowk to billion-dollar deals, would be noted. India's economy would boom. While the cashless economy would make fraud impossible, my tax reforms would dramatically reduce incentives to conceal wealth. People hide their money, the world over, because they do not want to— or cannot afford to—pay taxes.

Taxation

Background

In the first section of this chapter, I detailed how government money is squandered through criminally inefficient welfare expenditure where the efficiency of government welfare can be

---

*It is a mega gold market (or souk) district in this city of the United Arab Emirates (UAE), with hundreds of retailers dealing almost exclusively in jewellery, especially gold. With very low import duties and no taxation, gold comes for cheap—making Dubai the 'city of gold'—which makes Dubai Gold Souk one of the largest cash converters in the world.

zero. However, Indians have to bear the costs of a 'double whammy', as the government stymies growth through inefficient taxation. Last year, the company I run, paid Rs 540 million in taxes on a turnover of Rs 2600 million which amounts to 22 per cent.* I would be a willing taxpayer, if I knew my earnings contributed to the well-being of the country. It is painful to see hundreds of millions of rupees wasted. This money should be used to make a real difference in the lives of India's poor by funding more productive activity and fuelling the economy.

In this section, I have outlined a new system of taxation† that will encourage growth and ensure that government *doubles its revenue*. I argue that the current system penalizes productive activity. I am not 'anti-tax'; I propose a system where 'unearned profits', such as from inheritance and property, are taxed, and wages and productive activities are not. These proposals would actually double the current tax revenue *and* allow for rapid economic growth, encourage meritocracy and ensure the redistribution of wealth.

The current system

A famous businessman once told me, 'India survives today because its entrepreneurs have perfected the art of cheating on their taxes.' This is no glib statement. During the years of high socialism, profits were condemned as 'ill-gotten gain' by the government who raised the marginal tax rate to as high as 65 per cent.‡ *Those in the highest tax bracket—individuals making more than Rs 2 lakh (around US$5000)—accounted for virtually all the government's income. In 1973–74, it amounted to 97.5 per cent of its income.*[20]

---

*These include state sales tax, Central sales tax, corporate income tax, service tax, rental tax, fringe benefit tax, octroi, other municipal taxes on transport of goods, surcharge and cess on taxes, stamp duty tax on long-term rental and property transfer tax.

†The government has also attempted tax reforms post-1991. Among them, the recommendations of 1991 Tax Reforms Committee headed by Raja J. Chelliah, and 2002 Task Force on tax reforms chaired by Vijay Kelkar are prominent.

‡It was 57 per cent immediately before the 1991 reforms.

What this businessman meant was that with such crippling taxation, the only way Indian business could grow was through concealing income, otherwise there would not have been any surplus capital to reinvest. In such a situation and one where the government expenditure is wasted, the patriotic thing to do would be to avoid paying taxes. While this might sound dramatic, India's growth rate of 3 per cent in the 1970s and 1980s would probably have been even lower if businesses had not concealed income.

Taxation in India is inefficient. It imposes a drag on the most productive parts of the economy, while imposing little or no taxes on wealth from inheritance and asset inflation.

There are three categories of taxes as shown in Table 3.3.

Table 3.3: Three categories of taxes as a percentage of government revenues*

	Current	Percentage of Total Central Government Reserves (%)
1. Taxes on Income and Profit	Private Income Tax of 34%	17.5
	Corporate Income Tax of 34%	31.3
a) National Taxes on Income	Union Excise Tax of 17% on manufactured goods	25.1
b) National Taxes on Profit	Service Tax of 12.34%	8.2
	Customs Duties of 34%	17.5
2. State Level Transaction Taxes	Sales taxes accrue to state governments.	The percentage of total revenue coming from state-levied sales tax varies from state to state
	Octroi taxes accrue to municipal corporations	
3. State Level Wind-fall Taxes	None	0

*Union Budget of India, 2006–07.

The 'bad' taxes

I argue that taxes on income and profits are 'bad' taxes. They penalize productivity—vital to the well-being of Indians. These taxes are justified on the basis on redistributing wealth and limiting corporate power. But they do not work. *Progressive taxes on wages do not prevent disparities in income.* This is because the bulk of wealthy individuals' prosperity does not come from wages, but from dividends and capital appreciation.[21] Warren Buffet, the third richest man in the world, recently highlighted the inequities of the US tax system. He pays tax at a lower rate (at 17.7 per cent) than his secretary (who pays 30 per cent).[22] *Taxing corporate profits is an ineffective way of curbing corporate power.* A much better approach is increasing windfall taxes combined with increasing competition that drives down profits

At Fabindia it is crystal clear how taxing income, profit and transactions punishes enterprise. As a thriving business, we consistently create jobs and generate profits. For every Rs 166,000 (US$4150) increase in our annual sales, we create one full-time position. Craft production is a labour-intensive sector that gives jobs to people in rural communities where employment is vital. In terms of profits, *we give a 45 per cent pre-tax return on our capital employed.* The government taxes us in two ways: on our profits and on our transactions. Both have a 'stunting' effect on the growth of the business.

Taxing profit

With the tax on profits at 33 per cent, my company's return net profit growth drops by a third from 45 per cent to 30 per cent after taxes. If capital's 'job' is to move towards the highest return, the tax just reduced that return dramatically. You could argue that after taxes, the minimum return left would not justify the effort and headaches in running a business. There is a huge opportunity cost to the tax (a factor of compounding). Figure 3.1 shows that the long-term effect of such taxation stunts the accumulation of capital as each firm is deprived of the benefit of the compounding

Figure3.1: Long-term effects of taxation on the accumulation of capital

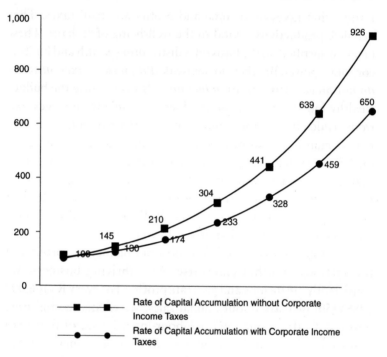

of that capital. Suppose I have a garden of plants each of which produces 100 seeds a year. Let us say, in this hypothetical garden, each seed in turn produces one hundred seeds. After five years, I have ten billion plants. Now assume I always remove thirty-three seeds from every single plant. After five years, I only have two billion plants. Now imagine we are not talking about plants but rupees. Imagine what I could have done with those eight billion rupees. Imagine all the productive uses I could have put that growth to, ploughing it back into the business, generating new jobs, assets and growth. This is the opportunity cost of the 33 per cent tax on profits.

This graph assumes two scenarios: one in which business is not taxed (profit before tax) and one in which it is (profit after tax). In both scenarios all profit is reinvested, the tax rate is 33 per cent and the return on capital is 45 per cent. The difference is telling.

The 'bad taxes': Taxing transactions

Now let us turn to another form of 'bad' taxes, those on transactions. Transaction taxes include sales tax, octrois, excise taxes, transfer taxes, etc.* Fabindia has invested in a factory that provides 250 jobs and is making furniture in India while many of our competitors are importing it from China or Malaysia. We generate our own power, have our own security force and manage our own water supply. So here is how the government rewards us:

Cost of furniture: Rs 100
Cost of furniture with excise tax of 19 per cent: Rs 119
Cost with federal government tax of 3 per cent: Rs 122
Cost with municipal octroi taxes of 6–8 per cent: Rs 130
Cost with state sales tax of 12 per cent: Rs 145.6

The end result is a 45 per cent increase in the base cost of producing one piece of furniture. Again we are punished for creating jobs and building the economy. It would be easier to import the furniture and get an obliging exporter in Malaysia to under-invoice the shipment.[†]

The 'good' taxes

Windfall taxes target profits that have nothing to do with productive activity. The most effective are property and estate taxes as they represent income that is earned through accident or privilege. India's super-elite class is growing fast. In 2008, a meagre 0.01 per cent of the population owned 35 per cent of the country's wealth. The top four richest people in India have the combined

---

*Sales tax is levied on the sale or purchase of goods by the Centre (Central sales tax) and by the states (state sales tax). Octroi tax is levied on the entry of goods into a municipality or any other specified jurisdiction for use, consumption or sale. Octroi tax is levied when goods enter the municipal limits where they are to be ultimately sold, used or consumed. Excise tax is levied on articles produced or manufactured in the taxing country and intended for home consumption. It is an indirect tax which the manufacturer or producer passes on to the consumer.
†A common practice as customs duties are charged on invoice values. So, if you can reduce a part of the invoice value and bill it separately, you save customs duty.

Table 3.4: Table comparing shareholding patterns of top ten Indian and US companies in terms of market capitalization

Indian Companies*	Largest Shareholder (%)	US Companies	Largest Share-holder in terms of Shares Outstanding (%)
Reliance Industries Limited (RIL)	45[†] Individual	Exxon Mobil	3.69 (IH) Institutional
Bharti Airtel	45.31[‡] Individual owned company	General Electric	3.29(IH) Institutional
Reliance Communications	66.12[§] Individual	Microsoft Inc.	8.74(OH) Individual
Infosys	2.85 Individual	Wal Mart Stores	43.24(OH) Family group
TCS	75.01 Family Trust	AT&T	3.74(IH) Institutional
ICICI Bank	28.58[**] Institutional	Chevron Corporation	4.50(IH) Institutional
DLF	87.43[††] One family	Proctor & Gamble	3.52(IH) Institutional
Reliance Petroleum	70.38[‡‡] Family owned through RIL	Johnson & Johnson	4.78(IH) Institutional
ITC	26.34[§§] Institutional	Google Inc.	6.76(IH) Institutional
Larsen & Toubro	15.98[***] Institutional	IBM	4.80(IH) Institutional

Sources: For rankings, see www.moneycontrol.com and www.corporatein formation.com.

Figures for Indian companies selected from the sections 'Promoter and Promoter Group' or '"Public" and owning more than 1 per cent of the total number of shares' of latest public disclosures of shareholding patterns available at the websites of the respective companies. Data for US companies taken from latest filings at Securities Exchange Commission and updated from http://finance.aol.com.

Note: IH—Institutional Holder; OH—Other Holder

*The shareholding pattern of Indian companies reveals why Indian business leaders are some of the world's richest. In a way this is false valuation because very little of their shares are traded.

net worth of 16 per cent of the total GDP.[23] Taxing wealth when rich people die would give the government an enormous source of revenue, even if the tax was only restricted to the highest levels.

Without windfall taxes, the government deprives itself of income and creates a powerful privileged elite who can manipulate democratic institutions. Comparing the ownership patterns of the top companies in India and the US shows the way that India's current tax system results in the concentration of wealth and ownership (Table 3.4).

In India, major shareholders own much, much more than in the US (because of high estate taxes). Giving this small elite such a huge amount of economic power poisons democracy. It also creates inflated stock prices as market capitalization is based on only a fraction of shares being traded (if the major shareholder owns 70 per cent of the company, only 30 per cent of the shares are left to be traded in the market). Reducing intergenerational transfer of wealth for the super-rich would ensure that the concentration of wealth is reduced. This would be good for democracy and good for the stock market.*

---

†Aggregate of share ownership split between members and organizations of the CEO's family.

‡From section '"Public" and owning more than 1 percent of the total number of shares'.

§Aggregate of share ownership split between members and organizations of the CEO's family.

**From section '"Public" and owning more than 1 percent of the total number of shares'.

††Aggregate of share ownership split between members and organizations of the CEO's family.

‡‡Owned by Reliance Industries Limited.

§§From section '"Public" and owning more than 1 per cent of the total number of shares'.

***From section '"Public" and owning more than 1 per cent of the total number of shares'.

*This is where corporate governance becomes important. It is defined as the general set of customs, regulations, habits, institutions and laws that help control, direct and administer a firm and determine the end to which it should be run.

The Right to Property

What happens to us in the absence of the right to property? The answer is provided in *Tintin in America*,[†] in a scene which perhaps makes the strongest political statement to be found in all of Tintin. In the scene, Tintin accidentally discovers an oil well on the ancestral land of a native Indian. A cigar-smoking entrepreneur enters in the next frame and offers Tintin up to US$100,000 for the well. Tintin insists that the oil belongs to the native American. At this revelation, the 'Blackfeet Indian' is offered US$25 and half an hour to leave his land. Soon, the bayonet of the National Guard ensures the native Indian is driven off the land of his forefathers. A petroleum company is established within hours and a traffic-congested metropolis comes up the next morning. Each time I see and read about the government acquiring land of the local, indigenous people, I am reminded of this scene from *Tintin in America*.[24]

The right to property is fundamental to the welfare of human beings. The Fifth Amendment of the US Constitution states that no person shall be 'deprived of life, liberty, or property, without due process of law; nor shall private property be taken for public use, without just compensation.' The framers of India's Constitution were aware of the importance of this right and, consequently, Article 14(f) guaranteed the right to 'acquire, hold and dispose' property as a Fundamental Right, which could be deprived only through state intervention in public interest. However, anticipating that an absolute right to property could work against land reforms—redistribution by the state of estates run as fiefs by large landowners—the ideas of 'due process' and 'just' compensation (in case alienation of property takes place) were distanced from this right. During the next three decades, in repeated conflicts between a legislature committed to social-economic equality and a judiciary upholding people's fundamental

---

India's corporate affairs ministry has set up the National Foundation for Corporate Governance in partnership with industry associations to promote and improve corporate governance.
[†]A Belgian comic book series.

right to property, the legislature progressively weakened this right through the first, fourth and the seventeenth amendments to the Constitution. Eventually, in 1978, through the forty-fourth amendment property ceased to be a Fundamental Right and found its place in Article 300A, which reads: 'No person shall be deprived of his property save by authority of law.' Thus, currently in India, property is a weak statutory right and no person can approach the Supreme Court under Article 32 (which allows recourse to the apex court on violation of Fundamental Rights) if her or his property is taken away by the state.

I argue for a reintroduction of property as a Fundamental Right. There are two reasons for this. First, land ceilings are profoundly undemocratic measures. They are similar to saying that one cannot hold stocks of a company beyond certain limits. The true market I outlined in chapter 2 cannot work under this skewed mechanism. Second, under the system I outline in this book, ownership of large estates works for social and economic good. For instance, a large landowner will be bound to pay 1 per cent annual tax on her or his property. The larger the property the greater the revenue generated from this tax. This revenue would go to the community and enable it to meet its TC obligations. Paying property taxes would impose a cost on large, unproductive estates. Additionally, the draconian Land Acquisition Act of 1894,* which gives the state unfettered power in usurping property, needs to be replaced with a more balanced law.

We need to recognize the fact that there may arise an extraordinary situation when the Nation, Region, Area or Community may have to acquire land for the larger public good. In such situations, two safeguards will be ensured:
1. 'Public benefit' would necessitate that the acquisition be recognized and passed through a resolution by the appropriate level of local government.

---

*The Land Acquisition Act, 1894, is a colonial law, which gives the Government of India absolute authority to unilaterally price and acquire any land for 'public purposes'. It is being used today to force people to sell their land for anything from dams to car factories.

2. It is also necessary to note that 50 per cent of the land needed must be bought willingly from the sellers and the average weighted price of that 50 per cent should be the *only* determinant in fixing the compensation for the remaining land to be acquired. These safeguards are necessary to protect the larger interest of the citizenry while not depriving the individual citizens' right to just compensation for their property.*,[25]

Taxing property is another way of limiting the power of the 'inheritance elite'. When my American grandparents died, my sister and I inherited their beautiful New England family home, a property full of memories and of great sentimental value to us both. However, we quickly realized that the property taxes were just too high to justify keeping a place that we used only for a week every year. Furthermore, the taxes were being spent on services for residents that did not benefit non-residents, such as the public school, the fire service and the snowplough. We sold the house. This was good for the community as it provided the opportunity for someone to live there who would contribute to the local economy. I am sure, that if property taxes had not been so high, we would have kept the family home. This phenomenon is common in Landour, Mussoorie. With zero opportunity cost to holding property and land values sky-rocketing, the place is full of absentee landlords and empty houses. At the same time, it is impossible for people who contribute to the local economy to afford living there.

The absence of property taxes is one of the key drivers of India's skyrocketing land prices. Money gets parked in real estate, which in turn drives up the price of property. A well-known lawyer friend of mine commented recently: 'We see property as our fixed deposit.' This mindset has made the cost of land in Indian cities so high that it bears no reference to earning capacity. In rural India, it takes land out of the reach of those who would like to put it to productive use. Agriculture becomes less and less viable. Once property taxes are in place, people will be compelled to use banks

---

*This would also necessitate repeals of Articles 285 and 289 of the Constitution which lay down that Union property cannot be taxed by states and vice versa.

rather than real estate for their deposits and property prices should fall dramatically.*

The new tax system

I propose a revolutionary approach to taxation. Taxes on wages and profits are eliminated and instead, windfall taxes are introduced. Table 3.5 shows the new taxation system.† The four-tier system of government is detailed in the next chapter, where I

Table 3.5: New system of taxation

Tier of Government	Revenue	Expenditure
Community	• 1% Annual Property Tax • Rental and Sales from Community assets	• Targeted Catalysts • Community • Government Administration • Community Courts
Area	• Rental and Sales from Area assets	• Area Government Administration Costs • Area Courts
Region	• Rental and Sales from Regional assets	• Regional Government Administration Costs • Regional Courts
Nation	• 1% Economic Activity Tax on all transactions • A flat 30% Inheritance Tax on any inheritance over 1000 times the prevailing GDP per capita • Rental and Sales from National Assets	• National Government Administration Costs • Constitutional Authority Administration Costs • National Legal Institution Costs

*Currently in India, property tax for urban areas is very low and negligible for rural areas.
†The proposed tax reforms would only be made when the proposals for expenditure as described above, and the new systems of government detailed in the following chapter, are in place.

describe a wholesale restructuring of the current system. Each tier will be responsible for its own revenue and expenditure.

Community level

ONE PER CENT PROPERTY TAX

Traditionally, citizens pay a property tax on their assets, and this tax is no different. In order to tax property, the first thing the newly formed communities (described in the following chapter) will need to do is to ensure the correct maintenance of land records and simplify the process of transferring property. In India today property records are a mess. The Peruvian author Hernando de Soto in his book *The Mystery of Capital* illustrates what happens to an economy and to the poor when land records and title deeds are incorrectly maintained. As community governments get their revenue from property taxes, there will be a strong incentive to improve title deeds and make it easy to buy and sell property.

Many of the reforms proposed in this new framework will not be viable if land prices are propped up artificially. The immediate effect of such a tax would be to deflate the value of land and give communities a consistent source of revenue and a strong incentive to develop their local infrastructure. The property tax will fund the entire Targeted Catalyst system described earlier in the chapter.

The 1 per cent property tax I have proposed is already being charged by state governments who levy a stamp duty on property. This varies from 6 per cent to 14 per cent from state to state and is levied each time a property is sold.[26] If we take an average levy of 10 per cent for the country, the interest on this amount equals to about 0.8 per cent to 1 per cent charge every year. In cases where property has never been sold this would amount to a new tax. But since urban India would be tripling or perhaps even quadrupling its housing stock in a decade, it is fair to assume that the effect of this tax is already taken into account.

I propose the creation of a National Cross-Subsidization Fund (NCSF), which will contain all property tax revenue above Rs 50,000 per resident. The figure is so high that it will affect only a very small portion of communities, and will not limit their capability to provide services. At 1 per cent, wealthy communities with high property prices and a few residents like those at Panchsheel Park in New Delhi or Malabar Hill in Mumbai would collect huge sums of property tax per head. If the amount of tax collected per capita exceeds a threshold of say Rs 50,000 the excess over that amount goes to the NCSF, which aims at transferring excess revenue from rich areas like Panchsheel, where people will pay more on property, to poor areas like Sewari. The surplus from communities like Panchsheel will be used by the Regional government to erase the deficit in communities like Sewari.

Area-level taxes

There are no Area-level taxes. Revenue comes from rental and sale of area assets.

Regional-level taxes

There are no Regional-level taxes. Revenue comes from rental and sale of area assets.

National-level taxes

THIRTY PER CENT ASSET TRANSFER TAX AT TIME OF DEATH

This inheritance tax will apply to assets* above a threshold of a thousand times the per capita GDP;† at the time of writing, it is around Rs 29.3 million (US$734,000). This tax would not affect 99.9 per cent of Indians. But the tiny percentage it would affect would result in important revenues for the national economy.

*Such as assets in wills or those gifted.
†Initially the revenue from this tax would be capped, with any surplus going into a Cross-Subsidization Fund created to counterbalance the differential in community budgets that would happen in the first 10–15 years of this plan. At

One per cent Economic Activity Tax

The national government will also be funded by a 1 per cent tax electronically taken off any transaction—from sales of goods and services to the transactions of investment funds. While in the past such a tax would have been impossible to monitor administratively, the ability to digitally calculate a person's total Aggregate Economic Activity, outlined earlier in this chapter, would make it possible. The tax will be levied automatically, electronically, leaving behind a digital record. The tax on each transaction would be tiny, but its cumulative effect enormous. This tax would be progressive, because the rich move larger sums of money and their money tends to move faster and more frequently through the economy. The *velocity* of money (the volume and frequency of transactions) is taxed, not its *productivity* (profits or wages). In the past such 'financial velocity' taxes have been proposed for different types of transactions from Keynes' proposals[27] on taxing stock trading in 1936 to Tobin's tax on currency trading in 1978.[28] Today there is growing support for a general, uniform flat tax on all types of assets.[29]

In the last two decades, financial trading has boomed. Large sums change hands every hour. This enormous trading volume means that even a low tax rate would yield substantial revenue. Furthermore, by curbing speculative activity, such a tax would actually have a positive effect on the unstable global markets, which are currently characterized by excessive liquidity and excessive price volatility.

There is an increasing discrepancy between the levels of financial trading transactions and the levels of 'real world' transactions. The volume of foreign exchange transactions is

this early phase, community incomes from property taxes would be very unequal. As the plan progresses and the 'assets' of poor communities appear on the balance sheet and richer communities begin to pay for things which are currently free, there will be a massive transfer of income from rich to poor. However, until that point poorer communities will need support that I shall detail in subsequent chapters.

almost seventy times higher than the world trade of goods and services. In Germany, the UK and the US, the volume of stock trading is almost 100 times bigger than business investment.[30] These trends are the result of the accumulation of extremely short-term transactions, they destabilize the global economy. The Economic Activity Tax would make such short-term transactions more costly.* Not only would it raise large amounts of revenue for government, but it would also act as a stabilizing force to world financial markets.

Economic development with unlimited supply of labour

Before I discuss financial projections to illustrate my proposals, a few words on some basic challenges confronting India's economic governance are necessary. India is an economy with what economists call an 'unlimited supply of labour'. The question is how we develop a society with this unlimited labour supply. This question is inextricably linked to two vital needs of the hour—generating more employment and raising wages for a better quality of life. It is important to highlight here that the TCs are, essentially, a way of helping the people of India reach the basic minimum standards that our Constitution guarantees. The rights to life and personal liberty become meaningless in the absence of these basic standards of life. Perhaps no one has showed the compounding effects of this problem of subsistence better than James C. Scott. In his classic, *The Moral Economy of the Peasant*, Scott argued that in subsistence-level societies the exaggerated fear of possible

---

*This would act as a damper on the volatility, which results from huge inflows of funds moving rapidly in and out of economies. As Henry Kissinger wrote on 30 May 2008 in the *International Herald Tribune*: 'With each decade, the role of speculative capital has magnified. For speculative capital, nimbleness is the essential attribute. Rushing in when it sees an opportunity and heading for the exit at the first sign of trouble, speculative capital has too often turned upswings into bubbles and downward cycles into crises.'

failure prevents people from innovation and risk taking. I have
realized the poignancy of Scott's argument through my own
experiences with rural artisans. Wherever I initiated efforts to
encourage rural artisans to innovate, I found that they hesitated to
take a lead. It was natural they could not risk their children's
education or health care by investing the little money they had in
something that could, theoretically, fail. I realized that if there was
a subsistence net of some sort, below which their incomes would
not fall, the rural artisans would be willing to risk innovation. The
TCs provide a subsistence net of this kind. That is the fundamental
purpose of the TCs. They cannot *create* wealth; not the real wealth
that is responsible for development of an economy and society.

How can *real* wealth be generated? The Nobel Prize winning
economist W. Arthur Lewis's pioneering treatment of the problem
of economic development with unlimited supplies of labour is a
helpful guide. Lewis recognized that neo-classical economics could
not fully address the development issues of economies like Egypt,
India or Jamaica which had surplus populations. 'An unlimited
supply of labour is said to exist,' wrote Lewis, 'where population
is so large relatively to the capital and natural resources, that there
are large sectors of economy where the marginal productivity of
labour is negligible, zero, or even negative.'[31] India is an ideal
example of this. With subsistence-level living standards prevalent,
people are averse to risk taking and innovation because of the
tension between innovation and fear of failure, and the
compulsions of sustaining a life. The return on risk is too high
for people to adventure. Without enterprise there can be no
increase in the marginal productivity of labour. Marginal
productivity of labour is the increase in output produced from a
given capital stock when an additional worker is employed.
Historically, the most successful economies—from great powers
to empires—have had greater marginal productivity of labour than
their historical competitors. Rise in marginal productivity leads
to increase in real wages. But increases in marginal productivity

of labour and real wages require capital formation at a rapid rate and its free availability. The process of wealth generation will have to ensure that these three interdependent conditions are met and allowed to operate in optimum conditions. In India, the class of speculative capitalists, which thrives on and creates asset bubbles, is a major impediment to real capital formation and circulation. The pattern of concentrated wealth ownership and shareholding stunts the flow of capital. Unless these disparities are addressed, no real wealth generation, which opens the possibility of economic and social development, can take place.

The Financial Projections

The aim of this financial projection exercise is to illustrate that my reforms are financially viable rather than to provide accurate predictions. The statistics that follow underestimate the positive impact of my reforms as they:

- do not take into account the huge accelerative economic effect that would result from eliminating taxes on productive activity;
- do not account for the full impact of legalizing the informal economy, which would result in a one-off 70–150 per cent growth spurt as the cash economy gets legalized;
- do not account for the positive impact of costing and trading environmental assets, and how this will dramatically reduce the numbers of people living in poverty.

Instead I have applied my fiscal reforms to India today. As such, the figures grossly underestimate the benefits from these suggested reforms. They show that even if directly applied to the current economy, the proposed revenue is more than sufficient to balance expenditure. Furthermore, my tax reforms would actually result in a doubling of tax revenue, despite the fact that all taxes on income and productive activity would be eliminated.

The new system of taxation would dramatically increase government revenue, as illustrated in Table 3.6 and Table 3.7.

Table 3.6: Current tax revenue of the Indian government 2006–07

Item	Value (Rs Cr)	Percentage (%)
Union Excise Tax (17% on all manufactured goods)	117,266	25.1
Customs Duties (34%)	81,800	17.5
Corporate Income Tax (34%)	14,6497	31.3
Private Income Tax (34%)	82,510	17.6
Service Tax (12.34% on all services)	38,169	8.2
Taxes of Union Territories	1341	0.3
Other	265	0.1
Gross Revenue	467,848 US$117.18 billion	100.0

Source: Union Budget of India, 2006–07

Table 3.7: Proposed tax revenues in new economic framework (Assume GDP of US$1 trillion)

Item	Value (US$ billion)	Percentage (%)
Property Tax for Community Government (1%)	294.00	93
Economic Activity Tax for National Government (1% of GNP)	18.13	6
Inheritance Tax for National Government (30% of value of a person's net worth at the time of death) on assets of more than 1000 times the per capita GDP	7.92	1
TOTAL	320.05	100

As is evident from tables 3.6 and 3.7, tax revenue would increase from US$117.8 billion to US$320.05 billion and yet there would be no corporate income tax, no individual income tax, no stamp duty on the transfer of property (currently averaging 10–12%), no sales tax, no octroi taxes, no service tax, no royalty tax, no fringe benefit tax, no turnover tax, no cess or surcharge on taxes. Armies of accountants, tax officials, special shelter schemes, and

Table 3.8: Balance of accounts resulting from the new system

	Revenue (US$ billion)	Expenditure (US$ billion)	Balance (US$ billion)
Community	Property Tax: 294	Targeted Catalysts: 139.87	154.13
Nation	Economic Activity Tax: 18.13	Government Administration:[†] 35.52	–9.44*
	Inheritance Tax: 7.95		

*Figures are for General Services and Defense, taken from Government of India, Union Budget 2007–08, http://indiabudget.nic.in/ub2008–09/ubmain.htm.
[†]At a national level, using my calculations there is a deficit. This is partly due to the impossibility of calculating the Economic Activity Tax; the figure would be much larger than my calculation. However, any deficit would initially be funded by government borrowing. Such a situation would be short-lived as once the suggested proposals take hold, the economy would boom as new asset classes are traded, the poor get wealthier and the compound impact of eliminating taxes on income and profits takes effect.

questionable tax avoidance techniques will all suddenly disappear, along with the entire black market economy of India, because the incentives for such activity would be eliminated. The most exhilarating point is that we can accomplish this while doubling government revenue and eliminating poverty.

Community-level revenue and expenditure

The main expenditure at the Community level will be the Targeted Catalysts. The total cost of the Targeted Catalyst is US$301* per person per year (Table 3.8). The 'poverty-line' is below this amount. Using information from the National Sample Survey Organization on consumption distribution, I have calculated that the total cost of providing TCs at US$139.87 billion. This is an overinflated calculation, because it assumes that all individuals currently below the poverty line would receive TCs for the entire

*The basis for this figure is explained earlier in the chapter and in Table 3.9.

year, when many will be able to move above the poverty line after receiving TCs before the year end.

Recall that the costs of TCs will be fully covered by the property taxes gained from the community. Using gross calculations, the total national revenue from property taxes would be $294 billion.* This revenue would cover the remaining costs of the TCs. Communities will also have all the revenue from the rental and sale of community assets to contribute towards additional support for low-income citizens or local projects (e.g. capital investment in public assets).

Area-level revenue and expenditure†

The main costs of Area-level expenditure will be the administrative costs of the members of Parliament (MPs) and any other coordination expenses. This will be small and will be covered by the revenue from sale and rental of Area assets. Area, Regional and National levels of government and the distinctions between the two will be covered in detail in the next chapter.

Regional-level revenue and expenditure

The main costs of Regional-level expenditure will be the administrative costs of the governor and any other coordination expenses. This will be small and will be covered by the revenue from sale and rental of Regional assets.

National-level revenue and expenditure

The National-level income will come from the inheritance tax and the economic activity tax. I have estimated the total revenue from

*This was calculated using information about property values combined with World Bank data on land classification in India. Given the property boom occurring in India, these figures are underestimated. They are also undifferentiated and so lack accuracy. Nevertheless, they more than cover the cost of the TCs.
†Area, Regional and National levels of government and the distinctions between the two will be covered in detail in chapter 4.

the inheritance tax* to be US$7.95 billion (Table 3.8) in five years time.

The revenue generated by the 1 per cent aggregate economic activity tax on all financial transactions is impossible to estimate precisely as there is no way of measuring the total number of transactions. In order to come close, I doubled the GDP to take account of incorporating the informal economy (which is estimated to be 70–150 per cent of the current economy), and then took 1 per cent of this. This is a gross underestimation—as the GDP obviously does not equate to the number of transactions—and is the result of all final transactions. Therefore, while the figure I came to is US$18.13 billion (Table 3.8), the actual revenue generated would be much higher.

The expenditure of the national government would be US$35.52 billion (Table 3.8). This figure was calculated using data from the *Non-Plan Expenditure Budget, Volume 1, 2008–2009*.[32] Figures for General Services were added to the cost of the Defense Department.

I have already described how smart cards could seal the leaks in the legitimate economy. This new tax system is the other part of the push to bring the underground economy into the open. As the new system does not penalize productivity, India's vast number of undeclared businesses, would be able to enter the formal economy. Paying taxes and having a say in the way those funds are spent is one of the most effective methods of binding citizenry to a republic. The great rallying cry of the American Revolutionary War proclaims: 'No taxation without representation.' I use the word representation, in its profoundest sense, to encompass having a say in how those funds are to be spent. This necessitates a new system of government, one that will enable the citizens of India to have a real say in the issues that affect their lives. The following chapter outlines how this will work.

*This would be a tax of 30 per cent applicable to anyone with net worth of assets over 1000 times the per capita GDP at the time of death.

The calculations

Community level

EXPENDITURE: TARGETED CATALYSTS

On the basis of Table 3.9, the total cost of one TC catalyst is Rs 12,044 (US$301).

Table 3.9: Calculation of Targeted Catalysts

Targeted Catalyst	Price per Unit	Quantity for a Year	Yearly Value (Rs)
Nutrition	US$123*	1	4903
Water			
Drinking: 4.5 litres a day‡	Rs 0.25 a litre†	1643	411
Potable: 20 litres a day	Rs 0.05 a litre§	7300	365
Sewage: 20 litres a day	Rs 0.05	7300	365
Education	Rs 200 a month	12	2400
Health	Rs 200 a month	12	2400
Legal Services	Rs 100 a month	12	1200

*Estimate of nutrition price per year. The Indian poverty line at present is decided on the basis of the amount of money required to buy 2,400 calories of food per head every day in rural areas and 2,100 calories in urban centres. The government considers how much this amount of food cost in 1973–74. It then uses inflation figures to find out how much that amount would be at today's prices. Using this method the poverty line is set at Rs 356.30 per person per month in rural areas and Rs 538.60 per person in urban areas. The United Nations Funds for Popular Activites (UNFPA) estimates that 71.3 per cent of India's population is rural and 28.7 per cent urban. See http://www.unfpa.org/worldwide/indicator.do?filter=getIndicatorValues&show=1.

I used these figures to find a weighted average for the total amount required to provide nutritional support to all Indians. This result was Rs 4,903 (US$123).

†This is the World Health Organization-recommended daily amount for manual labour in high temperatures. See www.water.org.uk/home/water-for-health/medical-facts/adults.

In order to calculate the amount that would be spent annually in India on TCs, I used consumption data from the National Sample Survey Organization, NSS 61st round (July 2004–June 2005). I split the population into deciles and calculated the average annual consumption for each decile. I then calculated how much it would take to bring the average for each group up to the poverty line. I added all these figures together to come up with the total cost of TCs for the entire country. Remember that this is an underestimation, as the projections do not allow for:

- the positive impact of trading environmental assets, and how this will dramatically reduce the numbers of people living in poverty; and
- the fact that many recipients of TCs will not have them for an entire year, as they will cease as soon as their income rises above the poverty line.

REVENUE: ONE PER CENT PROPERTY TAX

Property prices vary dramatically and the estimates used here are rough. These calculations also do not account for the changing value of rural land that would occur as environmental assets would be incorporated into the economy. Common lands such as forests, sanctuaries and village grazing areas are not currently valued. This would change significantly once forest and biodiversity zones are traded. India's huge swathes of agricultural land will become much more valuable. Tables 3.10 and 3.11 present the calculation.

---

‡Price per litre of drinking water. Using the marginal cost of treating a litre of drinking water with ultraviolet (UV) and reverse osmosis (RO) filters, the Centre for Science and Environment (CSE) cites the figure on the following web page: http://www.hinduonnet.com/fline/fl2307/stories/20060421006702300.htm.

§Estimate of price per litre of potable and sewage water. This is based on the figure cited by the CSE for Tamil Nadu as Rs 25–50/cubic metre, using the higher figure, Rs 50/ cubic metre or Rs 0.05 per litre. See http://www.cseindia.org/dte-supplement/industry20040215/industry-improve.htm.

Table 3.10: Calculation of individuals eligible for TCs

Decile	Average Annual Consumption per Decile	Poverty Line (annual TC cost) (Rs)	Fraction of Population Targeted	Value of TC per Decile in Rs (million)
1	254	12,044	0.1	990,054,563,960
2	332	12,044	0.1	886,025,309,312
3	384	12,044	0.1	818,107,717,064
4	435	12,044	0.1	751,263,953,792
5	489	12,044	0.1	678,965,364,704
6	552	12,044	0.1	596,368,546,532
7	631	12,044	0.1	492,403,066,496
8	748	12,044	0.1	337,046,376,524
9	970	12,044	0.1	44,699,583,764
10	2025	12,044	0.1	0

TOTAL: Rs 559,493.45 crore (US$139.87 billion)

Table 3.11: Calculation of property tax

		Estimated Value		Estimated Value	
	Percentage				
Land Use	of Total	(Rs/sq acre)	Area (sq.km)	Acres/sq.km	(Rs cr.)
Urban Land	6.79	15000000	224000	247.11	83027280
Agricultural	60.60	700000	1999800	247.11	34591241
Forested	20.52		677000		N/A
Percentage of Land classified as used (%)	87.90[33]				
Unused			399200		
Totals	100.00		3300000		117618521
Tax at 1 per cent					1,176,185 (US$294 billion)

National level

EXPENDITURE: GOVERNMENT ADMINISTRATION

The expediture on government administration has been worked out as presented in Table 3.12.

Table 3.12: Cost of government administration

Services	Cost (US$ billion)
General Services (Tax collection, Elections, Secretariat, Police, External Affairs, Pensions, Public Works, Intelligence Bureau)	12.39
Ministry of Defence*	23.13
Total†	35.52

Revenue

INHERITANCE TAX

The inheritance tax would apply to anyone with assets over 1000 times the total per capita GDP. Currently, this would apply to any individual holding assets in excess of Rs 29.3 million (US$734,000), (with this tax cut off-point as a deductible).

I have used data concerning High Net Worth Individuals (HNWI) in India for these calculations.[34] These individuals are defined as having investable assets (financial assets not including primary residence) in excess of US$1 million. Given that my tax would apply to anyone with over US$734,000 (1000 times the

*This figure does not include defence pensions, as these will be covered by the dividend from the National Asset Corporation (NAC).

†This figure does not include interest payments and debt servicing as these will be covered by the National Asset Corporation. The first call on the NAC will be the provision of Pension Bonds and retrenchment expenses to government employees who lose their jobs. The second will be pensions and interest payments. While debt repayments can be met from selling of equity shares held by the NAC, the funds raised from these sales can be used to bring down the national debt.

Table 3.13: Total value of HNWI in India in 2013

Number of HNWI in India today	100,000
Total value of HNWI in India	US$350,000M
Number of NHWI in India in 2013, assuming a 20 per cent increase	248,832
Total value of HNWI in India, in 2013, assuming a 20 per cent increase	US$870,912M

Table 3.14: Calculation of death rates of HNWI

Death rates per 1000* (%)	0.66
Death rates of <55 per 1000 (%)	0.48
Death rates of >55 per 1000 (%)	7.86
Percentage of India's HNWI >55[35] (%)	24.00
Percentage of India's HNWI <55 (%)	76.00
Assuming death rates of half of the national rates for HNWI	
Death rates of HNWI <55 per 1000 (%)	0.24
Death rates of HNWI >55 per 1000 (%)	3.93
Number of HNWI who die in a year in 2013	7572
Estimated Estate Tax at Flat 30% on all inheritances above 1,000 times per capita GDP	US$7,950,294,374

total per capita GDP), in investable assets, the figures presented in Table 3.13 are an underestimation. I have halved the national death rates for the HNWI, as they will have a considerably lower death rate than the average (see Table 3.14). In order to calculate the amount that would come from this inheritance tax in five years' time, I then assumed that annual growth of HNWI will be 20 per cent,[†] and compounded the information accordingly. This is actually a slight overestimation as I have not subtracted the deductible, as it is not possible to predict GDP per capita for 2013.

*Data on death rates for Age categories from Statistical Register, Govt of India.
[†]In 2007, the number of NHWI in India increased by 20.5 per cent.

Table 3.15: Calculation of Economic Activity Tax

Current GDP (2006), (US$ billion)	906.30
Post-reorganization GDP (assume a doubling), (US$ billion)	1812.60
Calculated 1% tax on GDP after reorganization (US$ billion)	18.13

ECONOMIC ACTIVITY TAX

The 1 per cent economic activity tax on all financial transactions is impossible to estimate precisely as there is no a way of measuring the total number of transactions. Therefore, I doubled the GDP to take account of incorporating the informal economy (which is estimated to be between 70 to 150 per cent of the current economy), and then took 1 per cent of this. This is a gross underestimate as the GDP obviously does not equate to the number of transactions, and is also only the result of all final transactions. Therefore, while the figure I came to is US$18.13 billion, the actual revenue generated would be much higher (Table 3.15).

Notes

1. National Commission for Enterprises in the Unorganised Sector, *Report on Conditions of Work and Promotion of Livelihoods in the Unorganised Sector* (New Delhi: National Commission for Enterprises in the Unorganised Sector, 2007). Available at http://nceus.gov.in/Condition_of_workers_sep_2007.pdf.
2. A recent example of such overkill can be found in parliamentarian Rahul Gandhi's constituency Amethi in Uttar Pradesh. This poor town is all set to receive a Rs 10 million IT Research and Development park when there is acute want of basic infrastructure. 'Amethi to get Rs 100-crore R&D park to remember Rajiv', *The Indian Express*, 21 August 2006.
3. P. Sainath, *Everybody Loves a Good Drought* (New Delhi: Penguin Books India, 1996).
4. Jo Johnson, 'Western Donors Wrestle with the Contradictions of Rising India', *Financial Times*, 23 January 2008.
5. Ganesh Pandey and Ravish Tiwari, 'UPA Mega Drinking Water

Scheme is Also Going Down the Corruption Drain', *Indian Express*, 4 March 2008.

6. Sanjoy, a remarkable visionary, social-economic activist and an agricultural economist, was kidnapped by the militant, terrorist outfit United Liberation Front of Asom (ULFA) in July 1997 and perhaps killed in August that year by ULFA and others who were in cahoots with the local government. Conflicting reports over this abduction and killing posed some serious questions for the state government, local contractors and ULFA in Assam. See, Dilip D'Souza, 'Not a Pretty Reflection', *Rediff News*, 9 December 1997. Available at, http://www.rediff.com/news/dec/09dilip.htm.

7. Sumita Ghose, ed., *Sanjoy's Assam* (New Delhi: Penguin Books India, 1998), p. 85.

8. Jean Drèze and Amartya Sen, *India: Economic Development and Social Opportunity* (New Delhi: Oxford University Press, 1995), p. 13.

9. Every year the UK's department for education and skills publishes information on the achievement and attainment of pupils in all schools. These tables provide a guide to how well a school is doing. They list National Curriculum test results for each school in England and show how they compare with other schools. The information is available online. See http://www.direct.gov.uk/en/ Parents/Schoolslearninganddevelopment/ChoosingASchool/ DG_10038420?cids=Google_PPC&cre=Education_Learning_Franchise.

10. Interestingly, a New-Delhi-based non-profit organization has launched education voucher programme to encourage, in the long run, free-market competition among government and private schools. Delhi's education minister has also suggested the possibility of greater governmental support to education vouchers. See, 'Not Enough to Vouch For' by Jayant Singh, http://www.businessworld.in/content/ view/2721/2800.

11. Quoted in Zeenat Nazir, 'Just What the Hospital Ordered: Global Accreditations', *Indian Express*, 18 September 2006.

12. Ibid.

13. These ideas would not have been possible to implement without the recent advances in technology, especially in connectivity, database storage space and algorithm-driven search functions. They sound mundane, but they have driven transformations like Google, web

banking, and web travel. The advances in the last fifty years have been staggering: the price of storing a megabyte—the equivalent of 500 one-sided, single-spaced, typed sheets of paper—has fallen from 4 lakh rupees (US$10,000) in 1956 to under 7 paisa as of 2004 (0.00125 cents). See http://www.alts.net/ns1625/winchest.html.

14. 'Multipurpose National Identity Cards Being Issued in 13 States, Union Territories', *The Hindu*, 31 October 2007.

15. John Elliot, 'Riding the Elephant: Smart Money for India's poor', *Fortune Magazine*, 7 August 2007.

16. Martin Foster, 'Virtual Payments Catching on in Japan', *International Herald Tribune*, 24 March 2008.

17. Jost, Patrick, and Harjit Singh Sandhu, 'The Hawala Alternative Remittance System and its Role in Money Laundering', Interpol, January 2000. See also John F. Wilson, Mohammed El Qorchi and Samuel Munzele Maimbo, 'Informal Funds Transfer Systems: An Analysis of the Hawala System', International Monetary Fund, March 2003, pp. 21–23.

18. Ron Suskind, *The One Percent Doctrine* (New York: Simon and Schuster, 2007).

19. In her *India Working: Essays on Society and Economy* (Cambridge: Cambridge University Press, 2003), Barbara Harriss-White suggests that this huge informal economy generates 90.3 per cent of all livelihoods and 60 per cent of the country's net domestic product. An International Labour Organization report suggests that 93 per cent of the country's population is in the informal sector with 83 per cent involved in non-agricultural activities. *Men and Women in the Informal Economy: A Statistical Picture* (Geneva: ILO Publications), pp. 33–36.

20. M. Govinda Rao, 'Tax System Reform in India: Achievements and Challenges Ahead', *Journal of Asian Economics*, 16 (2005): 993–1011.

21. For example, the Forbes list of forty richest Indians (available at http://www.forbes.com/lists/2007/77/biz_07india_Indias-Richest_FinalWorth.html) clearly shows that for most of them, their personal wealth comes from market capitalization of the equity they own.

22. Tom Bawden, 'Buffet blasts system that lets him pay less tax than his secretary', *The Times*, 28 June 2007.

23. Figures taken from Forbes 2008 Billionaires List. See http:// www.forbes.com/2008/03/05/richest-people-billionaires-billionaires08-cx_lk_0305billie_land.html.

24. Hergé, *The Adventures of Tintin: Tintin in America* (London: Mammoth, 2002).

25. Recently, a few large corporate houses have managed to acquire vast amounts of land at a fraction of the prevailing market price by their ability to manipulate state governments to acquire land, ostensibly for the public good, but essentially as a thinly disguised land-grab. See, Sanjay Sangvai, 'Land-Grab by Rich: The Politics of SEZs in India', 5 July 2006. Available at http://www.thesouthasian.org/archives/2006/landgrab_by_rich_the_politics.html.

26. For detail of state-wise stamp duty, see http://www.helplinelaw.com/docs/stampduty/index.php.

27. J. M. Keynes, *The General Theory of Employment, Interest and Money* (London: Macmillan, 1936).

28. J. Tobin, 'Proposal for International Monetary Reform', *Eastern Economic Journal*, 4 (1978): 153–59.

29. See Stephan Schulmeister, 'A General Financial Transaction Tax: Financing Development and Enhancing Stability', The Austrian Institute for Economic Affairs, Paper presented to UN Economic and Social Research Council, 14 April 2008.

30. Ibid.

31. W. Arthur Lewis, 'Economic Development with Unlimited Supplies of Labour', *Manchester School of Social and Economic Studies*, 22 (1954): 141.

32. Available at http://indiabudget.nic.in/ub2008–09/eb/npe.pdf.

33. Land values for farmland changing to land for Airport used as proxy for urban land. See values at http://www.business- standard.com/common/news_article.php?leftnm=3&autono=317975.

34. Data for India's HNWI from Asia Pacific Wealth Report, by Cap Gemini and Merrill Lynch and summarized on http:// www.domainb.com/economy/general/2007/20071017_merrill_lynch.htm.

35. Ibid.

Power to the People

All politics is local

Thomas O'Neill Jr

*Basic to a free city was the right to speak back to the state, to
criticize its actions in the assembly, the courts, the theatre, or
conversation. If the state suddenly interfered with that right, it
was breaking its part of the contract. It was becoming a tyranny.
Socrates could have argued—and most of his judges, I believe,
would have agreed—that if the Laws broke the contract, they
released the citizen from the obligation to obey them. When he
lost the right to persuade, he won the right to resist.*

I.F. Stone, *The Trial of Socrates*

India is feted as the world's largest democracy but, in reality, we
face a huge 'democratic deficit'. Our political system is failing
us through its institutions, which are either too large or
bureaucratic, or too small to be effective. Meanwhile, the
corporate hijack of our democracy is under way. It is now so easy
to buy a place in the Rajya Sabha that people joke about putting
the seats on eBay to maximize the 'auction' revenue of the political
parties.

Epigraphs: Thomas O'Neill Jr was a member of the US Congress, Speaker of
the House, 1977–87.
I.F. Stone, *The Trial of Socrates* (Boston: Little Brown, 1988), pp. 225–26.

In this chapter, I have argued for the 'rightsizing' of representative forums to allow for meaningful, democratic participation. In the first half of this chapter, I have shown that our government is both over-centralized and overextended; in the second, I suggest an alternative. The following chapter looks at judicial reform. Having read these two chapters on government, you may well ask yourself, 'Yes, but how is all this going to happen?' I have answered this question in chapter 8, which focuses on how to achieve a popular mandate for change and the steps to be taken during the transitional period. The changes I suggest amount to overhauling the present structure of the government rather than rebuilding it. I am advocating reform, not revolution. All of my recommendations are consistent with the Constitution of India.

A Problem of Scale

> The strength of free peoples resides in the local community. Local institutions are to liberty what primary schools are to science; they put it within the people's reach; they teach people to appreciate its peaceful enjoyment and accustom them to make use of it. Without local institutions, a nation may give itself a free government, but it has not got the spirit of liberty.
>
> Alexis De Tocqueville[1]

One of the goals of this book is to bring democracy within the reach of the people. In India, democratic institutions are a misfit from the community to the national level. Wrong scaling means that Indians are being denied their democratic voice. Most Indians view the actions of government as purposeless, its regulations as tinkering and its attempts to govern as ad hoc. Right scaling for a deeper democracy is a concept that has been widely discussed in political theory, from Jean-Jacques Rousseau's arguments that citizens should be directly involved in government[2] to Alexis De Tocqueville's espousal of the importance of local communities in a vibrant democracy. India's citizens use the electoral process to regularly replace governments, but none of the political choices available today will significantly better the prospects of the majority. *This situation will continue for as long as the very structure of government itself works against the citizens of India.*

The centralized state

How it all happened

India's over-centralized government is a legacy of the dilemma the country faced at the time of Independence. Though the drafters of the Constitution had some sense of the dangers of over-centralization, they were much more concerned with the challenge of making a nation out of a patchwork of principalities, with a myriad of religions, languages and ethnicities. The formation of the modern Indian nation broke many of the rules of nation building, as there was neither a common religion nor a common language to unify it. Granville Austin, in his classic study on the debates of India's Constituent Assembly, reflected on the need for centralization immediately after Independence:

> Responsible Indian leaders, already confronted with a fragmented society, believed no new divisive forces should be introduced . . . Local allegiances, as they existed, for example, in the United States, were to be avoided, not encouraged.[3]

The members of the Constituent Assembly in 1947 were guided by the fear that the young nation would disintegrate into its historical components, the princely states. My vision for the future would not have worked in the infancy of the nation; however, it is appropriate for the present situation, and fits easily within the framework of the Indian Constitution.

Key features

A national government is a monopoly. While the ruling party might change, the essential nature of the state does not. As is the case with most monopolies, over time the Indian government has become increasingly inefficient. It is both over-centralized and overextended. It centralizes power and patronage, nurturing the privileged political and corporate elite. By extending itself into all realms of public life it has spread its inefficiency far and wide*

The Government of India is an amorphous beast sucking up huge resources and achieving little for its citizens. A maze of ministries strangles progress through overregulation, with those sectors that they leave relatively untouched, such as IT, showing rapid growth rates. The Government of India involves itself in everything, from microfinance to the appointment of scientists to earth moving to badminton shuttlecock production to the level of taxation on mops. The ratio of the resources consumed to the output generated is far higher than that of private industries. Take the example of the civil aviation ministry, which has just completed a merger between the government-owned airlines Air India and Indian Airlines, both known for setting global standards for inefficiency.[4] Before the merger, the minister promised to achieve efficiency without any reduction in personnel. Cabinet meetings were held, huge amount of government time was taken up. The resulting entity—Air India—has just posted a combined loss of close to a billion dollars in financial year 2008–09. Should public money be thrown away on inefficient attempts to run a company? Is this the real role of government today?

The bloated Indian government currently employs 23 million people, the size of a small country.[5] It administers fifty ministries and two departments (the departments of atomic energy and

*The inefficiencies of the government are magnified by a 'cycle of distortion'; the government continually justifies itself on account of the highly distortionary effect of its interventions, which then require new interventions to correct the earlier distortions, and so on.

space), overseen by seventy-nine ministers. The list of ministries is included in Appendix 1.

There is a huge amount of ministerial overlap. In Fabindia's case, there are seven ministries that oversee our work: the ministries of small-scale industry, agriculture, health, textiles, food processing, rural development, and commerce and industry. All have overlapping jurisdiction over many policies that cover our business. As a result, it is impossible to get a concerted response on these policies, because the ministers represent different parties and interests. This is a system that produces executive gridlock.

Take the example of the Food Safety and Standards Act (2006), which is of pivotal importance to Fabindia's organic food line. From its introduction as a bill in 2005 until very recently, a turf war existed between the food processing industries ministry and the health and family welfare ministry. Both ministries wanted to be the nodal agency for implementation of the Act. The dispute appears to have been resolved in the health ministry's favour, which was supposed to implement the act by the middle of 2008.[6] There is no certainty, however, that fresh contestations will not surface. When there are seventy-nine ministers, fifty ministries, and a seemingly infinite number of bureaucratic bodies, there is complete and utter confusion. I often think that India functions *in spite* of its government.

A side effect of a massive government is that it is seen as a cash cow; and everyone wants to milk it. A government job becomes the ultimate aspiration for the poor and the lower middle class as it generally means economic security and, often, the opportunity to take a second job. For as long as it remains the one gravy train in town, everyone will want a piece of that action, as the caste-based reservation system for government jobs demonstrates. The reservation and consequent anti-reservation lobby create an endless spiral of bureaucracy that consumes huge amounts of time and resources.* I suggest that it is time to drain the gravy

*For example, the Gujjar community of Rajasthan held long protests through the summer of 2007 and again in 2008 demanding reservations as Scheduled

train by minimizing the size of government and dealing with the root causes of inequality via the TC system detailed in the previous chapter. Throughout this book, I argue against 'large government machinery' at any level. My own experience has shown me that a large bureaucracy with its reach and overregulation becomes greedy and creates needless rules to enrich itself.

The federation of states

The problem of scale is illustrated by the huge disparities between the Indian states in terms of population and area (see Appendix 1). Such diversity in size makes for a very uneven democracy. Imagine the difference in representation I get as a resident of Lakshadweep, the smallest territory in the Union (both in terms of its 32 sq. km area and its population of 60,650) and Uttar Pradesh, the largest (population-wise, with over 166 million people.) That is roughly 2740 times more residents than the population of Lakshadweep. As a resident of Dadra and Nagar Haveli, with a population of just 220,490 and an area of 112 sq. km, I can easily make an appointment to see the chief secretary, whereas this would be impossible for an ordinary citizen of a neighbouring town which happens to fall over the border in Maharashtra (wig a population of nearly 97 million). That the quality of representation is an accident of geography in India dramatically weakens democracy. This is widely acknowledged by political leaders in India today. Even the Uttar Pradesh chief minister, Mayawati, favours the division of her huge state into three parts.[7]

There is a minimum bureaucratic apparatus that is created every time a new state is formed. Friends of mine run a white water rafting camp on the Ganga which until recently was part

---

Tribes. Their agitation has claimed many lives and caused damage to critical public infrastructure like the railways. Failed negotiations with the state government in 2007 and precarious dialogue this year have consumed fair amounts of the government's time and resources.

of the vast state of Uttar Pradesh. When the camp became part of the new, tiny hill state of Uttarakhand, my friends were initially pleased. But their enthusiasm was short-lived. The newly created state quickly pounced on their small business with rules, quotas for employment and attempts to extract bribes. At one point they even feared that the state might create a white water rafting and adventure sports ministry. They have been spared so far.

The community

Communities are the building bricks of a nation, effectively representing and binding the needs of the individual to the needs of the nation. Yet in India, uneven and inadequate representation continues down to the community level with flawed institutions providing vastly different representation in cities and rural areas.

Two of the communities discussed in this book illustrate this. In Panchsheel, south Delhi, the community-level institution is the Municipal Corporation of Delhi (MCD), responsible for the city's nearly fourteen million inhabitants and the world's second largest municipal corporation.*,[8] If I have a problem with a bench in my local park, I have to go to this huge organization. The result is that in Delhi we do not control any aspect of life outside of our homes. The civic associations that do exist have no significant power to change the life of the community.

However, the problem with the MCD is not only of scale, but also of procedure. It is nicknamed the 'Maximum Corruption Department'; its archaic and complex regulations provide cover for ferocious bribery.[9] Living and working in Delhi, I experience this only too often. Once we were looking for a three-floor retail space for a Fabindia store and found a place we wanted. However, the landlord had priced all three floors for retail, even though the MCD rules clearly stated that: 'selling' was allowed only on the ground floor, the basement was to be used for 'storage' and the first floor for 'offices/studios'. When I questioned him about this,

*The largest city in terms of surface area is Tokyo.

he simply smiled and said that he would give me 3–4 per cent discount on the rent, which would cover the costs of Fabindia paying off the MCD. When I refused to do this, he told me there were many others who wanted the property and had none of my compunctions. The regulations themselves were so ambiguous and contradictory that I took this case to six lawyers, and each of them came up with different advice. I realized that the confusing language gave the inspector enormous discretionary power with no oversight and very little liability. I did not rent the property. Once again, the law abider is penalized.

While community-level governance in Indian cities is characterized by oversized corrupt institutions, in rural areas the problem is a different one. Panchayats at the village level in India are hundreds of years old. These institutions were largely self-governing, operating in a rigid social structure. When India became independent in 1947, the Constitution of India mandated: 'The state shall take steps to organise village panchayats and endow them with such powers and authority as may be necessary to enable them to function as units of self-government.'* In reality, they were largely neglected and under-resourced, and their autonomy eroded. Efforts were made to revitalize the institution of the Panchayati Raj in the seventy-third amendment to the Constitution that came into effect in April 1993, but they remain weak. In Sewari, the local village council (the Gram Panchayat) only represents a little over 10,000 people,[10] and is too small and under-resourced to effectively represent the local population. This is something I have repeatedly seen in my work in rural India.

Some argue that there has been a deliberate attempt to cripple and eventually discard the panchayats by the bureaucracy, local vested interests and MPs in the state legislatures and in Parliament.[11] The elite do not want to let go of power. Today panchayats are plagued by poor participation, lack of democratic practices and shortage of funds. They lack the resources because of their size and tiny revenue. If panchayats are to be effective

*The Directive Principles of State Policy, Article 40.

they have tó have the tools, the ability to raise funds and a framework that recognizes them as fundamental to the success of government. Once again it is a case of decisions, authority and funding for projects being made a long way from the recipients of those policies.

The Role of the Government

India needs a national government that is a fraction of the size and complexity of the present system of governance. Throughout this book, I make a case for the national government to function as the umpire that will only intervene to correct an imbalance where the normal forces of demand and supply will not self-correct. Local government, on the other hand, will be vibrant, strong and noisy. Traditionally, a strong government was thought to be important because 'the masses' were not competent enough to make intelligent political decisions.[12] Moral issues aside, research demonstrates that diverse groups of people are often smarter than the smartest people in them. James Surowiecki has filled a book with examples of this.[13] He argues that it is not logical to confine political debates to experts and policy elites. Ordinary people turn out to be extraordinarily capable of understanding difficult issues and making meaningful decisions about them.

When Fabindia set up a community-owned company in Chanderi, a town in Madhya Pradesh, the elections for the board of directors electrified the artisan community. They nominated twelve candidates for the two positions and brought considerable enthusiasm and energy to the politics of the election. India will see extraordinary results when this kind of democratic energy is productively directed towards improving local communities.

Reducing the role of the government and acknowledging the value of citizens making decisions about issues that affect them are not new ideas. I first encountered them through the political philosopher John Stuart Mill when I was a teenager. At that time, his words seemed like they had been written precisely for India in the mid-1980s. Today they sum up my views on the role of government:

> The objections to government interference, when it is not such as to involve infringement of liberty, may be of three kinds. The first is, when the thing to be done is likely to be better done by individuals than by the government. Speaking generally, there is no one so fit to conduct any business, or to determine how or by whom it shall be conducted, as those who are personally interested in it. The second objection is more nearly allied to our subject. In many cases, though individuals may not do the particular thing so well, on the average, as the officers of government, it is nevertheless desirable that it should be done by them, rather than by the government, as a means to their own mental education—a mode of strengthening their active faculties, exercising their judgement, and giving them a familiar knowledge of the subjects with which they are thus left to deal. The third, and most cogent reason for restricting the interference of government, is the great evil of adding unnecessarily to its power. Every function superadded to those already exercised by the government causes its influence over hopes and fears to be more widely diffused, and converts, more and more, the active and ambitious part of the public into hangers-on of the government.[14]

The New Government

A complete overhaul in the structure of the government is required. Rightsizing our democratic institutions will bring real democracy to Indians. My proposals are designed to amplify the positive aspects of our current democracy and reduce the role of patronage in government. The era of over-centralized, overextended and uneven government will come to an end. The needs of the people must come to the fore and be the principal criteria for decision making. In today's inappropriately scaled government, leaders

Figure 4.1: Current and proposed structures of government.

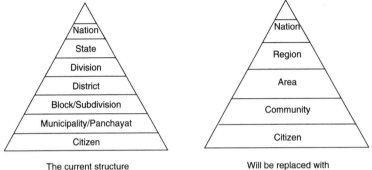

rarely know what people want, and fulfilling their needs is not a priority in government decisions. In reforming the administration my goal is to create a mechanism that enables citizens to communicate better with their leaders about their needs, who in turn will be able to respond with appropriate policies.

The new system (Figure 4.1) is designed to keep governance at the appropriate scale. Each level of government will be completely responsible for its own revenue and expenditure. The number of elected representatives at each level of government will be based on the size of the population. As the population size changes, a delimitation commission will determine new electoral boundaries.

A summary

A Community will replace the current administrative units of the panchayat, block, and subdivision. It will consist of approximately 25,000 people.* Its role will be management of the welfare of its members and administration of the Community's assets. Every citizen will be both a citizen of the country and a citizen of the Community.

An Area is a collection of 100 contiguous communities, which will collectively manage all works and administration. It will replace the current *district* and *division* classifications in the

---

*This figure represents the minimum population that can sustain the cost of an organization while remaining a player at the national level.

current administrative system with an administrative unit of a population not exceeding 2.5 million. The Area government will mediate between communities for the sharing of assets like airports, rivers, railways, or wildlife corridors.

The states will be replaced by a Region, and will consist of 1,000 communities (ten areas) covering a population not exceeding 25 million. Their primary role will be to facilitate inter-area projects, which impact a broader—but not national—geographic area such as ports and other large scale infrastructure projects.

The Nation, or federal government, at the top of this model will be reduced to a fraction of its current size. In this streamlined model, national government only performs a limited number of appropriate roles, and it performs them well.

The New Government in Detail

The Nation

The proposed leaner structure of the government will allow market economy and decentralized democracy to work and self-regulate

Figure 4.2: The new structure of the proposed government

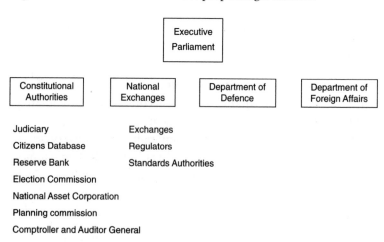

by themselves for the most part, but oversight is critical. The national government will serve primarily to ensure the smooth operation of each section of government (see Figure 4.2). My model empowers the Indian Parliament, whose elected representatives will oversee the work of the professional civil service.

The executive

In India, the President is the formal head of the state with the prime minister as the head of the Central government. Executive power is exercised by the government, while federal legislative power is vested both in the government and the two chambers of India's Parliament. The Lower House, the Lok Sabha (House of the People) consists of directly elected MPs, and the Upper House, the Rajya Sabha (Council of States) consists of members nominated by state legislative assemblies.* Seats are fixed for each state on the basis of population.

The bicameral model grew out of the monarchy system in Europe when there was a perceived need to represent both the aristocracy and the common man. Our Parliament has become increasingly skewed in favour of the corporate aristocracy. While the Upper House was created to provide representation for the states in the constitutional framework, its role has been eroded over time. Now it is the location of a growing number of 'surrogate MPs' who represent specific corporate interests in Parliament. Take the example of a new MP closely associated with one of India's corporate giants. He is going to represent a state which, by his own admission, he visited for the first time in his life only two months ago.[15]

It is time that we opt for a unicameral model of government, which only consists of directly elected representatives and merge the two houses. The presidential system will no longer exist, and

*There are an additional twelve members of the Upper House directly nominated by the President of India for their expertise in specific fields of art, literature, science, and social services.

the current classifications of 'President' and 'governor'* will be obsolete. In the current system, governors are appointed to office in states for a five-year term by the President on the advice of the prime minister, and their conduct is supposed to be above politics. However, this is rarely the case, in spite of the constitutional definition of a governor as a non-partisan actor. Take the example of 1989, when the National Front government replaced the Congress government. The new prime minister, V.P. Singh, asked eighteen governors to resign so he could replace them with his own men. In another instance, the governor of Jharkhand appointed a ruling party alliance member as chief minister, even though in the state elections his party won only twenty-six of the eighty-one assembly seats, compared to the opposition's tally of thirty-six.[16]

In the new model, a unicameral Parliament will have the following roles:

- To form the oversight boards: All current ministries will be abolished. All the departments listed on Figure 4.2 earlier will be overseen by Parliamentary Oversight Boards (POB). Each POB will consist of five MPs, with each MP representing 20 per cent of Parliament, selected on the basis of interest and capability.† Their job is to monitor the performance of the civil service. Each Standard and Exchange Authority (such as the Health Standards Authority, the Education Exchange Authority

---

*The governor has a similar role to the President, but at the state level. They appoint the chief minister, the advocate-general, the chairman and members of the state public service and the judges of the district courts. In terms of legislation, bills passed by the state legislature can only be enacted once the governor assents and he or she also has the power to reserve certain bills for the President. The judicial powers of the governor includes the power of granting pardon, or reducing or commuting sentences of any person convicted of any offence against any law relating to matters to which the executive powers of the state extends. This is not a comprehensive list of the powers of the governor but designed to illustrate the power of the position.

†Each POB MP will represent approximately 20 per cent of Parliament ensuring that these bodies replicate the composition of Parliament.

and so on) will have a POB. Below the Oversight Boards is the professional civil service of each division of the national government.

- To ratify and terminate key professional appointments.
- To make laws.
- To oversee approval of defence, foreign affairs and five-year plans.

The new structure of the nation

Constitutional authorities

Constitutional authorities are a vital check on misuse of power. At heart, they are institutions of accountability. Their competent and professional management is particularly crucial. My aim is to create mechanisms—to borrow from Madison's *Federalist Papers*— that pit interest against interest and ambition against ambition.[17] The Parliament, ultimately responsible to the voters, will administer the bulk of the accountability at the national level. The Parliament's power would be balanced by the constitutional authorities, which would be relatively autonomous from the politics of representative government. The Reserve Bank of India and the Election Commission are already exemplars of well-run constitutional authorities. Five of the seven constitutional authorities already exist and are protected by the Constitution. I propose adding two more.

I. Citizens Database: This would be the nerve centre of the republic and would need protection. I had mentioned in the previous chapter that the Citizens Database would only measure gross income. The collection of any other information such as where and when a transaction occurred would be a serious violation of privacy and this information will not be retained in the Citizens Database. Nevertheless, if foreign governments or organized criminals or terrorists or future authoritarian rulers obtained the information in the Citizens Database, they would have unparalleled information to monitor and control the lives of every Indian.

Three forms of protection would prevent this:

i. Access rights
   a) The Reserve Bank of India will be able to track single data parameters within the Aggregate Economic Activity (AEA) data.
   b) The Community board will be able to access basic information: name, address, age, and gross income level.
   c) The department of foreign affairs will issue passport information requests to the Community board for data verification.
ii. Coding controls: The data will be encrypted and will require a combination of programs to read it.
iii. Facilities protection: The physical citizen's database— facilities, servers, data hubs and national cable network— will be protected using advanced military security, such as the one used by the US at Cheyenne Mountain.*[18]

II. The National Asset Corporation: This will function as a government-owned investment fund (a sovereign asset fund). Its aims will be similar to a private equity fund: to maximize the return on the 'people's capital'. It is a model used very successfully by several other economies, most notably Temasek Holdings of Singapore† and Norway's oil fund‡ which today are among the

---

*Cheyenne Mountain Operations Center is the nerve centre of US defence, military and space missions. It comprises the largest and most complex command and control network in the world, using satellites, microwave radio routes, and fibre optic links to transmit and receive vital communications. It has thus far been completely secure to unauthorized interference. It has a self-contained warning system using stand-alone computers and dedicated communication circuits. In addition, cryptological (scrambling) devices are employed at both ends of every communication circuit.

†Temasek, which was founded in 1974, manages US$85 billion in assets. Its sole shareholder is the Government of Singapore.

‡Established in 1990, it is the largest sovereign wealth fund in Europe and second largest in the world with assets worth US$390 billion as of May 2008.

world's largest investors, with a hard focus on returns. In chapter 8 I detail the uses of the National Asset Corporation.

III. The Reserve Bank of India: This institution's management of India's monetary policy is commendable. It will continue to function as at present, with the added benefit of its head enjoying the same degree of independence and indefinite tenure afforded to all members of the executive branch. Aggregate Economic Activity (AEA) data will also provide the bank with a vast amount of information which will enhance the effectiveness of monetary interventions.

IV. The judiciary: This is detailed in the following chapter. The changes proposed will ensure that the enforcement of rights, the rule of law and timely justice is available to every citizen.

V. The Election Commission: Article 324 of the Constitution states that the 'superintendence, direction and control of elections [are] to be vested in an Election Commission.' This institution renders an extraordinary service to India. I have been witness to elections which have been conducted in conditions of violence, remote locations and difficult weather. The Election Commission has a reputation for fairness that is unmatched by other government bodies. They would continue to play their current role during elections.

VI. The office of the Comptroller and Auditor General: Article 149 of the Constitution describes the duties and powers of the Comptroller and Auditor General as follows: 'The Comptroller and Auditor General shall perform such duties and exercise such powers in relation to the accounts of the Union and of the States and of any other authority or body as may be prescribed by or under any law made by Parliament.' The CAG will continue to scrutinize public accounts through auditing of the finances of the Community, Area, Region and Nation. The head of the CAG will work to

General Performance Parameters (GPP), and measure the quality of accounting, transparency and critical expenditure ratios.

VII. The Planning Commission: After Independence, India's leaders decided that an overall planning body was necessary and they set up the Planning Commission in 1950 through a resolution. The scope of its work is presented in the following terms:

> The Constitution of India has guaranteed certain Fundamental Rights to the citizens of India and enunciated certain Directive Principles of State Policy, in particular, that the State shall strive to promote the welfare of the people by securing and protecting as effectively as it may a social order in which justice, social, economic and political, shall inform all the institutions of the national life, and shall direct its policy towards securing, among other things,
>
> (a) that the citizens, men and women equally, have the right to an adequate means of livelihood;
>
> (b) that the ownership and control of the material resources of the community are so distributed as best to subserve the common good; and
>
> (c) that the operation of the economic system does not result in the concentration of wealth and means of production to the common detriment.[19]

Under my proposals the Planning Commission will be both a planning certification agency and a professional membership accreditation agency that trains and certifies planners, civil administrators and managers who then seek appointments in the Community, Area and Regional governments. The Planning Commission will play an important role in the definition of habitat rights outlined in chapter 7.

NATIONAL EXCHANGES

The National Exchanges have three elements—the Standards Authorities, the Regulators and the Exchanges themselves as outlined in chapter 2. Every tradable commodity will have a National Exchange. In Chapters 2 and 3 I have shown how these elements will allow communities and individuals the free right of exchange and use the market for optimal resource allocation.

THE DEPARTMENT OF DEFENCE

The department of defence would ideally become obsolete one day as we recognize the frailty of the human condition and see the value of global unity for our brief tenancy on this planet. Unfortunately, with a nuclear subcontinent and dysfunctional neighbouring states, the maxim of 'trusting in God and keeping our powder dry' seems a more apt principle. The department will be presided over by a secretary, who will be a professional, not a political appointee. India's defence and foreign affairs policies are of vital importance to the future of the nation. This vast and complex area would require the space of another book to delve into.

THE DEPARTMENT OF FOREIGN AFFAIRS

The major components of the department of foreign affairs are strategy and implementation; these two divisions are designed to ensure that we engage with the community of nations based on a long-term strategy that is insulated from short-term politics while enjoying broad legitimacy among the various political parties. A secretary will head it in the same manner as the department of defence.

Staffing the civil services: Ensuring that the key civil service appointments be made on the basis of merit and not political value is essential for democracy. Candidates for key positions would be selected by the prime minister and then ratified by a two-thirds majority in the Parliament. This would eliminate purely political appointees.* Relying on a simple majority of 51

---

*Today many government appointments are made of individuals who have clearly stated political affiliations, even to bodies such as the Election Commission. This damages the legitimacy of such institutions.

per cent could subject the process to the ruling party or coalition, which by definition possesses a simple majority; only consensus candidates would be able to inspire a 66 per cent majority. The result would be a civil service run by the most competent, qualified individuals.

The key positions in the proposed national government are as follows:

- Chief justices of Regional courts and justices of the Supreme and constitutional courts
- Governor and deputy governors of the Reserve Bank of India
- Election commissioner and deputies
- Secretary and deputy secretary of the Citizens Database
- Director and deputy directors of the Planning Commission
- Director and deputy director of the Comptroller and Auditor General
- Managing director and directors of the National Asset Corporation
- Directors of National Exchanges
- Chief market regulators
- Commissioners of Standards Authorities
- Secretary of defence
- Secretary of foreign affairs

Security of tenure is essential for regulatory independence, consistency, stability and far-sighted policy making. Therefore, key civil service positions should have indefinite tenure instead, running for as long as the office holder meets a strict set of criteria (see Table 4.1), or the General Performance Parameters (GPPs). He or she could theoretically be employed for life, as long as they continually perform, thus affording protection from political interference.* (The POB will monitor the GPPs of all key civil

---

*There could not be a better example of how GPPs would build a culture of merit than E. Sreedharan, the current MD of the Delhi Metro Rail Corporation (DMRC). An engineer with the Indian Railways for fifty-four years, he was asked to come out of his retirement in 1990 to take over the construction of the Konkan Railway. He finished the immensely difficult project within time and budget

Table 4.1: Examples of the General Performance Parameters (GPPs)

Institution	Parameters
Head of Election Commission	a. Percentage of elections conducted that met the highest standards b. Ratio of violent incidents to elections held c. Ratio of funds spent per election
Chief Justice of a Regional Court	a. Caseload of court b. Waiting time between filing and hearings c. Case disposal ratio d. Ratio of disposal cases appealed e. Ratio of pretrial arbitration that results in an out-of-court settlement. f. Cases to appeal ratio

Revenue and expenditure for the National government

Revenue	Expenditure
Taxation • 1 per cent Economic Activity Tax on every monetary transaction	Rental and Sale of National Assets • National Frequency Spectrum (EXP) • Assets which are outside of inhabited areas
• A flat 30 per cent inheritance tax on any inheritance over 1000 times the prevailing per capita GDP (see chapter 3)	• National government administration costs • Constitutional authority administration costs • National legal institution costs

and it is considered to be one of the most technically complex railway projects in the world. After this, he was made the MD of the DMRC in 1998. Since he took over, each leg of the Delhi Metro has been either completed before time or saved on allocated budget, or both. At seventy-six, different governments have given him a series of extensions well past his official retirement age of fifty-eight because he has demonstrated that it is possible to create world standards in a system known for its debilitating corruption and red tape. Today, however, no political party can remove him from his position, simply because of his performance.

servants on a semi-annual basis.) Each POB will consist of five MPs selected on the basis of interest and capability. Each MP would represent 20 per cent of the Parliament. If civil servants' GPP score dips below a defined threshold, the Parliamentary Oversight Board would intervene to remove them. As James Madison wrote in 'Federalist No. 48' of the US separation of powers, the branches 'should not be so far separated as to have no constitutional control over each other'.[20]

The Other Tiers of Government

The rightsizing of the government is at the crux of my proposals. Part XI (especially Articles 245 to 254) of the Constitution provides for the separation of the areas of the responsibility between state governments and the Union government.* In this section I do the same, outlining a division of powers between the proposed different tiers of government. Each tier will have a limited revenue, and limited responsibility, resulting in streamlined, effective government.

Although there are four tiers of government (see Figure 4.3), general elections will only be needed for Parliament and for the

Figure 4.3: Effective streamlined government

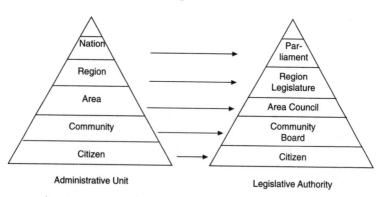

*More than separation, the distribution of powers is coded in terms of 'relations' between the Union and the states. Articles 245 and 246 are especially important in this context.

Table 4.2: Tiers of government

Tier Of Government	No. of Administrative Units	Head	Governing Body	Population	Current Tier	Equivalent Current Authority
Community Board	48,000	Chair	4 members + chairperson	25,000	Panchayat /Municipal Corporation	Sarpanch, SDM, Town Chief (Nagar Palika Adhyaksh)
Area Council (made up of 100 communities)	480	Local area MP is the Area Board Chairperson	100 Community Chairpersons	2.5 million	District/ division	• Member of State Legislative Assembly • District Collector • Pramukh Area Chief • Zila Pradhan District Chief
Regional Legislature is made from 10 Areas	48	Governor	10 MPs	25 million		Chief Minister
National Parliament has 1 MP representing each Area of approx. 2.5 million citizens	1	Prime Minister	480 MPs	1.2 billion		President

Community Boards. Members of the other two tiers—Area council and the Regional Legislatures—will be drawn from MPs and Community Board members as Table 4.2 illustrates.

The Region

This would replace the current classifications of 'state' and 'union territory'. India's 1.2 billion people would be divided into forty-

Revenue and expenditure plan for the Region

Revenue	Expenditure
Sales/ rental from 'Regional' assets	
• Terrestrial Right of Way; Road, water, rail etc.	• Area Government Administration Costs
• Large Infrastructure projects, such as ports.	• Area courts

eight regions of 25 million people each.* The main function of the Region would be to administer inter-area projects, and to re-demarcate the boundaries of areas and communities. This is to allow the governance institutions to adapt to changing population size.

The head of the Region, the governor, will be elected by the ten MPs and the chairpersons of the 1000 Community councils that belong to the Region. Each MP's vote will be equivalent to ten votes, so the total number of votes in this election is 1100.

The three main functions of the governor will be to act as:
  i) Head of the Regional Planning Authority, defining the Region's integrated five-year plan.
 ii) Chairperson of the Regional appellate court (equivalent to today's high court) to settle intercommunity/inter-area disputes about revenue sharing.
iii) Sole authority on re-delimitation of boundaries of communities and areas within the Region.

Geographical redistribution is very important. It will be carried out once every five years at the very beginning of an electoral term. When a Community's population exceeds a level of roughly 25,000 it will inform the government of the Region, which will carry out the re-districting in the following way:
  i) Calculate the population density per square kilometres in a Community.

*These figures are based on India's current population. As this increases so will the number of all governance institutions.

ii) Change boundaries based on population density, ensuring that the changes maximize the population density in the smallest possible land area, as illustrated in Figure 4.4 and its Note. The only caveat to this principle is that communities should not be extended to cross major geographical barriers such as large rivers and mountain ranges. This caveat will be explained in detail in chapter 8, under the Delimitation Commission.

Figure 4.4: Figure explaining changing boundaries according to population density in the new model.

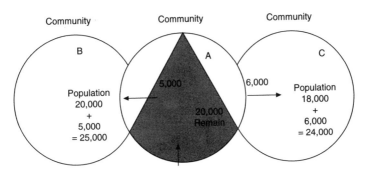

Shaded area represents highest density in a contiguous area

Note: Community A's population goes down from 31,000 to 20,000 with 5000 citizens now living in Community B and 6000 citizens now living in Community C whose populations are now 25,000 and 24,000 respectively. The land area of Community A was reduced while that of communities B and C increased.

If Community A's population grows to 30,000, and its two neighbours only have 20,000, the delimitation will work as demonstrated above. In this case the land area of Community A shrinks while that of communities B and C increase and population is evened out so that each Community now has 25,000 residents and no one is physically displaced. While Community A may lose some assets in this process, this will probably be offset by the increase in revenue from additional property tax. As the population density increases so too will property prices.

The Area

Each Area will represent 2.5 million people, who would be spread over 100 member communities. It will replace the current *district* and *division* classifications. The main responsibility of the Area is to facilitate intercommunity projects, such as investment in local airports, roads, rail links, mineral resources and large waterbodies.

Each Area will be represented by a member of Parliament, directly elected by the 2.5 million people of the Area. With current population figures, this means there will be a total of 480 MPs in India. This will rectify the current gross imbalances in representation. There are currently 543 members of Parliament in India representing constituencies with population, from 37,619 (Lakshadweep) to 3,103,525 (outer Delhi).[21] While there is currently a bill making its way through the Parliament to redistrict many constituencies, this will do little more than remove the most obvious distortions.

An MP will have four roles:
  i) Representing his constituents in Parliament,
 ii) Serving on the Parliamentary Oversight Boards,
iii) Chair the Area Council, and
 iv) Passing Laws.

Making an MP the chair of the Area Council ensures a strong link between national and local representation. The Area Council would consist of the elected representatives of 100 constituent communities. All decisions of the Area Council will be made by

Revenue and expenditure plan for the Area

Revenue	Expenditure
Sales/ rental from 'Area' assets	• Area government administration costs
• Area airports, roads, rail links	• Area courts
• Large waterbodies	
• Intercommunity mineral resources	
• Intercommunity forests and biospheres	

majority vote. The chairperson will have ten 'super' votes, the ability to delay votes for up to three months and under special conditions the ability to request a citizens' referendum. A citizens' referendum will be conducted by the Area government every time there is an issue which requires the coordination of several Community governments within the Area and the Community councils involved have different opinions. Take the example of the investment required by three communities to fence the area covered by their biodiversity zone. The investment is substantial and the gains long-term and therefore, two Community councils agree while the third does not. The biodiversity zone covers areas in all three communities. In such cases the Area government will call for a citizens' referendum to cover the citizens in each of the three communities as it is their money that will be used to make this investment.

The Community

This is the fundamental building block of government. It will replace the panchayat, block, and subdivision and consist of approximately 25,000 people.* Its role will be threefold:

Revenue and expenditure plan for the Community

Revenue	Expenditure
Taxation	
• 1 per cent Property Tax	• Payment for TCs issued to
Sales/rental from 'Community' assets	citizens below the poverty line
• Sale of water	• Purchase of forest or biodiversity
• Lease of common lands	• Credits if necessary to fulfil
• Leasing of 'surplus' assets like	the per capita quota
forests, biodiversity and right of way.	• Administrative costs and salaries
• Lease of mining licences	• Interest of loans for major capital
• Revenue share from Area assets	projects shared at an Area level
leasing	or for local infrastructure
	development

*This figure represents the minimum population that can sustain the cost of an organization while remaining a player at the national level.

i) Management of the welfare of its members via the TC system,
ii) Collecting information for the Citizen's Database, and
iii) Administration of the community's assets, such as land, local waterbodies, local mining, forests, biospheres.

The Community chairperson will be directly elected by the members of the Community, as will the four other members of the Community Council. The salary of the chairperson and the members will be a multiple of the per capita Community GDP* calculated according to Aggregate Economic Activity (AEA).† This links earnings to performance, and acts as an incentive for the council to maximize the Community's wealth.

The Community chairperson will have two key roles:
i) To manage the assets, budgets and development of the Community and
ii) To act as a member of the Area Authority.

This division of roles mean that communities have a voice in the overall development of their Region. The actual administration of the Community will be carried out by qualified professionals appointed by the Council. Every officer will have passed a certification standard administered by the Planning Commission. The list of the key personnel in the Community government is as follows:

• Targeted Catalyst Administrator
• Asset Manager
• Finance Officer
• Community Database Officer
• Land Records Officer
• Police Chief
• Magistrate
• Prosecutor and Enforcement Officer

While each part of the administration is run by appointed

---

*This could also be called Gross Community Product (GCP).
†For example, the chairperson's salary could be five or ten times the per capita Community GDP and Council members' three times this amount. The multiplier would be the same for all communities across the nation.

professional CEOs (those that have been certified by the Planning Commission) recruited much the same way as corporations hire management today, it is the elected officials who set the agenda for each part of the administration.

The Citizen

At the heart of the nation is the Community and at the heart of the Community is the citizen. In this new model every Indian is linked to a Community in which he or she resides. Residence equates to spending over 180 days in a calendar year in that Community or owning land or renting a place of residence.

In India a large number of citizens are stateless. My family home is in Delhi and we have a live-in staff of nine. My staff comes from across the country and over the last seven years, since establishing our household, we have worked hard to get them recognized by the state. The story of our nanny is an example. She is from Manipur, yet there is no record of her existence. In order to get her a passport, we had to use all our knowledge of how to navigate the Union home ministry, police department and state administrations—all this just to get her recognition of citizenship that should be her birthright as an Indian.

In this new system, any citizen can apply for membership of a Community by presenting:

i) Evidence of ownership or rent of a property: Almost every adult, living anywhere in India, pays someone something. Even the man sleeping on the pavement, the child who lives under a bench, the woman in the doorway, will be paying for it.[22] Within the new system, this will be recorded in the Aggregate Economic Activity and will be a valid evidence for residency.

ii) Evidence of employment of an entity or individual who resides in the Community.

Once an individual becomes a member of a Community the Citizen's Database records this change in residence. Their economic activity data will be linked to the Community and they will be eligible for TCs if their economic activity falls below the threshold.

This system will also be more effective in distinguishing citizens from aliens, especially in border areas where illegal migration is rampant. A Citizen's Database will enable verification of citizens. Aliens like economic migrants and refugees will be accommodated within communities of border areas *if* the Community leadership decides to offer them shelter. (Immigration most affects the Community the migrants live in. Hence it is the right of the Community concerned—rather than the national government— to accept or reject them.) For their contribution to the host Community, aliens would be duly recognized with residence privilege in the form of work visas. The issuance of the work visa would be the right of the Community governments in which they reside, as would be its renewal. This would enable the Community and the Nation to possess accurate information about aliens within the country. When immigrants decide to shift from one Community to another, they would have to be accepted by the new host Community before their visa status can be changed.*

Illegal immigration (from Bangladesh and Nepal) has become a major issue in India. From national security to adverse impact on local economies (illegal immigrants work for lower wages than the local workforce, which means the latter lose jobs), it is a problem that needs to be urgently addressed. My proposals would ensure that governments at various tiers have exact record of immigrants. This would enable better policy formulation, address legitimate grievances of local populations and prevent chauvinistic

---

*The genesis of this framework lies in my interaction with a head of a Swiss canton. During a conversation over our plans to expand our business in Switzerland, the canton head suggested that if we were to bring in a certain amount of investment, the canton would offer visas for two employees of Fabindia. The canton's autonomy enables it to recommend the issuance of visa to the federal government and the respective embassy. My system would give communities similar autonomy.

political impulses, which seek to prevent free movement of Indians within their country and capitalize on local fears and prejudices against legal and illegal migrants.*

Every citizen will have the following rights as a member of a Community:

i) Elect the Community chairperson and four counsellors every five years.

ii) Attend the annual Community board meeting and vote on the Community budgets and annual plan.

iii) Sue their Community Council if their basic habitat rights (outlined in chapter 7) are not met.

iv) Elect an MP during every general election.

v) Use the Community complaints system if they have a problem.

vi) Issue a citizens variance wherever applicable to their habitat rights (see chapter 7).†

Distribution of Resources between Different Levels of Government

Revenue for the different tiers of government will partly come from the taxes (detailed in chapter 3), and partly from the sale and rental of assets. The ownership of assets is divided between the different tiers of government, allowing each tier to gain revenue from the sale or rental of assets (as in Table 4.3). All assets would be traded and leased on the Exchanges, regardless of which administrative unit they belong to.

The logic of the system is to make an asset the property of the lowest level of administration possible without compromising

---

*It would be a solution apt for a country like India. It is part of a Region where illegal migration cannot be completely prevented. At the same time, South Asian regionalism has not shown encouraging signs of producing a cross-border movements regime. Yet, the country cannot shut itself off from such movements, given its pivotal role as the economic engine of the South Asian region.

†The last two points will be explained in detail in chapter 7.

Table 4.3: Asset allocation distribution between the different tiers of government.

Asset	Community	Area	Region	Nation
Land	■			
Local Waterbodies	■			
Local Mining/Quarrying	■			
Forest	■			
Larger Waterbodies		■		
Minerals, Oil, Natural Gas		■		
Biodiversity Reserves		■		
Major Transport Links—Railways, Airports, Ports		■		
Local Frequency Spectrum			■	
Terrestrial Right of Way—Road, Water, Rail, etc.		■		
Water Grid			■	
Power Grid			■	
National Frequency Spectrum				■
Assets that are outside of populated areas				■
National Public*				■

Some of these assets (e.g. major transport links) could be distributed to either the Area or Regional level of government. However, in the interest of keeping democracy as close to the Community as possible, I have tended to place them under the jurisdiction of the lowest level of government possible. Of course, in a situation where several areas were impacted by the construction of a new railway hub, for example, this project would be taken up at the Regional level. *This comprises assets that are part of national territory such as sea beds or assets that might be assigned by international bodies such as mineral rights in oceans, polar regions or space rights.

necessary access or asset viability. For example, local waterbodies are a Community-owned asset while a large port would be a Regional asset.

Here are a few instances of how this would work in the new administrative framework. Take the example of a large lake that covers three communities and needs to have its water catchment zones protected. In such a case, the investment required will be collected from the different communities in the Area. This would be managed by the chair of the Area administration, who would also be the local member of Parliament. Combining these two roles means that the individual will have strong incentives to both develop the assets and incomes of the Area in addition to giving communities a fair deal, as this is his or her vote base.

Now if we assume that four of the 100 communities (in that Area) pay for a total of 40 per cent (each pays say 10 per cent) of the cost of improving the water catchment zones that lie in their communities and they benefit from this investment as well, the other ninety-six communities all paid an equal amount of 0.62 per cent each. Let us again assume that because of this investment, the amount of water in the lake tripled, resulting in a tripling of surplus water available for trading. This water would then be graded by the Standards Authority and traded on the National Water Exchange. The Area administration would then work out a revenue share to ensure that the incremental increase in water sale profits are shared according to the ratio of investment made by the communities.

Caste and Minorities

Sceptics of the framework offered in the preceding pages would argue, perhaps legitimately, about the enormous arresting effects of the caste system on it. They may also question the impact it will have on the minorities—religious, linguistic, tribal—of the country. I have an answer, one that would eventually neutralize caste-based politics and hopefully reduce class barriers in Indian society.

The caste system and the politics around it have been one of the biggest reasons for the paralysis in India's governance, and the cause of many of its past and current woes. The framers of our Constitution hoped that the fissures the caste system created would heal through the specific affirmative action of reservations—

in jobs, representative institutions and educational institutes. This has not happened. Instead caste has infiltrated into electoral democracy, weaning it away from its liberal moorings. Political parties survive and gain power on caste arithmetic. While jobs in the public sector have augured well for many from the 'lower' castes, the humungous size of our government has turned into a parable of supreme inefficiency. There is a bigger problem with reservations in educational institutions. In the absence of a robust educational infrastructure at the primary and secondary level, reservations in institutes of higher learning are rendered meaningless as students from 'lower' castes often lack the training to cope with the standards.

There are two dimensions of the caste system that need revision: economic and social. It is beyond the mandate of this book to comprehensively address the social dimensions of the caste system. I will focus on the economic aspect of this malaise.

This biggest ground for caste-based discrimination in the economic arena is the lack of opportunities for groups with poor education and no skills which is almost always the case with people from 'lower' castes. I once had to refuse a job to a candidate because he did not possess adequate skills for the position. He responded by saying that I was refusing him the employment because he was a Dalit. I told him I did not know he was a Dalit till he informed me. I could not offer him the job because he lacked specific skills required for the nature of the work. This experience confirmed my conjecture that people from 'lower' castes are often denied the opportunity of employment in higher positions, especially in the corporate and private sector, where there has been the largest increase in jobs, because they do not possess adequate skills. This is especially true for jobs requiring technical skills which offer higher remuneration. The problem lies, as I argued in the preceding paragraph, in our country's embarrassing primary and secondary educational infrastructure. Inadequate and weak education in formative years put these students in a disadvantageous situation when they enter institutes of higher learning through reservations. Reservations have been targeted at the wrong level. Hence, they fail to produce desired results.

Providing equal opportunity—in democratic institutions, education, health care, civic responsibilities and environmental sustenance—is the core concern of this book. My proposals would effectively counter denial of opportunity and the resulting caste discrimination in the economic arena. One of the first areas where TCs would have greatest and most beneficial impact is education, especially at the primary and secondary levels. TCs incentivize service providers to deliver better services. The Education Standards Authority would ensure that school rankings based on transparent and quantifiable criteria are available to the public so that they can make the best decisions on where to send their children. Once we have a highly literate workforce—vocational and academic—discrimination in highly productive sectors of the economy would cease to exist. True market rewards efficiency. It has no place for primordial, obsolete identities.

I also propose a gradual, phased withdrawal of reservations from all sectors, at a rate of 5 per cent annually. Educational TCs would take effect in about a similar time span and the individuals who are no longer able to benefit from reservations will be supported by TCs so that they can acquire the necessary skills and have the legal vouchers to fight any caste-based discrimination in hiring practices. Over time, there would be no need for reservations. Table 4.4 illustrates this process. (Even the reservations offered by the Constitution were to be reviewed every

Table 4.4: Outline to end reservations.

Year	Current	1	2	3	4	5	6	7	8	9	10
Reservation (%)	50	45	40	35	30	25	20	15	10	5	0

ten years and it was hoped that they would cease to exist sixty years after the commencement of the Constitution.)* The smaller size of the government (at all levels) would make reservations redundant. Additionally, all the social security benefits that government employees currently receive would be available through TCs to every citizen of the country. Regions where caste discrimination is practised would linger. But once they are deprived of the 'oxygen' of reservations much of the social and political influence of caste-based politics would wither away. The politics of India will change for the better once caste considerations lose their power on the electorate.

Multicultural democracies face a peculiar tension between economic interests and ethnic identities.† Democratic distribution of limited resources on purely utilitarian principle, greatest good for the greatest number, invariably and effectively leaves minorities out. This has been true of India's democratic experience where minorities of all hue have found themselves alienated from the 'national mainstream'. They have remained at the margins of economic progress and find their identity threatened, primarily, by this economic marginalization. Opportunistic politics has turned them into convenient vote banks without ensuring their economic well-being or making them feel secure about their identities. Over the last six decades, armed movements and insurgencies have cropped up across the country mainly due to economic neglect and identity threats.‡

The denial of opportunity that abets and sustains caste also adds to resentments of the minorities. In the framework I advance in this book, the institutions providing opportunities counter this trend. Radical reorganization and decentralization would mean

---

*See, Articles 330, 332 and 334 of the Constitution.
†I use the term 'ethnic' in its broadest meaning to cover religious, linguistic, tribal and other variants.
‡The Naga and Assamese insurgencies in India's North-east, Kashmiri separatism, the Khalistan movement, are major examples.

that the mechanisms that work to eradicate caste would also give minorities a greater sense of control over resources and their allocation. I may illustrate it thus. The Dongria and Jharnia Kondh tribes of Kalahandi district in Orissa have been protesting against a London-based mining company which has an US$800 million project of mining bauxite from the Niyamgiri Hills. The local tribes consider the hills to be sacred and assert their right over the resource-rich mountains. Such protests against forest and natural habitats being harnessed without any direct benefits for the local communities go on across the country. Under my framework, with empowered Community governments, local residents would benefit in two ways: one, the decision to allow resource exploitation would be solely theirs; two, if they allow harnessing of natural resources, the accruing revenue will go to them and will be used, through the TCs, for their benefit. With the present governance structure I do not foresee India managing to achieve this, despite all efforts at decentralization and the rhetoric of empowering the minorities.

In this chapter, I have shown how to give power genuinely to the people. In the next chapter, I outline legal reforms to reinvigorate India's judiciary and ensure that all Indians, regardless of their social or economic status, are able to exercise their constitutional rights.

Notes

1. Alexis De Tocqueville, *Democracy in America*, trans. George Lawrence (New York: Anchor Books, 1969).
2. Jean-Jacques Rousseau, *The Social Contract*, ed. C. Frankel (Hafner: New York, 1947).
3. Granville Austin, *The Indian Constitution: Cornerstone of a Nation* (New Delhi: Oxford University Press, 2002), p. 189.
4. Air India has one of the highest employees to aircraft ratio in the world, 650 compared to the industry average of 350. 'Air India's Unions to Oppose Job Cuts after Sale', *Reuters*, 14 August 2001.

5. Gautam Bhardwaj and Surendra A. Dave, 'Towards Estimating India's Implicit Pension Debt on Account of Civil Service Employees', (Invest India Economic Foundation and Center for Monitoring Indian Economy, 2005), pp. 9–10. Available at www.iief.com/Research/BhardwajDave2005_ipd1.pdf.

6. 'Food Safety Act to be effective in 3 months', *The Financial Express*, 15 March 2008.

7. 'If centre agrees, I'm OK with UP's division: Maya', *Express India*, 15 January 2008.

8. See www.mcdonline.gov.in

9. MCD frequently tops the list of Delhi's most corrupt organizations. Two hundred and eleven complaints were launched against it in 2003. In 2005, the MCD decided to dismiss from service anyone caught accepting bribe. Crackdowns by the country's top intelligence agency, the CBI, have been very common, including a major one in 2006 involving the higher-ups of the corporation. Interestingly, reorganizing the corporation by breaking it into smaller bodies has been officially endorsed as one way of tackling rampant corruption. But opinions of those in charge remain divided and nothing has resulted so far. See 'Police, MCD Top Corruption List', *The Times of India*, 26 January 2004; 'MCD Crackdown on Corruption', *The Hindu*, 15 March 2005; 'Corruption in MCD: 17 Engineers, 15 Builders in CBI Net', *The Tribune*, 28 July 2006; 'MCD Division in Focus Again', *The Hindu*, 27 May 2005.

10. The 2001 Census puts Sewari's population at 8,844. Calculation for the year 2008 by World Gazetteer comes to 10,240 people. Available at http://world-gazetteer.com/wg.php?x=&men=gpro&lng=en&des=wg&srt=npan&col=abcdefghinoq&msz=1500&geo=414385328.

11. See 'Battling the Babu Raj', *The Economist*, 6 March 2008, available at: http://www.economist.com/world/asia/displaystory.cfm?story_id=10804248.

12. This point of view is articulated by Joseph Schumpeter in *Capitalism, Socialism and Democracy,* ed. T. Bottomore (London: Allen and Unwin, 1976), p. 262, where he states that it is the citizen's job to elect leaders to represent them, not to decide issues directly, because 'the typical citizen drops down to a lower level of mental performance as soon as he enters the political field.'

13. James Surowiecki, *The Wisdom of Crowds: Why the Many Are Smarter Than the Few* (London: Abacus, 2004). Surowiecki states that diversity and independence are key conditions for good collective decisions.

14. J.S. Mill, *On Liberty* (New York: Dover Publications, 2002), p. 92–93. First published in 1859.

15. 'After Surrogate Ads, Time for Surrogate MPs?' *Indo-Asian News Service*,17 March 2008.

16. Soutik Biswas, 'India's "Partisan" Governors', *BBC Online*, 4 March 2008.

17. James Madison, 'Federalist No. 51', in *The Federalist Papers*, 1788.

18. For more information, see http://www.norad.mil/about/CMOC.html.

19. Government of India, First Five-Year Plan (1952).

20. James Madison, 'Federalist No. 48', in *The Federalist Papers*, 1788.

21. Rediff.com, 'Election 2004', http://www.rediff.com/election/2004/apr/12espec.htm.

22. Rohinton Mistry illustrates this point in the following scene from *A Fine Balance* (Penguin: London, 1995, p. 307) where two of the protagonists find themselves homeless, and seek out a doorway for the night:
'Could you let us sleep here?'
'It's not allowed.'
'We could pay you.'
'Even if you pay, where's the space?'
'Space is enough. We can put our bedding near the door if you move your stool just two feet . . .'
They shifted the stool and unrolled the bedding. It fit exactly. 'How much can you pay?' asked the watchman.
'Two rupees each night.'
'Four.'

5

Justice for All

While every law restricts individual freedom to some extent by altering the means which people may use in the pursuit of other aims, under the Rule of Law, the government is prevented from stultifying individual efforts by ad hoc action. Within the known rules of the game, the individual is free to pursue his ends and desires, certain that the powers of government will not be used deliberately to frustrate his efforts.

F.A. Hayek, *The Road to Serfdom*

The Problem

On 29 September 2006, in Khairlanji, Maharashtra, a woman, her seventeen-year-old daughter and two sons were stripped, paraded naked through the village and beaten with bicycle chains and axes by a large crowd before being gang-raped. They were then brutally murdered. The victims were all Dalits.* Their crime? They

Epigraph: From F.A. Hayek, *The Road to Serfdom: Texts and Documents— The Definitive Edition*, ed. Bruce Caldwell (Chicago: University of Chicago Press), pp. 112–13.
*Dalit is the term used to describe the groups formerly known as 'untouchables' or 'outcastes' of Indian society. Historically, Dalits were, and many still are, engaged in jobs like 'night soil' scavenging, leather work, and the handling of carcasses. Following the political leadership of Dr Bhimrao Ramji Ambedkar, this group rejected the term 'Harijan' (children of God) given to them by Gandhi, and adopted Dalit, which characterizes honourable assertion of the

had witnessed a person from a higher caste beating up their relative who was mediating for them in a land dispute. They had reported the beating to the police who had arrested the culprits. Though the police were informed about the atrocity as it was happening, they did nothing to stop it. The case was not even registered until the next day. The doctors performing the initial post mortem did not check for evidence of sexual crimes. There have been numerous allegations of bribery and corruption in efforts to hush up the crime. It took a national uproar to galvanize India's law and order system into taking action. In India today there are over 200,000 pending cases of violence against lower castes. The conviction rate is just over 2 per cent.[1]

India's Byzantine legal system is riven with corruption, blindingly complex and excruciatingly slow. It is effectively a double-standard structure that allows the rich and powerful to manipulate it and remains virtually impenetrable to the poor. The result is a legal system that makes it impossible to enforce the Fundamental Rights as guaranteed by the Constitution. A quarter of members of Parliament (MPs) who themselves have criminal charges pending against them have little interest in promoting judicial reforms that might speed up their own trials and increase transparency.[2]

That independent India—an enormous, poor and diverse society—has managed to sustain a regime of constitutional liberty with any judicial protection of human rights has been described as 'one of the epic legal accomplishments of our time'.[3] This success is now in jeopardy.

India's grindingly slow wheels of justice are too often steered by corruption, with the public paying an estimated US$580 million a year as bribes to lawyers,[4] police and court officials, often to expedite or slow down paperwork in a largely non-computerized, under-resourced system. An overwhelming 90 per cent of Indians

---

self-identity. More recently, however, Dalit has come to be used more broadly for all persecuted and subaltern groups across India, and in some cases, across South Asia.

surveyed in a recent study said that they thought corruption would increase in the next three years.[5]

Judges ruling in a recent land dispute case, which had been in the courts for over fifty years, quoted from Charles Dickens's *Bleak House*, referencing the novel's epic court case 'Jarndyce and Jarndyce': 'This scarecrow of a suit has in course of time become so complicated that no man alive knows what it means.'[6] In 2007, the Supreme Court of India acknowledged the extent of the crisis when it said, 'People in India are simply disgusted with this state of affairs and are fast losing faith in the judiciary because of the inordinate delay in disposal of cases.'[7] The number of cases pending before the Supreme Court stood at 43,580 in June that year, up from 19,806 in 1998. There are 3.7 million cases lodged in the high courts and 25 million in lower courts. This is a system in which an employment termination dispute can take up to twenty years to be resolved.[8]

India's legal crisis is acting as a severe barrier to economic growth. The World Bank ranked India 173rd out of 175 countries for contract enforcement in 2006, ahead only of Bangladesh and East Timor. Commercial disputes in India are among the most time-consuming, costly and complex to settle in the world. It takes on an average 3.9 years to enforce a contract, compared to China where it takes less than ten months.[9] International companies are wary of working in a context where it can be difficult or impossible to oblige a firm to pay their bills, with some of India's largest and most profitable firms engaging in appalling credit and payment behaviour.

Contrary to popular belief, Indians are not genetically predisposed to lawbreaking and corruption. This is borne out by Indians who immigrate and the poor I have worked with, who demonstrate extraordinary honesty.[10] Indians break the law for many reasons:

- Many of the laws are complex, contradictory and frequently changing. This puts individuals in impossible positions where they have to make difficult choices between obeying the 'letter' and the 'spirit' of the law. In such an environment the law has little sanctity.

- There is a culture of impunity which means that the benefits of breaking laws far outweigh the costs.
- There is little social stigma against breaking laws.
- Government enjoys little legitimacy as its policies are seen as self-serving and its officers corrupt.
- Some laws are contradictory; thus by following one you violate another. This is often the case when the law has no underlying logic.*

In the previous chapter, I outlined a model of government that would restore power to India's citizens. In this chapter, I propose changes to India's legal system, to ensure it does the same. The rule of law is the sine qua non† (as my lawyer friends are fond of saying) on which my framework rests.

The conditions of law enforcement and the rule of law in India today have divided the country in two. In a small number of urban enclaves, the rule of law generally works and courts, while slow, do eventually take decisions. For the rest of India, patronage, social capital and sheer muscle power rule. Take the following example from the leafy heights of Landour, which provide magnificent views of the high Himalayas, pristine air and tranquillity, only a ten-minute drive from Mussoorie's noisy main bazaar. A government ruling has forbidden new building in the area; the result has been skyrocketing property prices. This has created massive incentives for 'squatting'. Rather than renting or buying property legally, squatters identify a property with an absentee landlord, bribe the chowkidar or watchman (US$100 should do

---

*A year ago the government introduced a fringe benefit tax—a tax on any unrealized gain in the price of the share—for unlisted private companies, like the one I run. The law defied its own accounting norms; additionally, it had to come up with a system of valuing unlisted private companies in order to levy this new tax. When I spoke to a retired head of India's tax service, the Central Board of Direct Taxes, he said that the tax was 'unethical' and violated all norms and principles of accounting.

†This Latin term literally translates as 'without which not'. Here, and generally, it refers to: an indispensable quality or thing; essential or non-negotiable; something without which something else cannot be.

it), and move in. Because the legal process for eviction is so convoluted and the bailiff system so inadequate, landlords are powerless to remove such squatters—without resorting to physical force*—and the squatters live with impunity. As a result, I have neighbours who live in million-dollar properties but have paid nothing for them (apart from a few small bribes).

I have spent time negotiating different levels of India's courts and observed that four main problems exist:

i. The sheer complexity of laws (as shown in Table 5.1) makes it impossible for the citizens to understand what is happening. The Government of India has wrapped its citizens in a veritable prison of thousands of laws. Unless one has the information on good lawyers and the financial resources to hire them, these thousands of laws are of little use in supporting one's case. They require a sophisticated system of implementation that simply does not exist in most parts of India. In the absence of consistent, transparent records it becomes very difficult to muster the amount of evidence required by the courts.†

ii. There exists a huge disparity in the nature of judgements made by courts. The law is so complex that it seems that 'no two cases are alike' and consequently the system of legal precedents falls by the wayside. When researching case law, there are often as many judgements supporting a position as there are opposing it. Here is one effort at compiling the various types of laws—'bare Acts'—and number of statutes they entail:

iii. There is often a contradiction between the effect and the intent of the law. Not a week goes by when I do not face this following dilemma. 'Do I obey that letter of the law when it clearly

---

*While most landlords do not resort to the use of physical violence, there are stories of those who have hired people or given a cut to certain political parties whose members specialize in evicting tenants and squatters and 'settling' land disputes.

†The Right to Information Act now addresses some of these issues.

Table 5.1: Types of laws

Type of Law	Number of Statutes
Banking	4
Consumer	3
Corporate	17
Criminal and Motor Accident	17
Direct Tax	6
Environment	6
Family	19
Foreign Exchange	4
Indirect Tax	8
Intellectual Property	3
Information Technology	1
Legal and Professional	12
Media	2
NRI-related	5
Property	19
Service and Labour	34
Miscellaneous*	16

Source: http://www.vakilno1.com/bareacts.htm#bank

violates the spirit of the law or generally acknowledged covenants, or is against the broader social good?' Take the following example. Several years ago the government introduced an arbitrary excise tax on our retail business. It was a tax that violated its own rules; being a value added tax, it was supposed to impose a proportional tax on each 'value addition'. However, in our business, most artisans lacked the means or could not be included in the value addition of the earlier stages of manufacture hence the entire burden of the tax fell onto the last payer and collector, which was our business.[†]

*Including the Constitution of India which is in itself a separate corpus of laws.

[†]Normally, such a tax would work as follows. An artisan would produce a quilt and sell it to a retailer for US$100. An additional US$5 (for a 5 per cent VAT)

In 2000, large, organized retail was still just starting to take off in India. Almost all retailers were small and quickly arrived at their 'personal arrangements' with the Excise Department, which meant that they did not pay taxes at all and therefore their prices were 16 per cent below ours. A group of retailers who did pay taxes fought the law, a task that involved 144 meetings with government (all of which I attended), before this rule was finally overturned.

iv. There is no method for evaluating the standards of a judge's work.

The New Legal System

The laws

Laws should be made with the purpose of protecting and enabling the exercise of basic rights. We need laws that guarantee the constitutional rights of every Indian citizen and enable markets to work by encouraging transparency and minimizing distortions. The ultimate aim of the lawmakers should be the realization of the potential of the citizens of India.

The Constitution of India provides for seven types of fundamental rights that are beyond constitutional review. One of them, The Right to Property, was amended in 1977, and was made a legal right:*

1. The Right to Equality
2. The Right to Freedom
3. The Right Against Exploitation
4. The Right to Freedom of Religion
5. Cultural and Educational Rights

---

would be added to that price. The retailer would pay US$105 for the quilt and then sell it for US$200 to a customer. The customer would owe US$10 (for a 5% VAT on the US$200 price). However, US$5 could be taken as a deductible since $5 in VAT is already built into the price.

*Constitution of India, Part III, Fundamental Rights.

6. The Right to Property
7. The Right to Constitutional Remedies

While these rights exist on paper, the quality of enforcement varies greatly depending on the wealth and social status of the citizen. For most of India, these rights are unenforced ideals. The changes I propose are intended to ensure that the Indian legal system operates as an umpire, enforcing laws that enable Indians to achieve their potential by exercising their constitutional rights, and allow the market to operate with the greatest degree of freedom and transparency. While my reforms suggest amendments to the Constitution, they do not affect its sanctity. The framers of the Constitution understood that its success depended on a balance between certain inviolable rights, and a flexibility to allow the government to respond to changing times. As one of its primary authors, Dr Ambedkar commented, 'One can therefore safely say that the Indian Federation will not suffer from the faults of rigidity or legalism. Its distinguishing feature is that it is a flexible federation.'[11]

I propose simplifying our complex web of legislation, as Table 5.2 illustrates:

Let us examine the types of laws common in India today. Most laws can be fit into four categories:

1. Laws intended to protect the rights of citizens, including family law, property law, human rights law and commercial rights;
2. Laws intended to raise revenue for government (that is, tax laws);
3. Laws intended to protect national interest, including immigration laws and restrictions on foreign ownership of national assets like telecom companies and airlines; and
4. Laws intended to redress social imbalances, including caste reservations and subsidy schemes.

Relevance of existing laws

Laws of the first type protect against the infringement of rights; they prevent classic crimes like murder and theft. They are essential

Table 5.2: Proposed laws

Existing Types of Law	Proposed Types of Law	Tier of Law
1. Constitutional and Administrative Law	1. Uniform Civil Personal Law	Individual
2. Criminal Law	2. Criminal Law Code	Individual
3. Contract Law	3. Community Administration Law	
4. Tort Law	and Property Law	Community
5. Property Law	4. Area Administration Law	Area
6. Trust Law	5. Regional Administration Law	Region
7. Family Law	· 6. Associational Law	Nation
8. Nationality Law	7. National Laws	Nation
9. Tax Law (excise, sales, income tax, others)	8. Constitutional Laws	Nation
10. Labour Law		
11. Factories Act Law		
12. Cantonment Law		
13. Food Adulteration Laws		
14. Cyber Laws		

to the functioning of any society. The second type of laws would no longer be necessary if my proposals for the four-tier tax system based on Aggregate Economic Activity (AEA) were implemented. The third type of laws are becoming irrelevant in our globalized world as ownership of companies changes and alternative providers exist for almost any type of goods or services provided.* The fourth type of laws would not be required if the TC system were introduced, as this would tackle the root causes of inequality directly.[12]

*As the enormous success of the mobile phone market in India has demonstrated, everyone wins—customers with low prices and many providers to choose from, companies with booming growth and profits, and government relieved of the burden of trying to manage this industry itself—when such markets are allowed to be large, competitive and open, rather than impeded by state control.

The new laws

Personal civil law

This would consist of a uniform set of laws that protect individual rights, including family law, worker's rights and TC rights. India needs a Uniform Civil Code. The presence of separate laws for Hindus and Muslims does not do justice to the idea of a republic in which all citizens enjoy equality under the law. Historically, separate laws for Hindus and Muslims have been the source of tremendous social tension and are frequently used by political parties to garner support from religious groups. Laws that are written to 'protect' different groups based on religion, ethnicity or caste weaken the claims of equality that all citizens must enjoy under law. They divide society and provide endless fodder for political parties to replace governance and value-based policies with cynical appeals to different caste and religious groups as a way of increasing their vote share. When I was growing up (my mother's family was from a kshatriya, or warrior, caste) I rarely heard people in our social group discuss caste or religious affiliation. Today when I travel through the country, I am often asked if I am a Christian and in some cases people have commiserated with me as my group (they assume I am Christian) has not gotten any special reservations from the government yet.* These experiences attest

*Reservations in India resemble a comprehensive regime of affirmative action aimed at creating a level playing field for the historically disadvantaged sections of the society. Caste-based reservations are the most common and politically sensitive. The Constitution prohibits discrimination on any grounds and abolishes 'untouchability', thereby guaranteeing formal equality. Further, it provides for political, educational and economic reservations. A fixed number of seats in Union and state legislatures are reserved for Scheduled Castes (SCs) and Scheduled Tribes (STs). Educational and economic reservations are provided so that 15 per cent and 7.5 per cent of seats in government-aided educational institutions and jobs in public/government sector undertakings are guaranteed for SCs and STs respectively. Another category, called the Other Backward Classes (OBCs), were given 27 per cent reservations in jobs in 1993. The government's effort to secure 27 per cent seats in institutions of higher

to the way in which the reservation system has—in spite of its intent actually functioned to keep the caste system alive.

The result of these laws is the rise of a new type of party politics that is based not on policy differences or the quality of governance outlined in campaign proposals, but solely on the practice of short-sighted pandering to different castes and religions that add up to a significant vote share. MPs who have a vision for the nation and its well-being as a whole are in danger of becoming a rarity.[13]

My proposals would eliminate the need for caste-based reservations by dramatically shrinking the size of government and encouraging quality educational institutions accessible to all through TCs. A uniform civil code would eliminate special privileges enjoyed by religious groups, ensuring fair laws that apply to all. Both these measures—equal access to quality institutions and equal treatment under the law—are necessary for the success of the reforms proposed in this book.

Criminal code

This is currently covered, in part, by the Indian Penal Code. However, the new criminal code would eliminate vague and archaic terminology[14] while inserting standards of evidence and witness protection programmes. With General Performance Parameters (GPPs) in place, prosecutors would be incentivized to win cases, as their success ratios would determine their promotions to senior lawyers and judges.

Community administration law and property laws

This would deal with community administration, the protection of AEA data, property management and title transfer laws.

---

learning for the OBCs was approved by the Supreme Court in April 2008. Besides caste, the state of Andhra Pradesh offers 4 per cent reservations to Muslims in government jobs and educational institutions. At the Union level, the total percentage of reservations for positions in the legislature comes to 49.5. The Supreme Court has put a ceiling of 50 per cent as the aggregate of all reservation initiatives.

Area administration laws

These laws* would concern the rules for capital expenditure and revenue sharing, project planning, and intercommunity dispute arbitration.

Regional administration laws

Regional administration laws would deal with the rules for capital expenditure and revenue sharing, project planning, and inter-area dispute arbitration.

Associational Laws

Associational laws are covered in detail in Chapter 6. They include governance standards for corporations, trusts and all form of associations (both shareholder and stakeholder), accounting/audit standards, ownership regulation, traceability standards, investor transparency standards, shareholder and stakeholder rights.

National laws

These laws would include issues such as national security, laws related to the cross-subsidization fund, the GPP formulation criteria and laws governing regulators, exchanges and standards laws.

Constitutional laws

This set of laws would deal with the Constitution itself and the provision of safeguards, especially for the Citizen's Database.

The structure of the judiciary

The rightsizing of government described in the last chapter would be accompanied by the rightsizing of the judiciary. Each Community would have a criminal and civil court. Each Region would have a Regional Appeals Tribunal, where citizens could appeal the decisions of the Community courts. Additionally, each Region would have an intercommunity arbitration court to settle

---

*Please refer to Table 4.3 to see which laws—Area or Region—would apply. Depending on the asset in question, either the area or the Regional government would have jurisdiction.

Table 5.3: Comparison of the current and proposed judicial system

Current		Proposed	
Administrative Unit	Equivalent Judicial Unit	Administrative Unit	Equivalent Judicial Unit
Panchayat/ Municipality	Sub-divisional district courts	Community Council	Community Court
District	District Court	Area	Intercommunity Court
State Government	High Court	Region	Inter-area Court Regional Appellate Tribunal
National Government	Supreme Court	Nation	National Court Supreme Court

Table 5.4: Area of jurisdiction in the proposed judicial system

Level of Government	Principal Jurisdiction
Supreme Court	Constitutional Law
National Court	National Law
Regional Court	Regional Administrative Rules Law Governing Associations Appeals
Area Court	Area Administration Rules Personal Civil Law Criminal Law Code
Community Court	Community and Property Law

issues that arise when communities enter contracts with one another over assets. Finally, the national government would have both a National Court to settle interregional conflicts and a Supreme Court to decide constitutional issues. An overhaul of the courts and the introduction of GPPs would prevent cases from languishing in the system, as they do today. See Table 5.3 for a comparison of the existing courts with the proposed new system of courts, and Table 5.4 for the proposed principal jurisdiction of these different levels of courts.

Aside from the change in the hierarchy of courts, each level of the proposed courts would have a clear area of jurisdiction in which their judgements would be final.

Employment in the new system

The head of the judiciary would be subject to GPP performance-based criteria. Tenure would be indefinite, providing he or she met

Table 5.5: Employment in the judiciary under the new system

	Qualifications	Ratification of Appointments	GPPs (common criteria)
Magistrate of Community Court	Certification in personal, criminal and Community law	Majority of Community Council	• Case disposal ratio and pending case load • Standard of evidence ratio • Appeals rejection ratio • Speed of contract enforcement
Justice of an Area Court	Certification in Area Law	Majority of Area Council	• Similar to those for the Community Court Magistrate.
Justice of a Regional Court	Certification in Regional Law	Majority of Regional Council	• Similar to those of a Community Court Magistrate
Justice of Appeals Tribunal	Certification in Regional Law	Majority of Regional Council	• Similar to those of a Community Court Magistrate
Justice of Associational Court	Certification in Regional Law	Majority of Regional Council	• Similar to those of a Community Court Magistrate
Justice of National Court	Certification in National Law	2/3rd majority in Parliament	• Similar to those of a Community Court Magistrate
Justice of Supreme Court	Certification in Constitutional Law	2/3rd majority in Parliament	• Similar to those of a Community Court Magistrate

the GPPs. The combination of a two-thirds confirmation majority and performance-based tenure would ensure that only candidates capable of delivering on their roles would hold posts in the judiciary. As with all other constitutional authorities, the judiciary would be overseen by a Parliamentary Oversight Board consisting of five MPs as members. Table 5.5 shows the qualifications, ratification and GPPs for the different tiers of the judiciary.

Law making in the new framework

Currently, laws and ordinances* are enacted at the state and Central government level by the state and Union ministries that are then passed either by the state legislatures or the country's Parliament.

If my proposed reforms were carried out, formulating laws would be the responsibility of the Nation, Region, Area and Community. The Supreme Court will intervene if any of the proposed laws infringes constitutional rights.

Rights and contract enforcement

Contracts are the bedrock of a legitimate property and business system and only work when they can be enforced. In my field of work, I see many finely worded contracts that are unenforceable in Indian courts. Without the enforcement of contracts, constitutional protections and rights are effectively nullified. This lack of legal protection creates incentives for violence and vigilante justice. In a recent poll of citizen's views on the extrajudicial killings or 'fake encounters' that police officers carry out, almost 77 per cent of those polled condoned the killings because they believed there was no other way for justice to be done.[15] The recent murder of a well-known 'encounter cop' Rajbir Singh highlights the prevalence of such extrajudicial killings. He alone was known to be directly responsible for 42 'encounters',[16] and there are others

---

*Ordinances are laws passed in lieu of Acts, when the Parliament is not in session. The powers of ordinances are temporary, and each ordinance has to be taken up by the Parliament, when the Houses reassemble.

like him in Delhi Police's 'encounter unit' (a term used frequently in the press to describe police killing squads). Meanwhile, mob justice is also on the rise, as frustrated citizens take the law into their own hands.[17] On one day in March 2008, an angry crowd in a small Bihar village lynched two men after they allegedly shot a villager in a land dispute, while in another district, a man was beaten to death for allegedly murdering a child. In the same state,* in September 2007, ten suspected thieves from an underprivileged group were beaten to death. Villagers complained they were fed up with rising theft despite regularly informing the police. The murdered men were later found to be innocent.[18]

A less dramatic example of poor law enforcement is the enormous backlog of landlord–tenant cases clogging the courts. Clients who have access to good lawyers are able to insert seemingly innocuous phrases into contracts that mean disputes will take decades to be resolved in court while the clients continue their exploitive behaviour. In my business life, the difficulty of enforcing a contract often outweighs the effort and we are forced to do business without one. This creates a warped and distorted working environment. Instead of doing business with the best operator, one deals with the operators one knows. Trust, not quality, becomes the deciding factor. This constrains the ability of entrepreneurs, who are not already well connected, to enter the market, thus resulting in reduced competition, less incentive for innovation, and higher prices for consumers.

I propose that contracts be graded for enforceability. This would encourage well-written, fair contracts. There is no need for a forty-five-page rental agreement or a seventeen-page employment contract. In most situations, contracts can be templated so that users know their rights if they offer or receive these templates. In addition to being enforceable, every basic

---

*Bihar is one of the poorest states in India. The per capita income in Bihar (Rs 6610 per annum) is a fraction of India's average (Rs 33,299 per annum) and the percentage of Biharis living below the official poverty line (42.6 per cent) is also above the national figure (26.1 per cent).

type of contract, along with the enforceability guidelines, would be available in the public domain. One reason for the backlog of landlord–tenant cases is that it is easy to bring a case to court in an effort to stall justice. For example, this is the advice I received when I wanted to extend a lease for a property. The lawyer actually told me we could just pay a few witnesses to say that the landlord had not fulfilled his part of the bargain and it would take at least ten years for him to fight it out. In a well-run system, such frivolous issues should take no more than a minute of a judge's time to dismiss. A friend who worked for a government-run company was implicated in a scam, which granted certain well-connected individuals 'out of turn allotments' of cars made by this quasi-public company. Although she was ultimately acquitted, it took fifteen years for a decision on the case, which was investigated by India's Central Bureau of Investigation (CBI).*

I propose that any sale or transfer of any goods, assets and/or services that has significance to the public be recorded such that every citizen has the right and ability to access information detailing the process and the outcome of that exchange. Technology has made it much easier to provide these records through the Internet. Records will be available for:

1. Changes in rights to ownership such as land titles or intellectual property titles;
2. Legal and regulatory decisions; and
3. The requisition by the Community, the Area, the Region, or the Nation of any goods or service (except for certain types of military equipment, which are covered in chapter 8).

All of these records can be linked with any of the participants' Citizen's Database entry. Such radical transparency makes legal action, if necessary, much clearer. For a public transaction to be

---

*The CBI, founded in 1963, is India's 'premier investigation agency' similar to the Federal Bureau of Investigation (FBI) in the United States. Its mandate has evolved from the investigation of financial offences to include other conventional and special crimes over the past two decades.

valid, the following steps need to be taken anytime a transaction is carried out:

1. A clearly delineated and recorded unit of measurement, which would be standard across the nation, would have to be specified;*,[19]
2. Each citizen would have access to this record without payment;
3. The sale or purchase of the goods, services, or title would be made in an open auction with the record of the auction filed;
4. Where applicable, a record would be filed with the Standards Authority, which would provide public access to all records;
5. Where applicable, a trading history would be filed with the Exchanges, which would provide public access to all records;
6. Where applicable, a decision would be filed with the Regulatory authority, which would provide public access to all records.

Any asset transfer would have a record attached to it. For example, if the Community government of Sewari sold some of its water, the value of that transaction and the date it took place will be available in the public domain. The entire system would integrate seamlessly with the cashless economy described in chapter 3; only the scale would be different.

Legal Aid and legal TCs

Unfortunately, even when armed with information, the poorest members of society cannot afford to defend themselves against more powerful citizens. Lack of access to legal rights is a part of

---

*India does not have a standardized measurement for a parcel of land, for example. In the revenue records, each unit of measurement is localized and the same name for measurement is a different area between regions. In fact, local units of land measurement vary across South Asia. The British tried to standardize these measurements, but little of that effort survives. While *bigha* was supposedly standardized as 1/3 of an acre (0.1338 hectare), it is nevertheless used to refer to anywhere between 5/8 and 1.67 times of an acre. A *marla* comes to about 25.3 square meters, and a *kattha*, or *katta*, equals 20 *dhur*s or 1/20 of a bigha. However, these vary from region to region as well. Other units, which baffle further, include the *kanal*, or *canal* (roughly equal to 20 *marla*s), the north Indian *biswa* and west Indian *guntha* and *vaar*.

my definition of poverty. When legal troubles arise, the system I propose would encourage citizens to get involved in the defence of their own rights. The TC system would level the playing field by ending dependence on pro bono work and the abysmally paid public defender system. Citizens in legal trouble would receive legal rights TCs, which they could spend on legal assistance. Lawyers would be graded by the Legal Standards Authority on the basis of the ratio of TC and non-TC cases taken, client feedback, success rate, etc. The legal TC credits would pay for lawyers' fees. The amount a lawyer would receive from the government would depend on their standards rating, as described in chapter 3. The access to legal services that the TCs would provide, in combination with the legal amendments to allow for class action suits* and the establishment of a contingency-based payment system,† would newly empower the poor of India.

Such a system of 'Law for All' is premised on four key reforms:
1. The publication of a league table of lawyers by the Standards Authority, based on quantifiable GPPs.
2. Legal changes to allow for class action suits. These would be used when a group right, such as a clean air standard, is not met; so that groups of citizens would be able to bring governments (Community, Area, Region or Nation) and corporations to court, if their rights were violated. The poor would be able to file class actions by pooling their vouchers to

---

*Class action suits are civil lawsuits filed by one or more people on their own behalf and that of others who are similarly situated. All claims in such suits are heard in a single trial. Contracts, security claims, hazardous and defective products, among others, have emerged as the most common sites of class action suits in the United States. In India, Public Interest Litigations (PILs) come close to class action suits, but are not similar to them.

†Contingency fees emerge from the practice of lawyers handling cases on contingency basis. In such cases, clients do not pay the legal fees unless and until they win the case. If clients win, lawyers receive a percentage of clients' recovery as their fee, the contingency fee. If clients lose, no legal fee is to be paid to the lawyers under the contingency fees arrangement. This allows people without money at the outset of a case to obtain competent legal representation.

pay for a larger team of lawyers—yet another way to protect the voice of the poor and ensure the protection of their constitutional rights.

3. The availability of legal services based on a contingency—'no win–no fee'—basis. This will enable the poor and middle classes to have access to competitive legal services as it transfers the financial risk to lawyers. Lawyers, in turn, would be unlikely to take frivolous suits to court, because this would adversely affect their GPP rating and force them to bear the costs of losing the suit.*

4. The introduction of whistle-blower laws,† similar to the False Claims Act in the United States, which allows whistle-blowers to bring *qui tam*‡ lawsuits. These are basically civil fraud lawsuits that allow employees to bring cases on behalf of the federal government, and receive 15 to 30 per cent of any damages paid out.[20]

With these rules in place, the inhabitants of Pali in Rajasthan, who have suffered greatly from the pollution of their groundwater

---

*Remember that under this arrangement, lawyers get paid *only* if they win cases. If they lose, they do not get paid. Assuming lawyers are rational individuals, we could safely concur that they would be inclined to handle genuine cases wherein their chances of winning, on legitimate arguments, are more than the chances of losing.

†Whistle-blower laws draw from the norm and tradition of accountability, especially of organizations and agencies whose operations directly or indirectly affect public interest. They accord legal protection to whistle-blowers from victimization, though their scope and effectiveness varies from country to country. The UK's Public Interest Disclosures Act (1998) is a recent example. The US, arguably, has the most comprehensive corpus of such laws. For more, see *Concepts and Procedures in Whistleblower Law* by Stephen M. Kohn (Westport: Quorum Books, 2000).

‡An abbreviation of a Latin phrase, which translates: 'who sues on behalf of the king as well as for himself.' In common law, a writ of *qui tam* is a writ whereby an individual who assists a prosecution can receive all or part of the penalty imposed. Under the False Claims Act, *qui tam* allows a private individual, or 'whistle-blower', with knowledge of past or present fraud committed against the federal government, to bring suit on its behalf.

and rivers, would be able to sue the multinationals and local dye industries whose toxic dyes are responsible for the pollution. By pooling their legal TCs together, the poor would be able to file a class action suit using the water standard as their right. Such cases would be easy to prove as there would be a quantifiable transparent standard that would make it easy for the courts to assess the extent of violation.[21]

Corruption

The goal of this book is to create a more egalitarian society, in which the basic guarantees of the Constitution are available to all citizens of India. My proposals would dramatically reduce the corruption that plagues the country. Eliminating patronage, corruption, and the inheritance elite would empower a meritocracy, in which success was the result of enterprise and hard work.

My grandfather used to tell me that a Third World country begins with a Third World mindset on the part of its rulers. Such a mindset is characterized by cronyism and incompetence. The USA, under President Bush, was a First World country ruled by a leader with a Third World mindset. The tragically incompetent handling of the aftermath of Hurricane Katrina and the cronyism and corruption[22] that underpins many of their overseas military interventions[23] are workings of a leader of a banana republic, not the world's largest economy. Regardless of the headlines, India is still a Third World country. I believe that if our leaders ruled with a First World mindset, the country would quickly follow.

One of the characteristics of political leadership in Third World countries is that simple things are made complicated and done so in the name of the people. As Indian citizens we have come to believe that most processes need to be complex, difficult to understand, and therefore, require an army of expert bureaucrats to create reams of legislation. This is the greatest lie of modern governments the world over and India is no exception. During the course of the last ten years that I have been running Fabindia,

I have delved into some of the most complex areas of governance and resource management—from oil exploration to defence material procurement. I have consistently found that while some of the details are complicated and require specific domain knowledge, the underlying principles could not be simpler.

My first experience of corruption was in class 9, during a morning assembly. I was listening to a teacher wax eloquent about virtuous qualities when I overheard some seniors gossiping about who had paid how much to get admission. Regardless of their veracity, such frequent allegations introduced a cynicism in my mind that, once planted, it grew over years. The result is a deep-rooted sense—a common feeling among many Indians—that things are 'rigged' and there is no level playing field. Success is perceived to be the result of palm greasing, or its more sophisticated variations, rather than the fruit of hard work and dedication.

In India, the blanket term 'corruption' is used to describe a plethora of different activities. Here I categorize them into four types.

Type 1: Bottleneck corruption

Government frequently creates artificial shortages, using regulation to prevent supply from meeting demand. The resulting bottlenecks allow the perpetuation of a patronage culture. The 'goodies' are handed out to those who are politically or commercially influential. This is very common. Take the example of trying to rent a 'commercially zoned' building in most Indian cities. By any kind of ratio of urban planning and population, Indian cities lack adequate commercial and office zones. People are expected to set up stores and offices in violation, paying bribes that are a fraction of the rents for legally zoned commercial spaces.

Type 2: Rule-induced corruption

This is the result of creating laws so complicated that interpretation becomes highly subjective and the system of precedent is obsolete. Success is only possible if you can navigate the complicated legal and regulatory web. The complexity hides all manner of irregularities. This is combined with a perpetual fear of a vigilance inquiry* amongst bureaucrats, which means that honest ones often prefer not to make decisions. There is no penalty for delay or missed opportunities, whilst every timely decision or file notation carries a risk. Again, urban planning in Delhi is a good example of this kind of corruption, where complicated, impractical rules, requiring subjective interpretation, are combined with ad hoc interventions by the court. The result is an unnecessary shortage of supply and huge corruption, as the returns for those who can manipulate the rules are enormous. Consequently, there is either decision-making paralysis, or decisions are only taken after sustained lobbying and bribery.

Type 3: Tender-bending corruption

This form of mega-corruption is globally on the rise. If you want to make money and avoid prosecution, the best way to do it is to influence the criteria used in government contract tendering or procurement in your favour. It is highly lucrative and virtually impossible to detect. The result is a huge loss to the public purse.

Whenever a government contract is open to bids there are always three sets of criteria: financial, technical and the pre-qualifications. These pre-qualifications, which are generally detailed and highly subjective, specify who can apply and how to do the job. They may say the applicant has to have twenty years' experience or be able to use a certain type of equipment. Pre-qualifications are the equivalent of saying that all prospective

*A vigilance enquiry is initiated against public servants by either the Central Vigilance Commission (CVC), or concerned vigilance officers at the state level, when they receive a reference either from the government or complaints from people. Vigilance enquiries seek to determine whether an offence has been committed under the Prevention of Corruption Act, 1988, and falls under the Code of Criminal Procedure, 1973. In practice, this has created ample room for vendetta politics, which, coupled with the fear of becoming entangled in complex set of laws, acts as a deterrent to bold, timely and positive decisions.

marathon runners have to have a certain body mass index, a certain leg length or a height no taller than 2 metres. But what matters is how fast you can run 26.2 miles; anyone using other criteria to judge participation would be viewed as insane. Yet time and time again, it is on the basis of irrelevant criteria that government contracts are tendered.

These qualification practices are rationalized as protecting citizens and guaranteeing efficient public expenditures, such that the company with the most experience and best equipment gets the job. In reality, pre-qualification criteria are a window for corruption. By paying bribes to have the criteria tailored to fit their profile, companies are able to ensure that they will get the bid. Take the case of defence equipment or oil exploration. While governments the world over are moving into an 'open auction system' for such procurement and assignment activities, in reality, these auctions are anything but open. Many are rigged using weighted pre-qualification criteria that are lovely pseudo-technical ways to eliminate competitive bidders.

This insidious form of corruption is very difficult to prove in courts. In the few cases where legal action has been taken, the highly technical arguments often leave the courts baffled, or, as my judge friends tell me, the judiciary often simply cannot afford to pay for independent panels of experts. The greatest irony is that once issued, it is very rare for tenders to be cancelled, even if the criteria are not fulfilled. Some 'well-managed' state governments, seeing the potential of this kind of corruption, have reduced their crude, type 1 corruption (that is, bottleneck corruption) and concentrated on this, as it is much more lucrative. The result is that they look 'clean' as type 3 corruption (that is, tender-bending corruption) does not directly affect most citizens.

In order to abolish this kind of corruption, I argue for open competitive auctions, which would eliminate pre-qualifications completely.[24] Instead, there would be a set of simple technical specifications (including safety standards) and financial criteria. Provided the technical criteria are met, whichever company puts in the most competitive bid would always get the contract, regardless of their political connections and other such factors. While some might object stating that without pre-qualification criteria, inexperienced companies would waste public money and do shoddy jobs, I argue that risk is essential to the flourishing of any economy. Pre-qualification criteria are attempts to limit risk; yet they de-incentivize competitive bids and quality results by making it possible for existing players to prevent the entry of new firms. There are better means of reducing risk. Specifically, governments can protect themselves by linking payments to contractually defined deliverables.

Type 4: Gunpoint Corruption

This form of corruption affects underprivileged citizens of India from whom—by threat of physical violence, arbitrary imprisonment and loss of livelihood—the state extracts money. Twenty years ago, as a student, I was returning to Delhi with two friends from a trip to the hills in the northern state of Himachal Pradesh. We arrived, scruffy and bedraggled at the town of Pathankot (located in the neighbouring state of Punjab) and had boarded the train to Delhi, when my friend suddenly realized that her camera was missing. There was a group of policemen standing around observing the scene. (It later turned out that they had masterminded the theft.) I went to them and tried to get them to register my complaint. The policemen took one look at us and immediately started shouting, threatening to beat us, saying that we might 'disappear' if we kept complaining. This was during the period of terrorism in Punjab. Police-engineered disappearances were frequent occurrences. Fearful, we backed down and managed to convince them not to take us in. The mother of one of my friends was a powerful judge. Once in Delhi, she had the officer who threatened us and his constables summoned. I was there, in the garden of the family's government house, when the officer and his constables arrived. The officer started physically trembling as he entered. On his way out he saw me in the garden and kept repeating: 'Why did you not tell me you were so well connected? Why were you travelling second class? . . . If only I'd known . . .' The response of a family friend, a senior bureaucrat, was, 'Now you know what the poor have to endure.'

Removing corruption

A key benefit of my proposed policies is that they could eliminate all of these four kinds of corruption by:

a) Removing the arbitrary rules that create types 1 and 2 corruption, as outlined above;

b) Introducing standards, exchange and a degree of transparency along with reforms to social and corporate organizations (chapter 6) that will eliminate type 3 corruption;

c) Eliminating taxation on profits and income, which will dramatically reduce incentives for concealing income; and

d) Ensuring law enforcement is conducted at the Community level and that legal TC catalysts are available to the poor. Once rights are known and enforced, type 4 corruption will cease.

In this chapter, I have described how to make India's legal system work for its people, ensuring that Indians are guaranteed their constitutional rights. These measures would ensure that justice in India is available to all, in a timely and consistent manner. The rule of law would—as it should—reign supreme, across the country.

Notes

1. Sudeep Chakravarti, *Red Sun: Travels in Naxalite Country,* 2008, (New Delhi: Penguin Viking, 2008), p. 110.

2. *Citizens' Report on Governance and Development 2006,* (Social Watch India: New Delhi, 2006).

3. Marc Galanter and Jayanth K. Krishnan, 'Debased Informalism: Lok Adalats and Legal Rights in Modern India', First South Asian Regional Judicial Colloquium on Access to Justice, New Delhi, 2002. Available at http://www.humanrightsinitiative.org/jc/papers/jc_2002/background_papers/galanter%20krishnan.pdf.

4. Centre for Media Studies, *India Corruption Study:Corruption in the Judiciary*, vol. 11 (CMS: New Delhi, 2005).

5. Transparency International, *Global Corruption Barometer 2007*, (TI: Berlin, 2007).

6. Quoted in 'People Losing Faith: Apex Court', *The Hindu*, 4 September 2007.

7. Justices A.K. Mathur and Markandey Katju, quoted in 'People Losing Faith: Apex Court', *The Hindu*, 4 September 2007.

8. Jo Johnson 'Engaging India, Crisis in the Courts', *The Financial Times*, 6 September 2007.

9. Ibid.

10. Take the example of the poor who participate in microfinance schemes. The Grameen Bank, which initiated the microcredit boom, has a 99 per cent recovery rate, much higher than that of commercial or national banks. Dipal Chandra Barua, 'Microcredit, Microfinance, Pension Schemes', paper presented at the Workshop on Extending Pension Coverage to Informal Sector Workers in Asia, Government Pension Fund, Thailand and World Bank, 2006.

11. Cited in *The Indian Constitution: Cornerstone of a Nation by Granville Austin* (New Delhi: Oxford University Press, 2002), p. 255.

12. Recent reforms to open up legislative review will significantly aid such a process. Until 2007, a legal loophole, the Ninth Schedule (of the Constitution), had provided blanket immunity for hundreds of laws. The Ninth Schedule was created in 1951 to help protect progressive laws on land reform and to end feudalism. However, it was misused and effectively became the equivalent of a vault that laws were locked into. Initially, there were only thirteen laws included in the Schedule; by January 2007 this figure had risen to 284. Opening up these laws to scrutiny will allow for greater accountability ('India opens laws to review', *BBC Online*, 11 January 2007).

13. Six national parties (recognized by the Election Commission) contested for the fourteenth Lok Sabha in 2004. One of them, the Bahujan Samaj Party, is avowedly caste-based. A total of thirty-five state/regional parties contested along with 173 registered but unrecognized political outfits! Regional parties like the All India Anna Dravida Munnetra Kazhagam, Telugu Desam Party, Shiv Sena, Asom Gana Parishad, Indian National Lok Dal, the various

Janata factions, and the All India Muslim League, among numerous others, have adopted religious, caste-based, regional-chauvinistic platforms to gain electoral prominence. This proliferation impacts national policies adversely as these parochial parties have neither the imagination nor the will to think of the nation's long-term economic, defence and international interests. Hence the national parties keep these portfolios to themselves, even in fractured coalition governments. Statistics on seat share in the Lok Sabha tell the story: in the fourteenth general elections, the national parties fielded 1351 candidates and had 364 elected and state/regional parties secured 159 of 801 seats they contested from. The figures for 1999 returned 369 of 1299 contested seats for national parties and 158 of 750 for regional/state parties. National parties won 466 of 1822 vis-à-vis 50 of 490 contested seats by state/regional parties in 1991. The year 1984 saw national parties winning 451 out of 1244 contested seats as against state/regional parties' tally of 58 wins of 151 contested seats. An average of 545 Lok Sabha seats were contested for through this period. See, Statistical Reports on General Elections for the years 1984, 1991, 1999 and 2004. All available at www.eci.gov.in. For broader perspectives on changes in India's party system, see Sudha Pai (1998), 'The Indian Party System under Transformation', *Asian Survey*, vol. 38, no. 9, pp. 836–52; Aditya Nigam (1996), 'India after the 1996 Elections: Nation, Locality, and Representation', *Asian Survey*, vol. 36, no. 12, pp. 1157–69.

14. Archaic and equivocal terminologies make laws confusing and difficult to comprehend for common citizens. For example, the word 'settlement' may mean a defined area populated by citizens or the procedure of fixing rights of individuals to property. To offer an example, the surge in non-performing assets in the banking sector—result of rising default cases—has led bankers to blame the archaic and ambiguous legal system of the country. Mahua Venkates, 'Wilful Defaults on Rise; Bankers Blame Archaic Legal System', *The Financial Express*, 21 February 2008.

15. *Hindustan Times*, 28 March 2008.

16. 'ACP Rajbir Singh: 42 Encounters', *The Times of India*, 26 March 2008.

17. Amarnath Tewary, 'Where Lynching is the Order of the Day', *BBC News Online*, 13 September 2007.

18. An official enquiry report clarified that the ten men were not thieves. See 'Vigilantes Deliver Mob Justice in Bihar' at http://www.southasianpost.com/portal2/c1ee8c4419bf54a30119ca65b8c00154_Vigilantes_deliver_mob_justice_in_Bihar.do.html.
19. For a convenient online conversion table, visit http://www.indianground.com/calculators/area-conversion-calculator.aspx.
20. As a series of market abuses rock global markets the existence of whistle-blower laws becomes increasingly important. The UK government recently announced a US-style whistle-blower system that will grant immunity from prosecution in return for evidence about market manipulation. See Larry Elliot, 'New Laws to Prosecute City Cheats', *The Guardian*, 28 March 2008.
21. In 2004, the Central Groundwater Board found that pollution had seeped into Pali's groundwater and contaminated wells in the region. See http://www.blacksmithinstitute.org/search3.php?project_id=124. In April 2008, the Rajasthan High Court ordered closure of 126 industries operating in non-conforming areas in Pali. See Esha Sekhar, 'Court Asks to Close Polluting Industries in Pali', *Down to Earth*, 15 May 2008.
22. The US defence establishment appointed a shady company run by a twenty-two-year-old and a licensed masseur to supply weapons and ammunition to the Afghan army, most of which were unusable and obsolete. See C.J. Chivers, 'Supplier Under Scrutiny on Arms for Afghans', *The New York Times*, 27 March 2008.
23. Unfortunately, there are numerous examples of this. A report by the US Inspector General for Iraq about the Coalition Provisional Authority (CPA) which governed Iraq between April 2003 and June 2004 stated that between April 2003 and June 2004, $8.8 billion went missing. In separate cases, one US$500 million outlay was justified by one word in the record books—'security'—while ten disbursements ranging from US$120 million to US$900 million were undocumented, as if they were petty cash. See 'The Fog of Accountability', *International Herald Tribune*, 8 February 2007. Meanwhile, contracts were awarded to US companies with no financial safeguards and no competitive bidding. They were issued in the form of 'cost-plus' deals where companies were paid both for the expenses they incurred, in addition to a percentage of the

profits. The result was a powerful incentive to 'spend' as much money as possible.

24. Interestingly, as this book was being written, a news report appeared highlighting the critical need and importance of open auction policy. The CVC had sought an explanation from the Department of Telecom (DoT) for not allocating scarce radio spectrum to mobile phone service firms through an open auction. The CVC wanted a convincing reply from the DoT as to why and how the spectrum could be allocated *without arriving at a market-driven price* (emphasis added). That some tender-bending had taken place appeared from a CVC official's comment: 'A logical next step for us would be to identify the people behind these decisions.' Pankaj Mishra, 'CVC Asks DoT to Explain Non-auction of Spectrum', *Mint*, 24 May 2008.

6

The New Organization

The principle of liberty holds that individuals have certain rights which a just society ought not violate. The principle of democracy holds that a just society must ensure popular sovereignty: people ought to have a voice—and in some sense an equal voice—in the substantive decisions that affect their lives. Liberal democratic theory generally supports the application of both liberal and democratic principles to the state, but only the principle of liberty to the economy.

Samuel Bowles and Herbert Gintis

A key principle of this book is the 'right scaling' of institutions for a deeper democracy. We have seen this applied to the economy, the government, the judiciary, and now it is the turn of business and civil society. The growing power of corporations has not been balanced by increased accountability. In this chapter, I offer a series of reforms with the purpose of making all types of social organizations more responsive to the needs of their members and more accountable to those who are affected by their work. Take mining, for example. The shareholders of mining companies would like the management to maximize profits, and therefore, their returns, while the

Epigraph: Samuel Bowles and Herbert Gintis, *Democracy and Capitalism: Property, Community, and the Contradictions of Modern Social Thought* (New York: Basic Books, 1986), p. 66.

Community government wants to ensure that adequate safeguards are in place, so that the effects of mining on the local population are minimized. This chapter is an attempt to see how these two competing interests can be balanced without sacrificing economic development.

There are two basic types of organizations: corporations and trusts. Most entities formed by groups of individuals take one of these two general forms. The distinction made between these in Indian law is defined in terms of aims and ownership. Corporations are made up of shareholders who own distinct, quantifiable portions of the corporation called shares. In trusts, the members collectively own the organization in 'trust'. Tax policy in India has favoured keeping activities that generate a profit in corporations, while activities that do not generate a profit are reserved for some form of trust.

The proposals made in this chapter, which would make corporations and trusts more responsive to the needs of the people affected by their work, can only happen when there are appropriate forms of representative political organizations, such as the ones I have proposed. The rightsizing of representative political institutions into Community, Area and Regional governments means that there would be appropriate forums to represent the interests of those affected by these organizations. To return to the example of mining, the people most affected by the operation of a mine— both in the short and long term—are those who live in the community where the mine is located. Therefore, this would fall under the jurisdiction of the community.

Corporations are divided into private and public (that is, those that are listed on a stock exchange for the public sale of shares) with more regulatory oversight focused on public corporations. Civil society in India is represented in various forms of trusts which include societies, non-governmental organizations (NGOs), trade unions and cooperatives. Many are also classified as not-for-profit organizations which have a tax-free status. Corporations are the property of their shareholders and exist to further their interests.

Trusts do not have shareholders; their power is vested in the general body of members. Both types of organizations are operated by a management which is appointed by shareholders or members. For corporations, these managers are called directors and for trusts, they are called trustees.

I propose a single structure and governance standard for all corporations and trusts: the association.

I have already suggested the removal of corporate and individual taxes on revenues and profits, thereby dissolving the distinction between for-profit and not-for-profit organizations. The association would ensure accountability and transparency across the full spread of India's corporations and social organizations.

The Problem

It may be surprising to some that as the CEO of a corporation, I am wary of corporate power. However, it is precisely because I passionately believe in the positive contribution business makes to society that I make these criticisms. Corruption and corporate concealment negate the beneficial impacts of business. In early 2008, this point was being felt across the world with the sub-prime mortgage crisis in the US that is still destabilizing the global economy. The former chairman of the Federal Reserve, Alan Greenspan, recently commented that, 'The current financial crisis in the US is likely to be judged as the most wrenching since the end of the Second World War.'[1] At the heart of this crisis is corporate obfuscation.

Corporations are increasingly becoming skilled at concealing their activities. As part of my work, I am constantly researching other companies, and time and again I find myself blinded by corporate smog. Once, I tried to figure out who owned an airline by following the money as it moved through the organization. The amazing thing was that each thread ended in a brick wall: one ended in the Isle of Man, one in the impenetrable web of Gulf holding companies and a third in a private investment fund.

On another occasion, I discovered an even more tangled web in the ties between a parent company and its subsidiaries. I was only able to untangle this with the help of an insider. The parent company had rented properties to its retail subsidiary—its largest business—at a value I could not discern. Suddenly, the subsidiaries were profitable and the company went public at an extraordinary valuation. The company has since been doing rather poorly, declaring a loss for the last few quarters. Given that rentals represent an enormous portion of the costs of any retailer, I would guess that there was some attempt at inflating profitability by 'deflating the rent' that was charged by the parent, a real-estate company. As rent is the single largest expense and, at the time, the markets were rewarding retail companies with profits up to fifty to seventy times on earnings, this savings on rent got magnified some fifty to seventy times when the company listed. The temptation to cheat in this way can overcome even the most honest CEO and board, especially when the chance of detection is minimal, as is the case in India.

The very structure of corporations hinders transparency.* One of the main problems with company boards is that they are self-perpetuating and members can be cajoled with both monetary and non-monetary benefits. Combined with a sense of fraternity, it becomes difficult for board members to 'rock the boat'. The new habit of appointing committees to look into potentially controversial issues is only the newest, politically correct form of smokescreen. The boards I have seen in India function with very little oversight. Currently, a company planning a public listing

---

*As Galbraith eloquently put in his *The Economics of Innocent Fraud* (London: Penguin, 2004), pp. 28–29: 'The myths of investor authority, of the serving stockholder, the ritual meetings of directors and the annual stockholder meeting persist, but no *mentally viable* observer of the modern corporation can escape the reality. Corporate power lies with management—a bureaucracy in control of its task and its compensation. Rewards that can verge on larceny. This is wholly evident. On frequent recent occasions, it has been referred to as the corporate scandal' (emphasis added).

has to issue a red herring prospectus* as a note of disclosure. I asked a prominent analyst who advises investors what he thought of this practice and he said that while it disclosed some major issues, the real dirt lies with those on the inside. In another instance, a prominent tax officer once told me that his best tips on tax evasion come from insiders. Therefore, we need a system that would empower the insiders to hold the management accountable.

Our increasingly networked society is already heightening the scrutiny of corporations. We were recently considering purchasing a US company. The company said they had recently 'completely made the transition' to a 'seamless' inventory management system, which would 'dramatically increase their profitability and cash flows through better inventory management'. I decided to check the employees' Orkut profiles to get another perspective. 'New plan a disaster', 'Hi Ron, I'm a manger in Albuquerque and I'm experiencing exactly the same problem', 'They don't know what they're doing', were just some of the posts. Once I delved a little further, I found these complaints to be substantiated. Needless to say, we decided not to buy the company.

The proposals outlined in this book would increase transparency which I have always felt is the most effective check on the authority of organizations. The best source of information about what a company is actually doing or not doing is often its own employees. Whistle-blowers play a vital role in alerting regulators and the public when corporations break laws.[†,2] Increasing transparency

---

*A red herring prospectus is a document submitted by a company (issuer) which intends on having a public offering of securities (either stocks or bonds). In India, this preliminary registration statement is filed with the Registrar of Companies (RoC) after the approval of the Securities and Exchange Board of India (SEBI).

†Take, for example, Sharon Watkins and David Franklin. Watkins was a senior executive at Enron who spoke up about the company's corrupt accounting practices. Several former Enron executives have been convicted since her revelations. *Time* magazine named her one of its 'People of the Year' in 2002. She went on to become a consultant and high-profile public speaker. Franklin, a

is part of the solution for increasing accountability; the other part is activism, or what you can do with that information.

The Solution

Today, in India, there is a plethora of trust organizations. Most of these are registered as societies formed under the Societies Registration Act of 1860,‡ which entitles groups with a common interests and agendas to form legal entities in pursuit of those interests. While corporations are subject to a certain amount of regulatory approval, trusts are largely unregulated. Many have thousands of members, control substantial funds and undertake activities that affect numerous people. While in corporations, directors on the board have varying degrees of power depending on the shareholding they represent, in trusts, the trustees rarely represent a specific number of members of the general body. Trustees are almost always appointed by the head of the trust and are supposed to have, in theory, their appointments ratified by the general body of members on a one-member-one-vote basis.

In the case of corporations, the maintenance and growth of profitability give shareholders a single point of reference with which to assess the leadership of the corporation. This makes it easy for shareholders to intervene, when there is a fall in profits, and change the management. For trusts, with varied aims and often multiple goals (which are hard to quantify) intervention by the general body is difficult to achieve. It is even harder when there are several thousand members and a majority of them have

---

scientist at Pfizer, won a US$27 million settlement in a lawsuit accusing the company of defrauding Medicaid by encouraging doctors to prescribe a drug for unapproved uses. The introduction of *qui tam* (or whistle-blower) laws, as outlined in chapter 5, would support the proposals I outline in this chapter to increase accountability.

‡This is one of the oldest Acts of the country. Societies established as non-commercial, non-industrial and non-profit entities for literary, scientific, charitable and/or cultural purposes need to be registered under the Act to be legal.

to cooperate with each other in order to pass a resolution to change the management.

Many of the large trusts in India are religious trusts. Because trust records are not easy to obtain and membership of these trusts is tightly controlled, information on these types of trusts is limited. A tax officer once told me that the largest private owner of land in India, apart from the government, was a trust set up by a religious cult.* When I asked one of the prominent members of this cult the aims of the trust, nowhere in his explanation was the accumulation of vast amounts of property defined as an objective. This disconnect between the objectives and actual workings of trusts is endemic and hard to oppose because of the lack of direct oversight by members of the general body.

Religious trusts control vast amounts of wealth and have the lowest standards of organizational governance.† Religious and educational trustees are often hereditary. As a result, relatives and children begin to treat the institutions as hereditary fiefdoms rather than public institutions as envisaged in the memorandum and articles of association or the trust deeds.

With the intention of increasing accountability in corporations and all types of trusts, I have proposed a single legal entity, the association. It is possible to do this as the removal of taxes on profit proposed in chapter 3 removes the major distinction between these two forms of organization.

There would be two types of associations: stakeholder and shareholder. As with corporations and trusts, all associations would be treated as individuals under the law. Every association would have a memorandum, or mission statement, detailing the organization's purpose, and articles of association, defining the terms of membership. All members would have to sign both the

---

*In the absence of official records, this information needs to be treated as anecdotal.

†For example, many state Wakf boards (Wakf is a permanent endowment of movable and immovable property in Islamic jurisprudence) in the country are parties to property disputes with claimants from within the community contesting their own boards' authority over disputed land.

memorandum and the articles of association, whether there were 400 or 40,000 members.

The shareholder

As the name suggests, this mode of membership is very similar to that of a shareholder in a corporation. A shareholder would have a divisible and tradable holding in an association, specific voting rights, rights to dividend, and rights of transferability, as defined in the memorandum and articles of association. Voting rights would depend on proportion of ownership.

The stakeholder

This form of membership carries no expectation of direct monetary return. The value of the individual's holding would not be divisible from the whole. Stakeholders would include members of trusts and societies, professional bodies, and not-for-profit institutions. For example, wildlife enthusiasts who form a conservation association would not be able to claim any monetary dividends, but as stakeholders they bear part of the responsibility to manage organizational funds to meet the aims of the association. In stakeholder associations, each member would have one vote. As a result, these types of associations would be better suited to trusteeship roles.

The difference between a stakeholder and a shareholder association relates to the type of capital and the aims for which the association was formed. Shareholder associations would have capital in the form of equity and debt, whereas the capital of stakeholders would be in grants and endowments. The standards of internal democracy and rights would be common across both types of associations.

Member rights

Beginning with the most basic accountability measures and proceeding upward towards the organization's mission, the following types of rights would be universal for members of all associations:

1. Individual rights
2. Group Rights
3. Referendum Rights
4. Majority Rights

Individual rights concerning access to information would be granted to every member of a stakeholder or shareholder association. All documents concerning the organization's conduct and activities would be published on the internet. Every individual, who wantèd to, could 'drill down' and see if the organization was true to its mission and following its prescribed operational procedures. A part of the audit procedure would include a review of the extent to which the association's work was in keeping with the objectives stated in the memorandum and articles of association.

An individual member would have two recourses in the event of a perceived deviation from these standards by the management of the association. One would be legal; the other would involve addressing the issue within the framework of the association itself. Both avenues of action would bring the issue to the attention of both the regulator and the wider membership.

If the member feels the association has failed to follow the conditions laid down in the memorandum or in the articles of association, he or she could seek legal clarification—using their legal vouchers, if necessary—and bring the matter under review. The identity of the member would always be apparent, unless protection was requested under the whistle-blower laws covered in chapter 5.

If the matter is less serious, but still affects the conduct of the organization, the member could post a grievance on the association's website or any other medium with widespread access. The posting would serve as a rallying point for a group of members, who could file a petition for debate upon receiving signatures or letters of support from 10 per cent of the membership. By taking such an action, a member would be able to inform others of the issue and strengthen their impact on its resolution by using the aggregate rights they have as a group. Upon crossing the threshold of 10 per cent of the members, they would be able to exercise their 'group rights', and their petition would then have to be included on the agenda of the board meeting. Minutes of the ensuing debate would be made available in the archives of the association. Group rights would serve as an intra-association process of alerting management, board members and regulators to the concerns of the membership.

Of course, such privileges carry the danger of misuse, resulting in frivolous debates that at best waste time and at worst spread discord. However, this is a small price to pay for improving the accountability standards of those who lead institutions. Shareholder or stakeholder activism is the best early warning system. I have seen so many instances in which leaders of corporations, trusts, and public institutions forget—in their machinations—that they owe their primary responsibility to their membership and to the aims for which the corporation, trust, or institution was founded.

In the case of a serious matter, with members supporting a petition growing beyond 25 per cent, group rights would be converted to 'referendum rights'. Referenda would focus attention on a particular issue such as management compensation or a specific policy of the association. Referenda would have significant value as a deterrent in an environment where all management information would be indexed and available in the public domain. The holding of a referendum would bring the issue to the attention of all stakeholders and shareholders, especially institutional shareholders, who, once alerted, could use the size of their holding to force a referendum. Until recently, institutional shareholders were 'passive', in that they rarely exercised power commensurate with their holdings. In 2001, the British government went so far as to reprimand pension funds and other institutional investors for failing to take a sufficiently active interest in the companies in which they invested.[3] This situation has shifted rapidly. The winds of change have become a virtual hurricane of pension fund activism in the USA, known as the 'CalPERS Effect'.* This mighty Californian public pension provider has become a corporate watchdog, bringing lawsuits and demands against businesses in which it is invested.[4]

The referendum would be a potent mandate to expose and halt corporate wrongdoing, well before it becomes a public hazard. An insider recently told me about a corporation transferring certain critical assets from the company to the founding family. The whole transaction was cleverly disguised in the verbiage and complexities that modern technocrats can create. In such an instance, a notice by a single shareholder could quickly develop into a movement of 25 per cent to call a single-issue referendum to force debate and vote on the issue. It would highlight to the outside world the intentions of the management and the complicity of the board, which in this case, was well compensated for its 'support'.

This model is designed to make shareholder actions easier. These are already a powerful force in corporate life. In 2004, after a year of mediocre performance, 43 per cent of shareholders at

*The California Public Employees' Retirement System (CalPERS) releases, every year, a 'Focus List' of companies it intends to engage in 'shareowner activism' over corporate governance problems. The activism pays—around $3.1 billion in the short run and estimated $89.5 billion in the long run, as a study by Professor Brad Barber of the University of California Davis puts it. The CalPERS Effect is this link between activism and financial performance. The seventy-six-year-old organization provides pension and health benefits to more than 1.5 million people, active and retired. At US$207 billion, it is the US's largest public pension fund. Its pension fund activism has challenged basic assumptions of long-term corporate performance, and, as one study put it, 'without question, it has contributed to many changes in how corporate managements now behave.' I emphasize the CalPERS story because I believe that the scale of its operations and the measure of its success testify, once again, that with collective determination, my proposals for reforms and right-scaling in India are possible and will benefit all Indians. As an aside, I must mention that CalPERS has set benchmarks for corporate governance standards and public welfare, while being fairly open about its decision making. It publishes a monthly compilation of useful information for its board members, staff and general public.

the Walt Disney Entertainment group's annual meeting withheld their votes at the re-election of the CEO. As a result, the company was forced to restructure its leadership.[5] Or take the example of Japan's first successful shareholder revolt, which blocked the takeover of a specialty steel maker by a unit of Nippon Steel because it offered no incentive to investors.[6] Additionally, social and environmental organizations, and even some sovereign wealth funds,* are using stock ownership to promote reform in corporate behaviour. Norway's Sovereign Wealth Fund recently sold its entire US$13 million stake in Vedanta Resources plc on the grounds of 'environmental and human rights violations' by the firm and its subsidiaries in India.[7]

Association obligations

Each association would have to submit an annual 'statement of accounts' that would be audited. The management would then be obliged to prepare a business plan or blueprint, which would be debated and agreed upon by majority vote at a meeting to which all members would be invited. Combined with periodic status reports, the plan would allow members to track the progress and hold management accountable. These safeguards would be particularly important in Community governments where the actions of elected and appointed officers would have a direct bearing on the citizens. Having served on the boards of trusts and other not-for-profit organizations, I have never seen a coherent vision plan presented, because doing so would make the heads of organizations accountable to the deliverables in the plan, and this is something they resist. When I took over the management of Fabindia, we introduced vision plans which were four to five year plans with detailed notes on what we hoped to accomplish and in what time span. Once approved by the board, the plan was communicated to the shareholders, employees and the public. It became much easier

*Sovereign Wealth Funds are state-owned funds, which focus on maximizing investment return.

to focus the organization and I found that we were able to complete the first two plans in half the time we thought we needed.

With these safeguards and rights in place, distinctions such as whether a company is publicly traded or not would be irrelevant. This would make it possible for all shareholder associations to list themselves on the stock exchanges without the onerous, burdensome regulations that currently exist. While the purpose of listing requirements currently mandated by the securities and exchange regulator* is to increase investor confidence by making corporations more accountable, this could be better accomplished by the new standards for transparency proposed in this book. The downside of the current regulations is that the compliance burden makes it expensive to publicly list a company's stock in India, imposing a significant barrier for small companies in their efforts to raise capital.[8] The protections these regulations afforded would be better met, and without the costs, by the measures proposed in this chapter. The stock exchanges would be just another kind of exchange working much like those described in chapter 2. In my proposals, once the disclosure norms, shareholder rights and transparency standards are operational, any shareholder association would be able to list its shares for trading. The standards authority would rate the financial security and disclosure norms of the company, enabling the investors to make informed decisions about where to put their money.

Legal framework

In any type of association, members would voluntarily agree to be governed by a set of memoranda and articles. These could not

---

*Presently, SEBI performs this role in India. It is an autonomous regulator that was created by the Government of India in 1992 to protect investor interests and create an efficient securities market. It has been moderately successful due largely to its partially legislative, executive and judicial powers. It drafts regulations, conducts investigations and enforcement actions, and passes rulings and orders. These powers are balanced by a two-level appeals facility, the second directly to the Supreme Court of India.

violate constitutional rights or national law. The Regional and National courts would enforce this.

Transparency

Once associations are subjected to public scrutiny and shareholder–stakeholder intervention is facilitated through the individual, group and referendum rights, the management would be forced to be more accountable. The boards and executives of associations would have little or no incentive to pursue policies that were either against the interests of the general membership, or break the law, as the risk of detection would be too high. If irregularities were detected, shareholders could exercise their rights to mobilize others and, if necessary, use legal TC vouchers to push their case. The increased chances of detection would reduce the temptation of management to pursue policies that either benefit one group of shareholders over another or simply break the law.

The Return of Social Censure

Once our lives are correctly scaled, the powerful force of social censure would come into play. 'Rightsizing' means individuals would have a context to their lives.

Our reputation means a great deal to us when we are part of a tight-knit society with strong social bonds. When we live a life without context, we become disconnected from our reference points, whether these are our local community, business associations or social leaders. These 'peers' have a powerful effect and act as a deterrent against individual members breaking a social contract.

Today our lives lack this wider context. Panchsheel, the 'colony' of Delhi where I live, is no more than a collection of houses inhabiting a common geographical area. We have no common representation, no sense of community, no citizens' forums. The result is that there is neither a sense of belonging nor responsibility. People conduct their lives with no consideration for either their neighbours or their community. Instead, there is a culture of 'see how much you can get away with', with those who have political clout, muscle or cash coming out on top.

My grandfather always spoke of individuals with reference to their character. People's personal credibility was held in such esteem; and in those days, there was apparently no shortage of role models who had a working moral compass. However, today the situation is very different. A friend of my parents, who was at the time the CEO and owner of a large family business, was caught evading huge amounts of taxes and siphoning money into private offshore accounts while shutting down one of the company mills, laying off thousands of workers and declaring bankruptcy. Because of its size and its role in the local economy of a rural area of one of India's poorest states, its sudden closure caused great economic hardship. There was no consultation; and, to be fair to the company, there was no forum or way to involve the local community—a decision was made in Delhi and that was that. Surprisingly, this person continued to be socially feted in Delhi, where the corporate offices were headquartered. He later became head of one of the national professional business associations. Social censure does not work when the impact of one's actions takes place in a context different from the milieu one lives in. I am not arguing for every CEO to live in the community where their factories are located. But once communities become empowered, such actions will have to be taken in consultation with them, as they will be the ones most affected.

When I lived in a small community in rural Rajasthan, I observed how strong social censure was. Many years later, when we were working on Fabindia's third five-year vision plan, we agreed to create local community-owned companies as a way to partner with our producers in building our supply chain. The idea was to bring the benefits of shareholding to artisans, many of whom were from the 'backward and Dalit communities' and had no concept of what it meant to be a shareholder. What I observed was amazing. Once they became shareholders, the perspective of the artisans began to change. They now had a second collective interest—that of maximizing their return (in the form of dividends), which would also increase the value of their shareholding. It took six years of experimentation with the first community-owned company before we were able to figure out a way to fairly value these companies and then let artisans trade their shares, a very difficult feat in the absence of an exchange. I did this because I felt that over time such community-owned companies would be able to develop the assets of their local communities in a way that shared the benefits with the shareholders who are the same group as the local community. We developed these companies by giving them access to the markets through the brand of Fabindia, which would make them viable as business entities. At a later stage, I expect that they will grow to a point where they can undertake local development projects as a viable alternative to corporations, which will also be bidding for the same development rights, be they for water, mining, land development and other such schemes. The difference will be in the legitimacy enjoyed by the community-owned companies whose boards are local and whose shareholders are drawn from the community in which they operate.

The most interesting aspect of appointing local boards in these companies was that I watched people who became board members make decisions that were often against their individual interests while supporting the greater interest of the company. It happened because of the social pressure exerted on them by the fact that they were locals and therefore accountable to their peer community for their actions. I had finally found a solution to the problem that had caused my first efforts at building a cooperative movement of rural artisans to fail.

In a nation where social status is of the utmost importance, one reason for the lack of social opprobrium could be that the Indian government faces such a crisis of legitimacy that cheating is considered 'socially acceptable'. I remember a dinner table conversation with an American who was expressing his indignation at the campaign of deception that led to the war in Iraq. He lamented the loss of trust in his government, saying 'they lied to us.' The Indians at the table found his holding the government to a standard of truth amusing. We no longer expect our government to be honest. The unreasonableness of the regulations and demands placed by the Indian state upon its citizens and the large scale avoidance of these rules, especially in the 1970s, 1980s and 1990s, created a nation of lawbreakers. This, in turn, 'delegitimized' the state, resulting in a loss of social censure. The result is that we are operating in a moral vacuum.

The intent of these proposals is to have a profound effect on social behaviour. The transformation of government, combined with transparency and tax reforms would mean that the Government of India would become less corrupt, less amorphous and less greedy. As such, it would gain legitimacy. Reforms to corporations and civil society combined with the right-scaling of government, would result in individuals operating in much more tightly knit circles. Social censure would become a powerful force in encouraging honesty and ethics amongst the citizens of India.[9]

Notes

1. Quoted in Larry Elliot, 'A Financial Crisis Unmatched since the Great Depression, Say Analysts', *The Guardian*, 18 March 2008.
2. As a news report from Japan put it, whistle-blowers in that country have shocked everyone in the past decade by revealing scandals as diverse as a car maker that hid dangerous flaws to avoid embarrassing recalls, to a meat company that sold ground pig hearts as beef, and a fancy restaurant chain that served customers other customers' leftover sashimi. Martin Fackler, 'Loyalty No Longer Blind for Salarymen in Japan', *International Herald Tribune*, 7 June and 8 June 2008.
3. This came in the after the government asked for a report on institutional investment in the country. See Paul Myners, 'Institutional Investment in the United Kingdom: A Review', available online at http://www.hm-treasury.gov.uk/media/1/6/31.pdf.

4. For more on various aspects of the CalPERS story, see 'The CalPERS Effect: Is the Power of Pension Funds Waning?', *Ethical Corporation*, 2 February 2005; Andrew Junkin, 'The "CalPERS Effect"on Targeted Company Share Prices', 2007, available at: http://www.CalPERS-governance.org/alert/selection/wilshirerpt.pdf; Bred Barber, 'Monitoring the Monitor: Evaluating CalPERS' Activism', *The Journal of Investing*, Winter 2007, available online at http://www.iijournals.com/JOI/default.asp?Page=2&ISS=24401&SID=698965.

5. 'Shareholder Revolt Stuns Disney', *BBC Online,* 4 March 2004.

6. 'A Former Morgan Stanley Banker Led Japan's First Successful Shareholder Revolt,' *International Herald Tribune*, 22 February 2007.

7. 'Norway's Global Pension Fund Drops Mining Group Vedanta on Environment, Ethics Concerns', *International Herald Tribune,* 7 November 2007.

8. Deregulation, on the other hand, facilitates financial innovation. As Raghuram Rajan and Luigi Zingales point out, deregulation of the New York Stock Exchange in the 1970s led to a very low cost of trading for financial institutions. This encouraged the growth of the market for derivatives, which reduce financial risks; and lead to institutionalization of stock ownership, thus allowing investors to organize more easily to 'force management's hands'. *Saving Capitalism from the Capitalists* (Princeton: Princeton University Press, 2004), pp. 73–74.

9. The success of the Grameen Bank is evidence of the power of social censure. The pressure of the social network plays a large part in the 99 per cent payback rate. The borrowers are encouraged to assist each other, and all loan disbursements and repayments are made publicly, in front of other groups. See Hal R. Varian, 'In a model for lending in developing nations, a Bangladesh bank relies on peer pressure for collateral', *New York Times*, 22 November 2001.

7

Sustainable Living

The mistake of the progressive commercial mind was to give undue importance to those modes of circulation that promised the highest financial return: this led the planner to overlook the role of the footwalker, and the need for retaining the flexibility of mass movements that only pedestrian circulation can ensure. At the same time it committed him later to the one-dimensional solution of private transportation by motor car, and to giving transportation itself priority over many other urban functions, quite as essential to a city's expense. Thus the overgrowth of the traffic network, bent on increasing the profitable congestion on the center, produced in fact, even technically speaking, an exceedingly primitive solution. Except at its congested core, the resulting city lacked many of the happy amenities of social life, which much smaller and seemingly more backward cities still possessed.

Lewis Mumford

R ecently, while travelling for work, I found myself walking down the narrow streets of a large Indian city. The air was filled with the stench of sewage. The road was crowded by the encroachment of buildings, and potholes and garbage made walking a challenge. Each building seemed to have been constructed with no plan or no reference to the others; often the

Epigraph: Lewis Mumford, *The City in History* (New York: Harcourt, 1961), p. 431.

owners had even cantilevered the buildings out on the upper floors in the hope of getting more space. Loud music and religious sermons blared out of homes with no regard for neighbours. Children played on the street because it was the only open space. An hour in this city was about all my senses could handle. Yet these are the conditions that roughly 300 million Indians call 'home'.[1]

The future of India will be defined by the quality of its habitat planning. The country is changing at a dizzying speed. By 2030, more than 40 per cent of India's population will be living in urban areas compared to the 28 per cent at present.[2] This amounts to the relocation of more than a hundred million people. Every month over 30,000 people migrate to Delhi alone. A denial of the magnitude of the problem, combined with ad hoc planning and widespread corruption, means that such dizzying migration could cripple India.

Most Indians live in squalor whether in a village hut or an urban slum, without access to reliable water, roads, electricity, proper sanitation or green spaces. In Delhi, a majority of inhabitants live in substandard housing.[3] The wealthy manage to create oases within the city, but even the wealthy in their gated communities cannot escape the toxic air pollution, traffic gridlock, power cuts and water quality that is well below any standard deemed fit for human consumption. However, for most Delhiites, this is just the tip of the iceberg, with millions living without running water, electricity or sewage facilities at all.[4] Meanwhile, in Sewari, raw sewage runs in open drains by the street, women collect water from the village pump, rubbish rots on the village outskirts and electricity supply is extremely erratic. In Mussoorie, the summer stench from the untreated sewage which runs in the storm drains, the piles of rubbish that trickle down the hillsides and crippling water shortages stand in stark contrast to the five-star hotels and plush mountain retreats that sustain the luxury tourism industry.

Given that migration is often catalysed by the pursuit of opportunity, my earlier proposals that facilitate the generation of wealth outside the metropolises would curb much of this movement. It is not possible to quantify what might happen once communities take charge of their own development, as Community governments would have the funds and the mandate to develop their local resources. *However, rural employment would likely be created on a massive scale, stemming the migration that is currently moving millions of Indians from rural to urban areas each year.*

Nevertheless, our cities, towns and villages will continue to grow. The planning of India's towns and cities is haphazard and poorly managed—following a set of archaic urban planning rules that create vast opportunities for corruption. It has resulted in an urban India that is a living hell. I argue for a series of reforms that will transform the way we live. My ideas revolve around a form of planning based on population density and infrastructure. The foundation is a set of 'habitat rights', which relate to air quality, green spaces, water, sewage and power supply.

The Problem

Urban planning in India is in a shambles. The nation has failed to meet the demands of a rapidly urbanizing country and there is currently a shortage of 22.4 million homes.[5] Analysts say that this massive failure could snowball into conflicts about water, housing and electricity in the future. As the size of cities balloons— and with hundreds of millions living in slums across the country— a solution is urgently needed.

However, urban planning is woefully inadequate; the new Urban Development Plan, the Master Plan for Delhi 2021,[6] is no exception.* Although its 172 pages (plus an additional 211 in the newly released 'Supplement') cover everything from badminton shuttlecock assembly to the maximum floor area permissible for atria, the complex web of regulations does not address the real needs of the city. While some of the attempts to combat noise

---

*But then, Delhi at least gets a 'plan'. In most urban centres, there is no plan.

and air pollution are admirable, the plan itself does not deal with the practicalities. Without clear, implementable policies, it is worthless. Furthermore, the bureaucratic rube c fr equently fails to keep up with a changing economy. I once asked a planner how he would classify a hypothetical nanotechnology company that employed tabletop machines to manufacture its product. Although I asked him to imagine that the machines were automated and hummed away silently, his answer was still 'heavy industrial'.

Planning in India is riven with corruption. It is so deep-rooted that one city has decided that the best approach is to institutionalize it. The Municipal Corporation of Ghaziabad* (MCG) now officially accepts bribes paid through cheques that would otherwise have gone into the pockets of its officials. The Municipal Commissioner, Ajay Shankar Pande has told the media:

> Corruption has gone so deep into the working of government departments that officials cannot dream of handing out work, or payments for it, without taking bribes. So, we have adopted this method of officially taking the bribes, by cheques, into the MCG account. Now, any contractor who gets a tender for a government project has to pay 15 per cent of the quoted amount to MCG. That is, the kickback money he would ordinarily have paid to individual department employees. Now the municipality gets it.[7]

Mumbai is a graphic example of how corruption and ad hoc planning laws lead to unplanned, unbridled development that is driven by private profit. The poor lose out and public spaces and historic buildings are destroyed. Here are some examples:

*Ghaziabad is an industrial city located about 19 km (or 12 miles) east of Delhi in the state of Uttar Pradesh. Industries located there include the manufacture of railway coaches, diesel engines, bicycles, tapestries, glassware, pottery, paint and varnish, and heavy chains. Recently, a number of malls and multiplexes have come up in the city and considerable investment has gone into improving roads.

- *Crawford Market*: This Grade 1 UNESCO-listed, one-hundred-and-thirty-eight-year-old market was sold at a flagrantly low price to a private developer who will convert it into a twin towered, multi-storeyed mall. There were no public tenders or discussion, and the Brihamumbai Municipal Corporation (BMC)* has rejected protestors' demands.
- *Public Grounds*: The BMC is handing over 25 per cent of Mumbai's public grounds to private clubs, gymnasiums, restaurants and bars, under a 'Caretaker Scheme'.
- *Mill Lands*: 273 acres of the city's 320 acre mill lands have been transformed into glossy malls, skyscrapers and offices, leaving only 47 acres for parks and low-cost housing.[8]

Such stories are replicated across the nation. Development in India is haphazard and ad hoc, with high costs both to Indians and the environment. The country is expanding on crumbling foundations.

The Solution: Dense Development

A revolution in habitat planning that pivots around the concept of dense development can change this haphazard, unplanned growth. It is important to distinguish between dense development and overcrowding. As Jane Jacobs clarifies in her classic work *The Death and Life of Great American Cities*:

> One reason why low city densities conventionally have a good name, unjustified by the facts, and why high city densities have a bad name, equally unjustified, is that *high densities of dwellings and overcrowding of dwellings are often confused*. High densities mean large numbers of dwellings per acre of land. Overcrowding means too many people in a dwelling for the number of rooms it contains . . .

*Officially, the BMC is now Brihanmumbai Municipal Corporation.

real-life high densities have nothing to do with overcrowding. (Emphasis added).[9]

High density makes power transmission, water supply and sewage management more efficient. Contrary to popular belief, a skyscraper can be a very 'sustainable' form of living while a fully serviced suburban lifestyle is prohibitively expensive. Think of all the extras that such a lifestyle demands: miles of power line, wells, personal septic systems, extra distance for postal delivery and increased capacity from emergency services.* Urban dwelling, if properly serviced by infrastructure, is the most efficient form of living. Residents can collectively recycle grey water, share power, and take public transportation.† It is infrastructure that should be the key planning determinant.

Unfortunately, such dense development is not happening in India. A ban on building above fifteen metres in Delhi means that density is confined to slums while suburbia extends further into the countryside. In developed countries, where people see infrastructure as a fundamental right, this has led to invisible subsidies, creating strange distortions and profound environmental inefficiencies. Suburbia is the perfect example of these distortions, and it is a recent phenomenon because it depends on private transportation and subsidized services. In the West, these costs are often hidden by subsidies, as described in chapter 2. However,

---

*This is not a description of the situation in rural India where millions of village dwellers have a very low ecological footprint, because they are denied access to essential services.

†To demonstrate the relationship between density, efficiency and cost, let us look at power distribution. Power is generated and transported through a grid that transports electricity at high voltage that is then stepped down to lower voltages through a series of transformers, ultimately reducing it to a voltage that households can use. With density you have many users in a small area, so if you put a transformer in that neighbourhood you do not have to carry the electricity over long distances that leads to transmission losses, a form of evaporation, which is directly proportionate to the distance between transformer and user.

India—with a population nearly four times that of the United States—cannot afford to take a similar path to development.

The challenge of India's future habitat development recalls the 'parting of ways' that urban society has come to, as Lewis Mumford wrote:

> Here, with a heightened consciousness of our past and a clearer insight into decisions made long ago, which often still control us, we shall be able to face the immediate decision that now confronts man and will, one way or another, ultimately transform him: namely, whether he shall devote himself to the development of his own deepest humanity, or whether he shall surrender himself to the now almost automatic forces he himself has set in motion and yield place to his de-humanized alter ego, 'Post-historic Man'. That second choice will bring with it a progressive loss of feeling, emotion, creative audacity, and finally consciousness.[10]

Our habitats are not merely a set of quantifiable assets, they are also the spaces in which we raise children, make friends, attend universities, build our resumes and find time to relax. Investing in the sustainable development of these habitats and the resources required to make them livable is a decision that is ultimately priceless.

Habitat Rights

One of the most important improvements that can be made to the quality of our habitats is to increase their density. The downside of high density, of course, is the loss of open space and the strain that it incurs on services and infrastructure. In order to counter this, I propose that every Indian citizen possesses a set of 'habitat rights', relating to air quality, water supply, sewage, power, transport, and access to open green spaces. Provided these basic rights are met, developers can build as densely as they desire, with high property taxes encouraging communities to support densification.

Certain habitat rights are inviolable and are the responsibility of the Community. Others are negotiable, to a certain extent, which is the prerogative of individuals who can agree to give up the 'negotiated component' of that particular habitat right. This holistic planning will ensure quality of life for all Indians.

Inviolable habitat rights will ensure that every citizen by law will be entitled to:

- *Adequate clean water*: Each member of a Community would be entitled to quantifiable amount and quality of water. These quantitative standards could be based on those established by the World Health Organization, for example, which ranks 'intermediate' access to water (for all personal and household uses) at fifty litres per capita per day and 'optimal' access at 100–200 litres per capita per day.[11] These standard measures, as with all habitat rights, would allow citizens and their communities to assess the quality of their habitat and to ensure their rights were being met.

- *Adequate sewage disposal*: Members of a Community would be entitled to have access to a public sewage system for the disposal of all waste water from domestic sources. This amount would be linked to the amount of clean water each resident is entitled to on a daily basis.[12]

- *Adequate power*: Each member of a Community would be entitled to a quantifiable energy allotment. For example, the world average for per capita electricity consumption was 2,436.3 kilowatt hours per person in 2003.*,[13]

*The average for the same year in middle-income countries was 1726.8 kWh per person. In Asia (excluding the Middle East) it was 1227.1 kWh per person, while in India, the per capita average was only 434.8 kWh. It is clear—as I have discussed elsewhere in this book—that India cannot afford to consume at the levels of countries with smaller populations, like Norway and Iceland, where per capita electricity consumption for 2003 was 23,195.8 and 27,716.3 kWh respectively. Nor can India—with a population solidly over one billion—afford to consume at the level of North Americans, with Canadians consuming 17,209.8 kWh per person in 2003 and Americans consuming 13,242.8. While electricity consumption compatible with the Millennium Development Goals is 75 kWh

- *Access to Green Space*: Green spaces will be located within a reasonable distance from the homes of Community members. For example, a recent study of spatial planning and green space access used two measures: 'less than 400 meters' and 'less than 1 kilometer'.[14] Once a basic minimum distance is ensured, the size of the green space each citizen has access to would be established on the basis of a per capita ratio. This ratio, which I shall now discuss, will encourage communities to invest in larger contiguous green spaces.

These inviolable habitat rights would work in conjunction with the density rights provided to each Community and its members. For example, the maximum permitted density of an area would be defined by the quality of infrastructure provided. If the infrastructure meets the standards prescribed, the population density permitted will be high. If it does not, only a low population density will be allowed. This would ensure that services are improved to the necessary levels before resident demand overburdens capacity. In the words of K.T. Ravindran, the dean of studies at the School of Planning and Architecture in Delhi, 'Issues like water, disposal of sewage, solid waste, groundwater conditions, must become thresholds of development, rather than just land.'[15]

Density would be defined as the number of people living in a square metre, which in terms of building regulations is known as the Floor Area Ratio (FAR). However, any increase in FAR would be permitted after the inviolate Habitat Rights have been met.

- Water supply pipeline and treatment capacity,
- Sewage pipeline and treatment capacity,

---

per household annually, this is sufficient only to provide reading light in one room for four hours each day. As income levels increase in India, a standard will have to be established that allows all Indians to have adequate access to reliable sources of electricity, while maintaining levels of consumption that are sustainable with respect to the size of our population and the capacity of our environmental resources.

- Availability of power,
- Access to green spaces, and
- The proximity and type of transport links.

These would constitute the density rights of the members of each Community. The combination of these five essential services would be mathematically expressed in a formula for densification, accessible to any citizen with a calculator. This would enable citizens and their communities to assess the quality of their habitat and to ensure that their density rights were being met. This would save government time and resources by enabling any developer who met these transparent densification requirements to require no further permission from any level of government.*

The transport vector

This parameter is intended to incentivize the development of public transport that facilitates efficient, high-density living (see Table 7.1). If a Community wanted to increase its density, it would have to ensure it had adequate transport links to meet the proposed density. In contrast to cars, mass rapid transit systems (MRTS), walking

Table 7.1: Relation between modes of transport and city density

Modes of Transport	Density Allows	Provisions
Walking	Very high	Walking paths, pavements,
Bicycle	Very high	Dedicated bicycle routes
Mass Rapid Transport Systems (metros, skytrains)	High	Stations to be close to housing and commercial developments
Common Public Transport (buses, trams)	Medium	Connecting local public transport to rapid transit stations
Cars	Low	Minimal private road area Minimal parking areas and high daily use congestion charges will discourage private car use.

*This measure would end one of the largest sources of corruption in India.

and cycling allow for denser development. Cycling and walking paths are viable transport options when accompanied by MRTS. As a company, Fabindia has realized the importance of transport and located its new north Delhi stores close to metro stations. We have also found that pedestrianization has a large positive impact on retailers. Our research has shown that in one hour 10,000 people passed our store on the largely pedestrian 'commercial street' in Bangalore. For our store in Delhi's Greater Kailash district, where most people travel by car, the equivalent figure was only 100.

Planning

Planning would be constrained and incentivized by the densification parameters described above. Developers would have to apply to the Community for confirmation that any project proposal was not in violation of the Community's density rights. Applications would be passed provided the infrastructure ratio meets or exceeds the level needed for the desired density. Applications could also be submitted for proposals that would impact the negotiable set of habitat rights. While the four habitat rights specified above (that is, those pertaining to clean water, sewage disposal, adequate power, and access to green space) are inviolate, the following habitat rights would be guaranteed to each member of a Community, but open to limited, democratically consensual negotiation. These six negotiable habitat rights include:

- Adequate air quality (with ozone, carbon monoxide, sulphur dioxide, nitrogen dioxide, and suspended particulate matter measured in terms of micrograms per cubic metre);
- Limited traffic (measured in terms of movements per hour and per day);
- Relative quiet (measured in terms of decibels);
- Adequate solid waste disposal (based on solid waste pollution credits);
- Adequate relative temperature (measured in terms of degrees Celsius); and

- Safe levels of electromagnetic radiation[16] (measured in terms of militesla or microtesla).[17]

There would be two indicators for each of the parameters limiting the negotiation of the six negotiable habitat rights specified above: 'standard' and 'inviolate'. For example, air pollution would be measured on a scale ranging from 'very good' (that is, clean) at the bottom to 'critical' (that is, very polluted) at the top. In the new model, the inviolate level would be positioned, for example, at the upper end of 'good' and the standard at the lower end of 'good'. (Delhi's air pollution is currently 'critical'.)[18] The space in between, what might be called a 'high good' and a 'low good', would be negotiable, but negotiation would be limited to this range. Therefore, if I want to set up an industry that would pollute beyond the air quality standard, I would have to apply for a variance from all the individuals affected.* Provided the level of pollution does not exceed the inviolate limit, and as long as two-thirds of the individuals concerned agree, I can set up my industry. Now, why should my neighbours agree to breathe substandard air? There are three avenues open to them: a one-off payment (in the amount of a mutually agreed sum) to compensate them for the reduction in habitat quality; an agreement on my part to reduce the anticipated levels of pollution through the use of different technologies, for example; or a refusal of my requested variance.

Let us assume that an individual applies for permission to establish a cellphone repair store and a variance is obtained from the Community office, subject to limits on certain externalities. Some time later, the business acquires a moulding machine that generates heat, noise and waste beyond the original limits.

At this point, the owner of the business has two choices:

1. Apply to those affected for an amendment to the variance, which may be granted in return for a one-off payment or significant investment in noise proofing and waste disposal;

---

*These individuals would be defined as those residing in the area where the particle levels were above the standard.

2. Move to another site where an additional variance would not be required or would be easier to procure because there is an existing cluster of such externality-generating industries and a collective waste management system is already in place as a result.

The power to grant a variance is the prerogative of the individuals affected and must be based on certain clearly articulated principles related to the type and quantity of externality generated. Because externalities such as noise pollution or solid waste generation can easily be measured, affected individuals would be able to make decisions based on the trade-offs between revenue generation and negative impacts the activity will have on their lives (see Table 7.2).

Habitat rights would ensure that adequate infrastructure is the prerequisite for development. As planning becomes decentralized, communities would compete to build new homes and therefore maximize their property tax revenue (their main source of income). Legally enforceable habitat rights would compel developers to maintain the necessary open area ratios and provide infrastructure according to the ratios for water, sewage, power

Table 7.2: Possibility of variance in habitat rights

	Quality of Life parameter	Negotiable sub-limits	Variance possible
Infrastructure to density parameters	Adequate clean water	No	No
	Adequate power	No	No
	Adequate sewage disposal	No	No
	Access to green space	No	No
	Transport	No	No
	Relative quiet	Yes	Yes
	Pollution (air, water and ground)	Yes	Yes
	Limited traffic	Yes	Yes
	Safe levels of electromagnetic radiation	Yes	Yes
	Adequate relative temperature	Yes	Yes

and transport. The local economy would be the beneficiary allowing developers to add much needed housing and commercial supply, while building urban infrastructure. If a developer does not follow the habitat planning rules and manages to get the FAR by bribing Community officials then citizens can enforce the rules by using their legal TCs to ensure the developer complies with their habitat rights.

Another example of how this model would work is the calculation of open spaces. This would be expressed as a ratio of the amount of open space per citizen. Let us say the minimum standard is 2 sq. ft for every urban citizen. In order to incentivize the development of larger areas of contiguous green space, the area allotment would be reduced slightly on a per capita basis as the size of the park increases. Therefore, if the park is larger than 40,000 sq. ft (approximately 0.4 ha), the per capita requirement would drop to 1.5 sq. ft. If the size of the park exceeds 400,000 sq. ft (around ten acres), the requirement would drop to 1 sq. ft per citizen. This means that an urban Community with a population of 25,000 would need to provide small parks totalling 50,000 sq. ft or it could provide one large park of 40,000 sq. ft. This would encourage Community governments and private developers to save land by making larger parks which serve a greater number. Instead of designing little postage-stamp-sized parks—as has been done by many of India's urban planners, so that only a cluster of households can benefit—this would encourage the creation of larger open spaces, which thousands could enjoy. Large urban parks like New York City's Central Park are an excellent example of how this would work in tandem with dense development.

In India, at present, complex rules and centralized decision making have created an ideal climate for corruption.* Within this

---

*A low-level (Category D) officer once told me the amount he needed to pay as a bribe to get transferred to a land registry office in south Delhi. It equalled eighteen months of his basic pay. Assuming he would be posted for thirty-six months and his basic pay is Rs 10,000 per month, and he would like to make a 50 per cent profit on his 'investment', the bribes he would need to collect can be

climate, restrictions on supply have resulted in the manipulation of land-use categories. In my model, once the criteria for densification have been met, no further 'permission' would be necessary. Community governments would support such high-density planning because more infrastructure and higher property values would result in increased property tax revenues. In order to manage taxation, communities will have to ensure that all property owners have marketable titles to their land. As Hernando de Soto aptly puts it, 'Without an integrated formal property system, a modern market economy is inconceivable.'[19] Giving all Indians formal ownership of their land will be a crucial step in recognizing the assets of the poor.

Property taxes will also end speculative land acquisitions and accelerate the settlement of land disputes. While it is difficult to quantify current levels of speculation in the real estate market or to estimate the value of disputed properties in India, it is a fair guess that these activities account for a significant share of the country's GDP. In the part of Mussoorie where we own a house, there are about fifty-five estates that are empty most of the year (including our own). Another owner of an absentee property once told me that his property was his 'fixed deposit' with its 20 per cent annual growth rate. A piece of land has become a veritable bank account with vertiginous interest rates. Because there is no cost of holding onto such land and because policy makers themselves have intervened in the real estate market resulting in false caps on supply,* property prices in India are among the highest in the world.[20]

---

expressed mathematically as: Rs $10,000 \times 18 \times 0.5$. This does not include upstream bribes paid to senior officers who are part of the chain of corruption. *The Rent Control Act in Mumbai is a classic example of this. Passed in 1947 as a temporary measure to keep prices stable for residents during a period of significant change, the Act has proven politically impossible to overturn. The result is that rent prices for many apartments are frozen at 1940s levels, creating no incentive for owners to invest in building upkeep. Meanwhile, the false control on supply has created a housing shortage, which drives up the prices for those not grandfathered into rent control apartments.

The same logic of making profit because of poor legal enforcement and inefficient land use policies applies to the prevalent issue of property disputes. There is an Indian saying, 'If you start a dispute today your grandchildren will resolve it.' One of the reasons for this, apart from the inevitable judicial delays, is that neither party has a strong incentive to arrive at a prompt settlement, as the property value will only increase, and there is no cost of holding on to the property.* Accumulating property taxes combined with the threat of seizure will be an incentive to settle disputes rapidly and put large amounts of property back into supply.

Zoning

In the new model I propose, only three zones would exist:
- Habitat,
- Forest, and
- Biosphere.

Habitat

Within the habitat area, there would be no zoning as it currently exists. No distinction would be made between land used for agriculture, residences, commercial, heavy industry or light industry. Instead, all development would be based on two factors: density rights and habitat rights. While these two factors would encourage certain patterns and clusters of land use, they would do so organically. For example, it would make sense for heavy industries to group together in non-residential areas, where a multitude of variances would not be required. The result of this approach to land use is a move away from top-down planning towards a more dynamic, organic, bottom-up form of development. These proposals would improve habitats by encouraging social

---

*A high court judge recounted this to me.

and economic forces that current zoning policies constrain. As Jane Jacobs expresses in work:

> One principle emerges so ubiquitously, and in so many and such complex different forms . . . This ubiquitous principle is the need of cities for a most intricate and close-grained diversity of uses that give each other constant mutual support, both economically and socially. The components of this diversity can differ enormously, but they must supplement each other in certain concrete ways.[21]

This approach would be reinforced by fiscal policy, as property taxes would incentivize dense development, triggering investment in the infrastructure necessary to ensure that density and habitat rights are upheld.

Take the example of Panchsheel. Currently, it is a residential colony consisting of mostly single-or double-family homes. We all drive cars around Delhi because there is no reliable and comfortable public transportation available. However, the area has tremendous potential for dense development as it is near a metro line that is currently under construction. In my model, once the local metro station is functional, the Community of Panchsheel could decide to pedestrianize the areas around the station— meeting one of the critical requirements for increased densification—which would entitle the Community to build up to fifteen floors for every plot of land. Since rental revenues would increase with the increase in density, property values would also rise. Property tax will increase correspondingly, dramatically incentivizing densification. Anyone who resists erecting a higher building could simply pay a higher tax, but most people will opt for the higher income to balance higher taxes. The system could also flow in reverse—if densities got too high, communities would have to invest in infrastructure, and the comparatively higher property taxes would help pay for the additional investment.

This new density-based planning system, combined with property taxes would force Community governments to continually compete with each other, and as a result invest in good schools, neighbourhood security and other quality of life parameters, in an effort to make their Community more attractive and therefore ensure higher property prices. This in turn would increase the demand for property in that Community by attracting migrants from other parts of the Region and Nation. It will also allow communities to negotiate from a position of strength when fixing rates with service and utility providers, as they will be seeking these services as bulk consumers.

Biodiversity and forest cover

The two other habitat zones—forest and biospheres—will be regenerated by the environmental per capita quotas (EPCQs), described in chapter 2. Each Community will have to purchase a defined quantity of forest and biodiversity for each resident in their jurisdiction. This will ensure that substantial amount of much needed revenue is transferred from urban to rural India as urban communities buy the surplus forest and biosphere EPCQs from rural communities in order to meet their thresholds. In this way, those communities in rural India that maintain and protect the country's environmental assets will be compensated for their work.

Conclusion

If these proposals were put into practice, planning in India would largely self-regulate. Cities would develop at high densities, but with the support of excellent infrastructure and the relief of mandatory open spaces. The implementation of real costing would move suburbia into the history books. India's forests and biospheres would be regenerated by the process of urbanization itself as urban communities invest in EPCQs and the huge differential between rural and urban incomes would be bridged with the transfer of wealth generated by the purchase of EPCQs, resulting not only in greater economic equality but greater political equality as well. All of this is possible with the implementation of a few significant policies; the rest would be driven by human ingenuity and the basic mechanisms of demand and supply.

Notes

1. According to the 2001 Census of India, 286,119,689 Indians (or 27.8 per cent of the population) were living in urban areas. See http://www.censusindia.gov.in/Census_Data_2001/India_at_Glance/rural.aspx.

2. This is from the United Nations' report on the State of the World Population 2007, published by the United Nations Population Fund in New York. According to a 2006 report by Jones Lang Lasalle on the investment future in India, the country is urbanizing at a rapid rate of 2.5 per cent per year with the number of cities over one million expected to double from thirty-five in 2001 to seventy by 2025. See http://www.jllm.co.in/en-GB/research/researchabstract?artid=2425

3. Estimates from a 2003 study published in the Bulletin of the World Health Organization suggest that there are over 1500 unauthorized colonies in Delhi without civic amenities and that as much as 60 per cent of the city's population lives in substandard housing. The living conditions of the residents in these colonies are very poor; 70 per cent are without any sewage facilities and 60 per cent are merely single rooms for an entire family and every household activity, without even a separate space for cooking. See http://web.iitd.ac.in/~tripp/publications/paper/planning/WHO per cent20Bulletin per cent20GT per cent202003.pdf.

4. Ibid.

5. Soutik Biswas, 'Why So Much of Delhi is Illegal', *BBC Online*, 4 February 2006.

6. The Master Plan for Delhi 2021 (MPD) was notified on 7 February 2007 and is available online at http://www.dda.org.in/planning/draft_master_plans.htm. In April 2008, a 'Supplement' to the Master Plan for Delhi was released which incorporates 'consolidated list of notified commercial, mixed use and pedestrian streets with alphabetical index to notified streets in Delhi; fixation of charges for mixed use and commercial use premises regulations 2006 along with text of relevant public notices; development control norms

for residential plotted development along with text of relevant regulations and public notices; National Capital Territory of Delhi Laws (Special Provisions) Ordinance 2007; Delhi Stamp (Prevention of Undervaluation of Instruments) Rules 2007; circle rates in Delhi; e-stamping in Delhi; up-to-date amended list of colonies/localities/industrial areas/urban villages/rural villages with category.'

7. Lalit Kumar, 'A Municipality that Officially Takes Bribes!' *The Times of India*, 11 September 2007.

8. Farah Baria, 'Whose Mumbai?', *The Indian Express*, 15 March 2008.

9. Jane Jacobs, *The Death and Life of Great American Cities* (New York: Random House, 1961), p. 205.

10. Lewis Mumford, *The City in History* (New York: Harcourt, 1961), p. 4.

11. These figures are taken from chapter 5 of the current edition of WHO's *Guidelines for Drinking Water Quality* report, accessible at http://www.who.int/water_sanitation_health/dwq/gdwq0506_5.pdf. The whole report, which includes detailed measures of water quality, is accessible at http://www.who.int/water_sanitation_health/dwq/gdwq3rev/en/index.html. For a comparison of different national standards and the WHO standards of water quality with respect to various contaminants and compounds, see http://www.nesc.wvu.edu/ndwc/articles/OT/SP03/Inter_DWRegs.html.

12. All industrial process waste waters (for example, lab wastes, shop wastes, cooling waters) would require an approved variance for disposal into the public sewage system. Any variance for industrial use of the public sewage system would require industrial waste water pretreatment standards to be met. See, for example, http://www.unep.or.jp/ietc/Publications/Freshwater/FMS10/8optimizing.asp. Injurious, toxic, flammable, radioactive, or nuisance-producing substances would not be deposited in any sewer, storm drain, ground area, or in any other place without meeting pretreatment standards as approved by the Community government in concert with the citizens affected.

13. For more information and sources for this data from the International Energy Agency (IEA), see http://earthtrends.wri.org/text/energy-resources/variable-574.html. For more information on the Millennium Development Goals project, see http://

www.unmillenniumproject.org/documents/MP_Energy_Low_Res.pdf and http://www.risoe.dk/rispubl/SYS/syspdf/Pacudan_electricity_development.pdf.

14. See the May 2006 report, *Urban Green Space: The Incorporation of Environmental Values in a Decisions Support System*, available at http://www.itcon.org/data/works/att/2006_14.content.01332.pdf; with additional information at http://www.ucd.ie/greensp/docs/final2.pdf.

15. Urmila Rao, 'Will Delhi's Master Plan '21 Solve Its Woes?' *Outlook Money*, 4 April 2007.

16. Electromagnetic radiation (EMR) can be classified into ionizing radiation and non-ionizing radiation, based on whether it is capable of ionizing atoms and breaking chemical bonds. Ultraviolet and higher frequencies, such as X-rays or gamma rays are ionizing. Both types pose potential hazards to communities. In particular, non-ionizing radiation is associated with two major potential hazards: electrical and biological. Most commonly considered are the biological hazards posed by EMR. While the preponderance of evidence shows that the low-power, low-frequency, electromagnetic radiation associated with household current is very safe, and no biophysical theories for the initiation or promotion of cancer have been substantiated, some research has implicated exposure in a number of adverse health effects. These include, but are not limited to, childhood leukemia, adult leukemia, neurodegenerative diseases (such as amyotrophic lateral sclerosis), miscarriage, and clinical depression. For more information on research implicating EMR in these adverse health effects, see http://www.dhs.ca.gov/ehib/emf/RiskEvaluation/riskeval.html.

17. See World Health Organization Fact Sheet for more information, http://www.who.int/mediacentre/factsheets/fs322/en/index.html.

18. Several years ago, Delhi was ranked as having the worst air pollution of major Asian cities. See http://cities.expressindia.com/fullstory.php?newsid=109621. Since then, policy makers have taken measures to change this. However, with increasing car ownership, these improvements seemed to have already been reversed. See the press release from the Centre for Science and Environment, http://www.cseindia.org/Aboutus/press_releases/press_20071106.htm.

19. Hernando De Soto, *The Mystery of Capital: Why Capitalism Triumphs in the West and Fails Everywhere Else* (New York: Random House, 2000), p. 147.

20. India's most expensive cities in terms of real estate prices, Mumbai and Delhi, are extreme examples of the market forces affecting real estate prices throughout India, which are significantly disproportionate to the country's per capita GDP. According to a report released in April 2008 by the Hong Kong-based consultants, ECA International, residential rents in Mumbai rose 21 per cent over the past year, making it the second costliest in the rental market in Asia and sixth in the world; Mumbai is now a more expensive city to rent an apartment in than Paris, Dubai, Seoul, Singapore, Shanghai, Dubai, Beijing, St Petersburg and Amsterdam. According to a Global Property Guide report, apartments in south Mumbai are priced to sell at US$9000 to US$10,200 per sq. m. Even for relatively well-paid call centre agents with annual incomes of around US$3000 to US$4500, the condominiums in Bangalore—India's Silicon Valley—which are priced between US$950 to US$2000 per sq. m, are clearly unaffordable. Cushman and Wakefield reported that Mumbai had the world's highest rise in industrial property rent in 2007, while the industrial area surrounding Delhi saw the fifth highest increase. According to ECA International, Delhi is the second most costly city in India, the ninth in Asia and twenty-second in the world in terms of residential rentals. Additionally, Mumbai and Delhi rank among the world's ten most expensive cities to rent office space, as evidenced by the results of the CB Richard Ellis Group's semi-annual global market rents survey released in May 2008. See http://economictimes.indiatimes.com/articleshow/3085792.cms. Also, see http://www.globalpropertyguide.com/Asia/India.

21. Jane Jacobs, *The Death and Life of Great American Cities* (New York: Random House, 1961), p. 14.

8

The Transition

Democratic mobilization, while it has produced an intense struggle for power, has not delivered millions of citizens from the abject dictates of poverty. Yes, the broad framework within which practices of popular authorization can be carried out remain intact, but politics itself has become an area where norms exist only in their breach . . . The very mechanism designed to secure the liberty, well-being and dignity of citizens, representative democracy, is routinely throwing up forces that threaten to undermine it; the very laws that are supposed to enshrine republican aspirations are incapable of commanding minimal respect, and their inaction subjects the entire political process to ridicule. The corruption, mediocrity, indiscipline, venality and lack of moral imagination of the political class, those essential agents of representative democracy, makes them incapable of attending to the well-being of citizens. The capture of the political process, by the meanest of interests, intermittently violent, occasionally unleashing uncontrollable passions, the lack of any ideological coherence, all suggest democracy has become a hollow shell. It is a ritual, albeit an engaging and spectacular one.

Pratap Bhanu Mehta

O nce, as a small boy, I complained to my father about not winning a lottery I had entered. He replied that I had already

Epigraph: Pratap Bhanu Mehta, *The Burden of Democracy* (New Delhi: Penguin, 2003), pp. 17–19.

won the biggest lottery of all, simply through my birth. I have been incredibly fortunate—born into India's elite with the privileges of a world-class education, social connections, top-quality health care, and a life of comfort. The older I get, the more my father's words ring true. One in every three malnourished children in the world lives in India; everyday, half of the children in this country go without sufficient food.[1] Every year, 2.5 million Indian children die, accounting for one in five deaths in the world.[2] Fifty per cent of Indian children between the ages of five and fifteen do not go to school.[3] It was indeed a lottery that I won. Throughout the previous pages, I have asked you to imagine a different India. I have put pen to paper only because I believe that everything I have described is possible. In this chapter, I lay out a transition, connecting the dots between the situation today, and what I believe India could be tomorrow. After explaining why such drastic changes are necessary, I outline the financial, legal and administrative aspects of the transition.

Many may read this book and question the need for such major reforms, arguing that while flawed, the current system is adequate and a gradual approach to change is appropriate. I believe that if we continue on our current trajectory, no amount of piecemeal change is going to affect the huge threats facing our development, the epic inequalities in our society, or the environmental havoc we are wreaking. These are not melodramatic predictions. Delhi is facing huge power and water shortages, Naxalite violence is gripping much of the country, and headlines about the melting of the Himalayas are commonplace. The chronic mismanagement of India can no longer be hidden. The cracks are becoming too big to paper over. We are at a historical tipping point.

The Problem

Globally, we are facing an environmental crisis. If we do not rapidly change our course, by the year 2030, the Himalayan glaciers will have melted by 80 per cent or completely disappeared, causing devastation to the billions who depend on them.[4] The Ganga, which directly supplies more than 400 million people—one-fifteenth of all humanity—with drinking water, may be reduced to a trickle. Floods and drought would result in food shortages and make environmental refugees of those who lose their homes due to flooding.[5]

In India, population is expected to continue to boom, nearing the 1.8 billion mark by the middle of this century and possibly exceeding 2 billion by 2100.[6] Within the next fifteen years, demand for water is expected to exceed supply.[7] Already, over 70 per cent of Indians—90 per cent in the rural areas—do not have access to adequate sanitation.[8] Shortage in electricity threatens to derail the country's growth with a peak-hour shortage of over 13 per cent. It is exacerbated by unacceptably high transmission and distribution losses, ranging from 30 per cent to 45 per cent in many states.[9] These failures are blamed on bureaucratic hurdles, policy uncertainty and lack of political will.

Poverty in India exists on an epic scale with 837 million Indians (77 per cent of the population) living on US$2 a day.*,[10] As it becomes harder to make a living in the villages, millions flock to the cities, with over 30,000 people moving every month to Delhi alone. The result is unsustainable, unplanned urbanization, straining already inadequate infrastructure. By 2020, the number of urban poor in India will exceed the entire current population of the USA.[11] Meanwhile, poverty is driving desperate rural Indians to violent solutions, creating what Prime Minister Manmohan Singh has labelled the 'single biggest security challenge to the Indian state'.†,[12]

Our politicians would have us believe these problems will be

*This is Rs 20 in purchasing power parity (PPP) terms.
†He is referring to the four-decade-old Maoist Naxalite movement which seeks to overthrow the 'comprador-bourgeois' Indian state and establish a 'People's Republic' through guerrilla warfare strategies directed by Mao Zedong.

solved by the market alone. But we are not seeing liberalization in India. The situation today is one in which a tiny corporate minority is able to manipulate the Indian government and economy to its own interest. As a result, one of the biggest threats to India's development is the elite who control the levers of government and have succeeded in hijacking the democratic nature of our polity to cater to the demands of a crony state.[13] It is 'cheap' to buy a seat in the Parliament today—apparently, Rs 10 million is the prevailing rate—a trifle for controlling the policy that will shape our future. Privatization on these terms can only result in greater inequalities. Policies today are enacted without anything like the well-being of our nation in mind.

I have written this book because I do not want to wait. I do not want to wait for the riots over water, power and food. I do not want to wait for millions to die unnecessarily. I do not want to wait for Naxalite violence to spread across rural India. I do not want to wait until we have emitted so much carbon that the earth reaches the point that we face a complete environmental meltdown.

The new system outlined in this book preserves and amplifies India's strengths but avoids the pitfalls of the Western development model. Growth built on infinitely increasing consumption will fail. As a nation, it is time to stop blindly following the development paths of others, which may have been appropriate to their historical and social contexts, but now have gone long past their expiration dates. It is time for India to show global leadership.

The Path to Change

The politics of transition

In this book, I propose a transformation of society. While such major societal reform generally takes place at gunpoint or in the midst of revolution, I believe it can occur in the context of a stable democracy. However, such a change would require an enormous political mandate—on the scale of Rajiv's Gandhi's 1984 electoral landslide (the largest mandate in India's electoral history) that put the Congress party in 80 per cent of the seats in the Lok Sabha.[14] As India has shown, such a mandate is possible.

The degree of change would also require new leaders to be guided by a vision. In contrast to the current political paralysis and ad hoc policy making that politicians are engaged in, our new leaders would need to see the bigger picture. They would need cast-iron conviction—the perseverance and tenacity to push the reforms through—the vision of Martin Luther King, combined with the resolve of Margaret Thatcher.[15] Finally, and most importantly, these new leaders would need to convince the citizens of India that this new system is the solution to their problems. This would require an immense publicity campaign to gain the support of the electorate for such a radical change. Such a campaign would be on the scale of Al Gore's climate protection campaign, on which he plans to spend US$300 million over three years on order to make global warming the most urgent issue for American leaders.[16]

Strong political will is essential. Too many politicians lack a clear direction. Policy making should not be an exercise in telling voters what they want to hear; it should be the proposal of a coherent political project.

Managing the Transition

Many of my reforms will require constitutional amendments. As I pointed out in chapter 5, the authors of the Constitution understood that the ability to alter the Constitution was an integral part of its longevity. In the words of Granville Austin, '[The amending process] has proved itself one of the most ably conceived aspects of the Constitution.'[17] There are three ways of amending the Constitution as laid out in Article 368:

1. A simple majority in the Parliament and presidential assent;
2. A simple majority in the Parliament with two-thirds of the members present and voting, and presidential assent;

3. Amendment method (2) plus ratification by the legislature of one half of all the states.*

Any one of these methods (provided in ascending difficulty) could be used to make the necessary amendments to allow the changes that follow. However, an enormous political mandate would be required and I believe that this is possible.

The major reforms to government suggested in chapter 4 will streamline India's bloated public sector, which was recently described by *The Economist* as suffering from a form of 'bureaucratic cancer'.[18] The first of these reforms would be to eliminate the offices of the President and governors and merge the two houses into one—the Lok Sabha, where each MP would represent approximately 2.5 million citizens.

This measure would safeguard democracy, ensuring that only directly elected MPs wielded power. In chapter 4, I described how the Rajya Sabha was degenerating into a club for special interest lobbies and corporate groups, resulting in immense corporate regulatory capture. There is a saying that in the old days, if you wanted to buy the election you paid the electorate; today you just buy a seat in the Rajya Sabha directly. Take the example, narrated to me by a local party leader, of how his party's top election strategist could not win his own parliamentary seat, so had to be accommodated in the Rajya Sabha.

The majority of Indians may not be educated, but they are remarkably politically savvy. I remember watching a puppeteer, in a small town in Uttar Pradesh years ago, perform a parody of a governor dancing to the tune of his political masters, aptly called '*guvarnar jaise naache*' (dances like a governor). The Constitution provides for conditions to facilitate political neutrality of the

---

*This method of amendment applies to the amending Article 368 itself and articles dealing with the election of the President, the extent of executive power of the Union and the state governments, the distribution of powers and the representation of the states in Parliament. See Article 368, *The Constitution of India*.

governor;* however, as I explained in chapter 4, today they are considered puppets of the political parties that appoint them. This undermines our democracy.

The three other major reforms I outlined in chapter 4 would:

- dismantle all ministries apart from defence and foreign affairs. This would reduce government size and employment at the national level to a fraction of the current numbers;
- replace the current system—twenty-eight states and seven Union territories—of widely diverging size and population with forty-eight regions each representing twenty-five million people;
- replace the district administrations and Panchayati Raj with Area and Community administrations at the local levels.

The new administrations, after these changes are carried out is outlined in Table 8.1.

Table 8.1: The proposed administrative system

Current tier of Government	Proposed tier of Government	Number of Administrative Units	Population in each unit	Head	Council
Panchayat/ Municipalities	Community	4800	25,000	Chair	4 members
Blocks, Subdivisions, Districts, Divisions	Area	480	2.5 million	MP and Area Board Chair	100 Community Chairpersons
States and Union Territories	Region	48	25 million	Governor	10 members of Parliament
Nation	Nation	1	1.2 billion	Prime Minister	480 members of Parliament

*Article 158, dealing with conditions of the governor's office, stipulates that the governor cannot be a member of Union or state legislatures and cannot hold any office of profit. These provisions aim to ensure his or her neutrality.

Funding the Transition

Once my proposals have been instituted, government revenue will be more than ample to cover expenditure. The transition itself, however, will require substantial investment. To cover this, I propose setting up a National Asset Corporation (NAC) that would function as a sovereign investment fund called National Asset Fund (NAF). It is a model used very successfully by several other economies, most notably, as I mentioned in chapter 4, in Singapore by Temasek Holdings, and in Dubai by Istithmar World. Today, they are amongst the world's largest investors. Each is run independently by a board of directors and a management team, with the key objective of maximizing shareholder returns on their investments. Their shareholders are their governments.

If the Indian government created such a corporation, its diverse portfolio of all public sector companies would make it a large and competitive player. The scale of these Public Sector Undertakings (PSUs) is truly incredible: Indian Railways is the world's largest commercial employer with more than 1.5 million people on its payroll,[19] while the giant Oil and Natural Gas Corporation (ONGC) is the most profitable company in India, and Bharat Petroleum Corporation Ltd (BPCL) and Hindustan Petroleum Corporation Ltd (HPCL) were among the fifteen global firms on the Forbes 500 list, for the extent of their increase in profits.[20] The top forty PSUs alone are valued at more than US$400 billion.*,[21]

Initially, the NAF would be used to cover the costs of transition. After the transition, it would be a valuable resource to help cover long-term investment in the public interest. I envisage three distinct phases in the use of the fund:

1. To cover the costs of dramatically reducing the size of the public sector, via a one-off payout to existing employees. This is detailed later in this section.

---

*Even though government does not have 100 per cent ownership of all PSUs, these figures show that funding the transition through the creation of a National Asset Corporation, would be possible

2. To fund research on diseases disproportionately affecting the poor. For example, this would research on forms of hepatitis, tuberculosis, malaria, cholera and dysentery, which have not seen significant research by pharmaceutical companies because there is little incentive for profit, but which kill millions. Governments have an important role to play in sponsoring research and keeping the fruits of it in the public domain. India could become a world leader in health care research for the poor, with funds going into establishing labs at universities and in private companies. By keeping the intellectual property rights in the public domain, the drugs would be owned by the NAC, which means it could control the price, ensuring that essential medicines were affordable. The NAC could recoup some of its cost through volume of sales and investment in generic drug companies. Such a use of the NAC actually represents a long-term investment in the future of the country.

3. Another use of the NAC—many years down the line—would be to fund pure scientific enquiry, which would dramatically raise India's profile on the world scientific stage. There are other advantages as well: funding such research has the potential to yield important commercial or national security-related results. With its reserves of scientists and engineers, India just needs strategic funding to unlock its creative scientific potential.

An example of the benefits of far-sighted investment in research and development is the Government of India's Centre for Development of Telematics (C-DOT). It was established by Rajiv Gandhi in 1984 as an autonomous body with total flexibility to develop state-of-the-art telecommunication technology to meet the needs of the Indian network. The key objective was to build a centre for excellence in the area of telecom technology. It consequently spearheaded the telecommunications revolution in India.

Changes to Constitutional Authorities

An essential initial step is drafting and establishing the general performance parameters (GPPs) for the heads of constitutional bodies, national exchanges, Standards Authorities and regulators. Once they are in place, the process of recruitment for these positions can begin. As described in chapter 4, the prime minister will select candidates and a two-thirds majority in the Parliament will ratify their appointment. The roles of the Reserve Bank of India, the Election Commission and the Comptroller and Auditor General would not change considerably.

- The Citizens Database: As soon as the new tiers of government are delimited, the details of all citizens will be registered in the database.
- The National Asset Corporation: The role of this body has been discussed earlier in the chapter.
- The Reserve Bank of India: Initially, the use of biometric cards that will be used to support the dematerialized cash system will run in parallel to the current system. The RBI will oversee this process and the subsequent transition to a completely cashless economy, while continuing as a banking and financial services regulator.
- The Election Commission: Once the temporary Boundaries Commission has delimited the new political constituencies, the Election Commission will continue its historical role of holding elections to all tiers of government.
- The Planning Commission: This will be transformed into the Planning Standards Authority that both provides guidance and audits the development plans of the Community, Area and Regional Authorities.
- The Comptroller and Auditor General's Office: This will set the accounting standards for the different tiers of government, in addition to the certification criteria for the finance officers and CEOs of each tier. It will also audit the accounts of each tier of the government.

The Transitional Commissions

A number of transitional commissions will need to be established for two to four years.

Government Employees Pension and
Re-employment Commission

This commission will ease the transition to a streamlined government, approximately one-tenth of the size of the current administration. I estimate that the government will be able to function with approximately twenty million fewer employees. In order to avoid protest by government employees, I propose a generous severance package in the form of pension bonds funded by the NAC. At the time of redemption, the amount payable to the retrenched government employees from their pension bond would be met by the selective sales of equity in the NAC. To give you a sense, the total market capitalization of all public sector undertakings, which are companies owned by the Government of India and which would now be owned by the NAC, is approximately Rs 14.5 trillion.[22] This figure does not cover the thousands of government companies that are not listed on a stock exchange and, while many of them carry accumulated losses, they also control some of the most valuable real estate in India.

I do not agree with the plan by certain political parties in India that envisage selling these assets to the private sector. These assets represent the accumulated wealth of the citizens of India and many of these companies can be run profitably just by distancing the management from the interference of politicians.[23] The creation of a NAC will accomplish this goal and keep these assets as part of national property.

The first lien on the income of the NAC would go to pay off the pension fund liabilities of the millions of government employees who were given a 'golden handshake'.* This process should not take more than four to six years as public sector employees are generally older than the Indian population as a whole,[24] but many of them will still have productive years left.

---

*A handsome payment made generally to senior executives of companies upon termination of their employment before their contract ends. Here, it would mean relieving government employees with a substantial severance package.

The payment of wages and the promise of retirement benefits will allow them great income security and freedom. They can run for election to their Community governments or apply their skills entrepreneurially. The buyout will be possible because of the enormity of the NAC. It will be a huge one-off payment, and then it is finished. The cost would be amortized over the thirty or forty years of remaining life expectancy of the current generation of civil servants. The former employees have the option of selling their pension bonds for a lump sum.* The creation of the NAC ensures that the process will continue without political interference because its funding will be independently secured.

The National Cross-subsidization Fund

This would correct the extreme imbalances that will occur when communities first collect property taxes. It would provide short-term 'grants' to help communities whose total property tax revenue is insufficient for them to issue TCs to their members who are below the poverty line.

The fund will operate by capping the per capita property tax level in every Community for a predefined transition period (two to four years). Any revenue collected above this will be pooled into the National Cross-subsidization Fund (NCSF), and made available to communities which are not able to meet their TC expenditure. If the expenses on account of TC are insufficient, any Community running a deficit can apply for an annual grant from their Regional government, which will be drawn from the NCSF. For example, initially, Panchsheel will have relatively high levels of revenue from taxation as property prices here are among the highest in the country. The property tax revenue that accrues to the Community Government of Panchsheel will be far above the per capita maximum with the surplus going into the NCSF. The NCSF will allocate this surplus as annual grants to the deficit communities such as Sewari, where revenue will initially be low

---

*The NAC can raise funds for this by selling equity in its companies.

and demand for TCs high.* The deficit situation in Sewari will be on account of the large number of TCs the Community Government of Sewari will have to fund. But, the situation will change dramatically as soon as Sewari's Community administration starts to develop, rent and sell its assets—most notably its surplus water, forests, biospheres and mineral mines. In Panchsheel—once the ludicrous town planning rules that limit Delhi's housing supply are removed—property values will drop, as supply will quickly rise.

This process would happen throughout the nation and over time would make India a more equitable society where the enormous gap between rich and poor is narrowed, as the 'free' assets of the rich get priced and the poor get a value for what they own.

India's poorest communities are frequently located in areas abundant in minerals, forest, water and biodiversity, as illustrated in chapter 2. Once these communities gain control over these resources and begin to trade them, their wealth will increase dramatically. However, it will take a few years for the value of such assets to gain currency, hence the need for the NCSF.

The legal review commission

This will review all the national laws and essentially remove millions of defunct laws from the statute books. Its second goal will be to make the process of rule creation simpler for the public to understand. Laws will be grouped into:
1. Uniform Civil Personal Law
2. Criminal Law Code
3. Community Administration Law and Property Law
4. Area Administration Law
5. Regional Administration Law
6. Associational Law
7. National Laws
8. Constitutional Laws

*Sewari will start with a low property tax base and large numbers of poor.

The Boundaries Commission

This will be responsible for delimiting the new boundaries, based on population, for Community, Area and Region, as detailed in chapter 4. The first step will be to delimit the 'Community' to as close to 25,000 people as possible, by identifying centres of population density using census data. Three criteria will apply:

1. All communities must be geographically contiguous;
2. No Community can be separated by a natural boundary such as a river, mountain range, major canal or a built boundary such as a major road;*
3. Communities must have the highest density in the smallest area.

The logic behind this it to use demographics and geography to create more equitable, mixed communities. The first and second criteria prevent 'islands' of wealth joining together to form a Community, so two halves of a wealthy residential colony in Delhi separated by the ring road, would not be able to join together. The third would ensure that the Boundaries Commission could carry out delimitation on a mathematical basis that is verifiable and transparent.

The Institutions of the New Economy

The system of standards, exchanges and regulators described in chapter 2 is essential to the functioning of the new economy.

The Standards Authorities

These essentially function as sector specific rating agencies. Their role will be to define criteria for assessment, undertake regular

---

*While this criterion makes sense for Panchsheel Community, there might be cases where it does not. An important consideration for the Boundaries Commission will be to consider each Community on a case-by-case basis. Preventing unnecessary 'islands' of wealth will require attention not only to geographic and natural boundaries—which in certain instances will matter less than others—but also to income distribution data from the Indian census.

evaluation of all organizations falling under their jurisdiction, and publish the results in publicly available league tables. There will be many standards authorities. I shall not detail them all here, but rather give two examples:

- *Education*: Existing institutions, such as the education ministry, University Grants Commission, National Council for Educational Research and Training, All India Council for Technical Education, state education boards, Central Board Secondary Education, the Council for the Indian School Certificate Examination, which currently have overlapping and conflicting jurisdictions, would all be merged into the Education Standards Authority in partnership with Regional and Area governments. This would administer standardized assessments of progress for all levels up to PhD,* evaluate all educational institutions periodically and publish the results, similar to the UK's educational league tables and develop criteria for the Targeted Catalyst scheme.

- *Health care*: A plethora of public health bodies will be merged into the Health Standards Authority, the Nutrition Standards Authority and the Drugs Standards Authority. These three institutions will instigate standard operating procedures, set the criteria for rating medical establishments and evaluate all such organizations periodically. The results would be used to publish and develop criteria for the Targeted Catalyst scheme. The Drugs Standards Authority would be responsible for drug testing and certification procedures. The Nutrition Standards Authority would issue guidelines for the Nutrition TC.

The exchanges

Each type of public asset would have one national exchange, similar to a stock market. All records would be available online. For example, a Water Exchange would trade water and encourage

*Education upwards of graduation would be the responsibility of the Universities.

investment by surplus regions in the water grid. These investments would allow regions to transport water over distances to meet the demands of communities that do not have enough water.* By pricing water, the exchanges would allow investors to calculate returns on investments on water projects. It would also give regions a price for when one Region consumes the entire freshwater supply carried by a river (such as the city of Delhi does today). Once these proposals are implemented, this pricing would evidence that this water is the property of the citizens of all regions that live along the river's banks.

The regulators

Each regulator, as discussed earlier, would cover a specific domain for which an exchange exists. For example, radio frequency spectrum (which is needed for mobile phones) would be traded between mobile phone providers. The regulator would monitor trading on the exchanges much the way an umpire monitors a game. They would intervene only when a single player controlled 50 per cent or more of the market.

Regulators have been introduced in India to cover certain sectors of the economy. They have functioned partly to set standards and over time expanded their influence in the sector they regulate by constantly introducing regulations to 'protect the public interest'. Policing these growing regulations has let the regulator assume huge discretionary powers and added a new dimension to corruption in government.

My reason for separating the standards, exchanges and regulators is that each performs a different and vital function which

---

*In the process, communities will get rid of what Sainath calls 'water lords' and he presents an example of acute water scarcity: 'To this day, close to 90 per cent of irrigated area here depends for water on the 1841 ancient tanks. For the rest of Tamil Nadu, the area dependent on rain-fed irrigation averages only 38 per cent. Ramnad's traditional irrigation system is its lifeline. But it is a lifeline in crisis. Most of the tanks desperately need repairs. But as one senior official put it, "The funds allotted for the upkeep of tanks are less than 40 per cent of what is needed."' See P. Sainath, *Everybody Loves a Good Drought* (New Delhi: Penguin Books India, 1996), pp. 344–45.

can often be at odds with the other. The idea of an insurance regulator stipulating financial norms to protect citizens from insurance companies that default is an important activity for government to perform. However, it should be done by the standards authority, not the regulator. Insurance is a commodity that will be traded on the insurance exchange and as such, if the standards are consistently maintained, the regulator will need to ensure that consumers get the best price through vigorous competition.

The pricing of assets—be they mining rights, radio frequency spectrum, air space, a life insurance policy, the right to ply a train on a track of rail—is best done on open exchanges. The state's role should be limited to establishing institutions such as the standards authority, the exchanges and the regulators and then letting them do their job. Oversight would come from the POBs which would use the GPPs as the sole means for judging the management of these institutions.

Once these institutions are established, all existing assets would be transferred to the appropriate tier of government, as illustrated in Table 4.9. All existing infrastructure and organizations would be converted into associations. For example, ownership of government hospitals will be transferred to the Community, while airports, train stations and rail tracks would belong to the Area. If the suggested changes are implemented India would lead the world in heralding a new age of an accountable, democratic capitalism.

Conclusion

In 1987, I visited Zimbabwe and was awestruck by its beauty, its resources, and its wealth. Today, the country represents profound human misery. It has taken only twenty years of bad leadership to destroy what was once a vibrant nation. I fear that the same thing will happen to my country as profound mismanagement, a crony corporate state, environmental constraints and a booming population take their toll. As I watch India's political leaders help themselves to the spoils of office, I remember a time when people who served this country would have considered such behaviour unthinkable. These were people who kept two ink bottles on their desks—one for their official letters and one for their personal ones. My proposals will have opponents, many of whom have a vested interest in continuing 'business as usual' approach. Whatever they think of the ideas in this book, they will not be the ones to push for change. This responsibility lies with the millions of young Indians who are coming of age and who perhaps are asking themselves why the tiny minority who benefit from the mismanagement of India should stymie the aspirations of over a billion people. These young people will be the next-generation leaders. The responsibility they inherit is enormous.

In this chapter, I have shown that with the political will and a mandate in the Parliament, the proposals in this book are feasible. The preceding chapters have not just been a mental exercise. I have outlined the financial, legal and administrative pathway to implement this framework. In the following, final chapter, I hope to give you a glimpse of this new world, by revisiting the three communities after my proposed reforms have occurred.

Notes

1. UNICEF India, 'Children's Issues: Nutrition', available at http://www.unicef.org/india/children_2356.htm.
2. United Nations Development Programme, *Human Development Report, 2005* (New York: UNDP, 2005).
3. UNICEF, *The State of the World's Children: 2000*, p. 97.
4. Experts differ on extent, and not the fact, of the glacial loss. See Emily Wax, 'A Sacred River Endangered by Global Warming', *The Washington Post*, 17 June 2007; 'Melting Asia: China, India and Climate Change', *The Economist*, 5 June 2008; Intergovernmental Panel on Climate Change, 'Fourth Assessment Report', 2007, available at http://www.ipcc.ch/pdf/assessment-report/ar4/syr/ar4_syr.pdf.
5. Take Bangladesh, for example. A one-metre rise in sea level will submerge about one-third of the country's total area, uprooting

25–30 million people. Statement by the permanent representative of Bangladesh to the United Nations, Ambassador Ismat Jahan, on 29 October 2007, available at http://www.un.int/bangladesh/statements/62/c2_protection_global_climate.htm.

6. Population Reference Bureau, *The Future Population of India: A Long-range View*, Population Foundation of India, New Delhi, 2007, p. 7, available at www.prb.org/pdf07/FuturePopulationofIndia.pdf.

7. John Briscoe, *India's Water Economy: Bracing for a Turbulent Future*, World Bank report, 2006. Available at http://www.worldbank.org.in/WBSITE/EXTERNAL/COUNTRIES/SOUTHASIAEXT/INDIAEXTN/0,contentMDK:20674796~pagePK:141137~piPK:141127~theSitePK:295584,00.html.

8. Asha Krishnakumar, 'A Sanitation Emergency', *Frontline*, 22 November–5 December, 2003.

9. '6 key dangers to the Indian Economy', *Rediff News*, 11 September 2007, available at 11/09/07http://in.rediff.com/money/2007/sep/11perfin.htm.

10. National Commission for Enterprises in the Unorganised Sector, *Report on Conditions of Work and Promotion of Livelihoods in the Unorganised Sector*, New Delhi, 2007, available at http://nceus.gov.in/Condition_of_workers_sep_2007.pdf.

11. Around 300 million people live in urban India. Official estimate for urban poverty is 49.6 million people (Tenth Five-Year Plan). But as I stressed earlier in the book, the official poverty line is skewed and gives a distorted picture. Almost doubling the official parameter of poverty reveals that 42.5 per cent of urban population lives below a poverty line of Rs 840 per month (Mohan Guruswamy and Ronald Joseph Abraham, 'The Poverty Line is a Starvation Line', http://infochangeindia.org/200610195662/Agenda/Hunger-Has-Fallen-Off-The-Map/The-poverty-line-is-a-starvation-line.html). India's urban population is likely to reach 620 million by 2020 (Ninth Five-Year Plan) and nearly half of that population—which is little more than current US Population of 304 million—will be poor even at Rs 840 per month (inflation adjusted). This is even borne out by the government's *India Vision 2020* report where it concedes that 'The face of urban poverty in 2020 is unlikely to be very different from what it is today'. See www.planningcommission.nic.in/plans/planrel/pl_vsn2020.pdf, p. 59.

12. Bibhudatta Pradhan, 'Naxal Menace poses biggest security threat to India: PM', *Bloomberg/Mint*, 21 December 2007.

13. Thomas Frank illustrated this point brilliantly in his book *What's the Matter with Kansas: How Conservatives Won the Heart of America* (New York: Metropolitan Books, 2004). He highlighted how the middle and lower-middle classes in the US consistently vote against their economic self-interest as a result of skilful manipulation by an enormously well-funded political public relations machine.

14. '1984: Rajiv Gandhi Wins Landslide Election Victory', *BBC News*, 29 December 1984.

15. Lady Thatcher, when prime minister and under pressure from her party to water down her economic reforms, famously said, 'To those waiting with bated breath for that favourite media catchphrase, the U-turn, I have only one thing to say: You turn if you want to. The lady's not for turning!', '1980: Thatcher "not for turning"', *BBC News*, 10 October 1980. In order for my suggested reforms to have a chance of success, they would need leaders of similar determination.

16. Suzanne Goldenberg, 'Gore to Recruit 10 million Strong Green Army', *The Guardian*, 1 April 2007.

17. Granville Austin, *The Indian Constitution: Cornerstone of a Nation* (New Delhi: Oxford University Press, 2002), p. 255.

18. 'Battling the Babu Raj', *The Economist*, 6 March 2008.

19. Anand Krishnamoorthy and Cherian Thomas, 'Indian Rail Expansion is Biggest in a Decade', *International Herald Tribune*, 26 February 2006.

20. Surojit Chatterjee, 'Indian PSUs fare well in 2007 Fortune Global 500 List', *International Business Times*, 21 July 2007.

21. At the same time, the failure of the political elite to pass the burden of the soaring global crude prices to consumers has affected the financial health of these PSUs. It is projected that revenue losses of Indian Oil (IOC), Bharat Petroleum (BPCL) and Hindustan Petroleum (HPCL) for the financial year 2008–09 would be Rs 246,000 crore. Indian Oil, controlling nearly half of the country's fuel market, was losing Rs 392 crore on fuel sales each day. Energy Bureau, 'Crude burns deeper hole in oil PSUs' pockets', *The Financial Express*, 4 June 2008.

22. This was the total market capitalization of listed PSUs towards the end of 2007. Yoshita Singh and Rakesh Pathak, 'Listed Public Sector Companies Post Big Gains in Market Cap', *Mint*, 26 December 2007.

23. Political interference and bureaucratic noose—from day-to-day management and managerial decision making of enterprises to township management and social overheads—have brought many PSUs in aviation, steel, textile, heavy engineering, coal, etc., to bankruptcy. The government either declares them 'sick' and disinvests or tries to revive. In July 2007, Prime Minister Manmohan Singh acknowledged the damage political interference has done to public sector enterprises and called for more liberal atmosphere for their functioning and autonomy to top management. See, 'PM Releases Book *The Indian CEO: A Portrait of Excellence*'. Available at http://www.pmindia.nic.in/speech/content.asp?id=564

24. For example, the average age of a public sector banker is close to fifty. Tamal Bandopadhyay, 'HR Dilemmas of India's Public Sector Banks', *Mint*, 25 November 2007.

9

The Citizen's Republic

*My notion of democracy is that under it the weakest should have
the same opportunity as the strongest.*

Mahatma Gandhi

It is mid-afternoon in Sewari, Rajasthan, and the main street is
bustling. Look inside the small houses and you will see a clean
drinking water tap in every one. The children are in their uniforms,
coming home from the schools. An ambulance drops off an elderly
man from one of the high-quality hospitals in Pali. Cows still
wander down the street and the chilli seller still sits under the
banyan tree chatting into his phone. Walk to the western outskirts
of the village and what was once a barren stretch of land is now
forested with the hills of the Aravalli biosphere in the distance.
Within the biosphere zone, which spans several communities in
the Region of Godvar, is an abundance of rare plant and animal
species. It is filled with small lakes and thousands of little gully
wetlands that are home to an extraordinary variety of birds. It
provides a large source of income for the local communities in
the Region of Godvar as they sell the environmental per capita
quotas (EPCQs) to city dwellers on the national exchanges. A
thirty-minute walk will take you to the community-managed
Sewari reservoir. In an otherwise desert environment, the water

Epigrapgh: Quoted in N.B. Sen (ed.), *Wit and Wisdom of Mahatma Gandhi*
(New Delhi: New Book Society of India, 1960), p. 69.

inside is 'blue gold'. Consequently, the Community government of Sewari ensures that the reservoir's catchment areas are maintained, leaks have been fixed and there is regular removal of additional silt.*

Meanwhile in Mussoorie, the summer tourists flock to the hills to escape the heat of the plains. Most of the town has been pedestrianized with a cable car transporting tourists from the car park in the Doon Valley 1200 metres below. The air is pristine—no fumes, no stench of raw sewage (installing a sewage system was one of the first acts of the Community council), no beeping car horns. Honeymooners still walk along the mall, children are still sticky with ice cream and stallholders selling trinkets still shout to passers-by. Stroll out of town and the hillsides are pristine. The disposal voucher system means that rubbish is recycled rather than left to rot on the outskirts. The dense forests stretching out into the distance are thriving, as much of the Community's income comes from selling forest credits on the national exchanges. The Community forest management scheme is the largest employer in the Community as they manage thousands of acres of regenerated forests and sell the surplus credits on the exchange. The revenue from the sale of EPCQs of the local forests is the largest source of income for the Community government, which uses these additional funds to supplement the baseline support given to the poor through TCs. Property tax revenue has boomed as more tourists visit and business from tourism-related industries has increased property values.

In Panchsheel, New Delhi, I walk my daughter to the local park, rather than drive as I used to. The streets are bustling. With a metro station nearby, safe walking areas and cycle lanes, the area is transformed. It is still full of parks, as they are essential for maintaining the green space ratio. In some areas, tall housing blocks dominate the skyline with restaurants and stores on the ground floor, offices in the second, third and fourth floors and residences

---

*Siltation—accumulation of silt on the water bed—decreases water-holding capacity of the reservoir by making it shallow. Hence its periodic removal.

above them. All the services we need are within a five-minute walk. Owning a car is a luxury with parking charged by the hour since the local streets are pedestrianized. Passing Shahpur Jat, I note that the Community has paved the streets, installed an adequate drainage system, and every household has clean drinking water on tap. The children of low-income families go to excellent local schools and receive quality treatment at good hospitals. There are plenty of choices, as service providers push themselves to increase their rating from the Standards Authority, in order to receive more for the TCs presented by low-income families.

In each of these places there is a strong sense of community. Citizens directly contribute to the management of their local resources, and the new system of planning means neighbours cannot be strangers. The TC system has lifted hundreds of millions out of poverty. India now leads the world with its educated, skilled population, its healthy environment and its high economic growth rates. The Indian development model is being emulated across the globe.

Having made it to the last chapter, I hope you will not dismiss these images as unrealistic fantasies. A future with such promise is within our reach. The previous eight chapters have outlined a way of eliminating poverty and ensuring rapid economic growth that is environmentally regenerative and socially inclusive. The system I have proposed would create huge incentives for building quality public services, protecting environmental assets, eliminating corruption and reinvigorating democracy—giving people a real say in the issues that affect their lives. In this chapter, I want to provide a window into this new world, by detailing the changes that could happen in the three communities we have considered throughout.

Let us start with the new boundaries that will have been put in place when the Delimitation Commission (one of the transitional bodies covered in chapter 8) divided the country into regions, areas and communities. The table below places these three communities within their new areas and regions.

Table 9.1: Division of the three habitations into Region, Area and Community

New Region (population 25 million)	New Area (population 2.5 million)	New Community (population 25,000)
Delhi	Siri	Panchsheel
Mewar	Godvar	Sewari
Himal	Garhwal	Mussoorie

The Region

In chapter 4, I outlined the responsibilities of the Regional governments. These were activities that involved coordination between areas. My logic in dividing up assets and responsibilities between the different tiers of governments was to allocate activity upwards in the administrative chain only when it could not be done at the Community level. This logic stems from a core conviction that those who are most affected by changes should have the greatest say in the decision-making process.

The Region will consist of a governor elected by ten Area MPs and 1000 Community chairpersons, one each from communities comprising a Region. Its jurisdiction would be over major transport links, rivers, highways, inter-regional rail links. Thus, Delhi would consist of twenty-five million people, which is a little less than the current size of the state.[1] The tiny part of the city (2–4 sq. km territory) that houses the Parliament and the national government will become the National District. Mewar would be approximately half of the current state of Rajasthan (current population of 56.5 million) spanning the western and southern parts of the state. Himal would cover parts of the sparsely populated Himalayan mountain regions and the densely populated western part of the Indo-Gangetic Plain, currently part of the state of Uttar Pradesh.

Activities

There would be four major areas of responsibility common to all regions:

Water revenue sharing arrangements.

One of the greatest challenges facing India is the sharing of river water. While it is an issue of great political sensitivity, I believe that the solutions are not political but mathematical. Adopting the policy framework outlined in this book would ensure that all 'users' of a waterway are compensated if they do not receive their calculated share, or if the water they receive is too polluted to use.

Take the example of the Yamuna that runs through Delhi. When it comes to water, Delhi gets a free ride at the expense of India. As the Yamuna enters the capital, it is still relatively clean after its 246-mile descent from the Himalayas. The city's public water agency then extracts 229 million gallons every day from the river, its largest single source of drinking water. As the Yamuna leaves Delhi, it becomes the principal drain for its waste. Residents pour 950 million gallons of sewage into the river each day.[2] Last year, a government audit found that the faecal level in the Yamuna was 100,000 times over the safe limit for bathing.[3]

In the new system, Delhi would pay Himal huge water charges for the water it received. It would then have to compensate those in regions downstream for extracting more than its allocated share of water and for the pollution it poured into the river.[*]

In the following calculations, I shall illustrate how costing and revenue sharing would work. I make a set of financial assumptions about the cost of water, for example, which are not definitive, but intend to demonstrate how this principle would work in practice. Let us assume that the Yamuna originates in Himal Region and then flows into Delhi and passes through, say, five other regions before it drains into the Ganga. The Yamuna passes through seven regions,[†] each with a population of twenty-five million. Therefore, 175 million people are official stakeholders in the Yamuna and thus have equal rights to its water. Himal uses very little of the Yamuna before it reaches Delhi. Therefore, the onus would be on

[*]A part of this compensation would be an investment in better pretreatment technology.
[†]Himal, Delhi and five regions downstream.

the Regional Government of Delhi to compensate the five other regions downstream and Himal for the water that Delhi extracts and the pollution that it pumps into the Yamuna.

Under the new framework, let us say that the going rate for 'sweet' drinking water on the National Water Exchange is Rs 1 per litre. I have assumed that Delhi consumes all the freshwater in the river and releases its waste water back into the river which is the water that goes downstream. Here is how the calculations would work:

Total water in river consumed by Delhi = 1 billion litres per day

Cost of Water consumed by Delhi at Re 1 per litre = Rs 1 billion per day or Rs 365 billion annually.

This would then be divided by the total population of the seven regions who have equal rights to the water (that is, 25 million × 7), who lose out on their water because Delhi effectively consumes all of the potable water coming from the source.

Total water share per Region = 365 billion ÷ 7 (the number of regions the Yamuna flows through).

Therefore, Delhi (and each of the other six regions) have a right to 52 billion litres per annum. But Delhi consumes the entire 365 billion litres. So, subtracting its credit of 52 billion litres (365–52) means that it owns each of the other 6 regions 52 billion litres × Re 1 per litre or Rs 52 billion each year for their share which Delhi consumes.

Total compensation for all 6 regions: Rs 313 billion per annum.

Under this arrangement water disputes in India would cease. Himal and the five downstream regions would receive Rs 52 billion each annually from Delhi, which they would share on a per capita basis with all communities within those regions.

Sewage would be priced in a similar way. The Regional Government of Delhi would compensate all regions downstream for cost of treating (say at Rs 2 per litre) the vast quantity of sewage (around 3.6 billion litres per day) it pumps into the river. The amount of compensation would be calculated using the cost of sewage treatment on the National Exchange, and dividing it by the population of the five downstream regions.

In this scheme of real costing, Delhiites, who receive water for a price that is so low that it is almost free and pay no charges for sewage, would now have to pay. Faced with these costs the areas and communities that are part of the Delhi Region might choose to look for alternatives for their water supply* and sewage treatment, which would eventually result in a clean river flowing out of Delhi.† In the meantime, all those living downstream who are losing out would be compensated.

Investment in water grid

Given that large cities often have a water deficit, Regional governments would need to work closely with the Area and Community governments to develop investment sharing agreements that would build a 'water grid', allowing communities to 'move' the water that they trade on the water exchange. A water grid would entail massive infrastructural investment that would require the users to share the cost of setting it up. However, once in place, it would make it easy for surpluses to reach deficit areas.

Take the Region of Mewar which is traversed by the Aravalli Hills. The communities on either side of the range would have a large surplus of water because the topography is ideal for rain water harvesting. The hills of the Aravallis serve as giant water catchments and by foresting these hills and building check dams

---

*They would have to start recycling Delhi's grey water immediately.
†For example, if the exchange priced the cost per litre of discharged sewage on quality as well as volume, communities that did more to pretreat sewage would pay less.

it will be easy to construct a series of reservoirs. Proper management of the forested catchments and reservoirs would allow large quantities of water to be collected. This can then be traded on the water exchanges and moved to the purchasing towns and cities within the Area via the water grid. The Mewar Region will have a number of water surplus communities and they would be able to use the grid to transfer their surplus both within their region and between regions. However, the price of water on the exchange would not cover movement charges per litre per kilometre on the grid; the buyer would cover these costs. With water consequently becoming more expensive, the further it travels, communities would focus on intra-regional sales. Eventually, efficiency improvements to the grid will result in lower water-carrying charges.

Coordination of investments and revenue sharing on major highways, waterways and rail tracks

The railways are currently run at a national level. Indian Railways have a monopoly on train services in India and are the world's largest commercial employer with more than 1.5 million staff, and cost to the government US$1.83 billion for the year 2008–09.[4] While it is a formidable logistical feat, it is nevertheless also incredibly inefficient.[5]

A railway consists of

- Infrastructural assets, the track, the stations and the real estate they are built on; and
- Rolling stock, which includes the train engines and carriages.

In my new framework, the track and the land on which it rests would belong to the Area where they lie. The Standards Authority would classify assets into two standardized segments:

- Track section
- Traffic rights

Let us take an example from the Mussoorie Community, which lies in Garhwal Area and Himal Region. The closest major rail station is Dehra Dun. Currently the train track forms a long loop from a town called Saharanpur via the towns of Haridwar and Rishikesh (in the case of Rishikesh it actually travels down a spur and then reverses) to reach Dehradun. While the road distance is 43km, the track is 170km,[6] taking trains three hours to cover what could easily be a one-hour journey, even with today's rather slow train speeds.[7]

The communities around Dehradun may decide that they want a more efficient train service, with a more direct track from Saharanpur to Dehradun. At this point, the Regional Government of Himal would step in to broker the revenue- and cost-sharing agreements between the different areas that will benefit from this new infrastructure. Once these agreements are finalized, the participating communities will contribute the capital and lay the track, conforming to the technical standards set by the Standards Authority. Alternatively, they could agree to give the contract to a corporation (now known as a shareholder association) to build on a revenue share basis. The rights to use the track would then be traded on the Railway Exchange, so that the user buys slot times on the track.

There are even more opportunities for profit with the two railway assets of track sections and traffic rights. Different qualities of tracks, whether single or double, as well as the quality and sophistication of the signalling equipment would affect the frequency with which it can be used, creating different types of investment options. The Standards Authority would have criteria that lay out the frequency allowed by the different quality parameters. Let us say the new Saharanpur–Dehradun track type allows one train per hour. Technically, it is possible to auction twenty-four slots a day. However, peak demand would be at 'rush hour' times in the morning and evening, while there would be moderate demand throughout the day and after the rush hour in the evening, with low demand at night. The result would be a great deal of bidding for peak hour slots, which would be auctioned by the Area for a higher price on the exchanges, while the night slots may only have a single bidder, who pays a low price to run freight trains during this time. This means that fares stay low because passenger operators profit through volume while freight operators benefit from a low barrier to entry.

Now let us say that the communities make a major investment in signalling equipment, which allows the track to be used in half-hour slots by the faster trains now being introduced by the train operating companies. Since such signalling equipment entails a large capital investment cost, the Area government would work out the cost and revenue share between the communities. However, as the major capital expense has already been made—that of land acquisition—this would be an incremental expense for communities; and already aware of the revenue from one-hour slots, communities would be able to make decisions based on the cost–benefit analysis, quickly and transparently.

In chapter 8, I covered the break-up of the Indian Railways into regional railway systems which would make it possible for regional governments to enter into agreements with different railway companies.

Coordination of investments and revenue sharing of the power grid

In the case of power generation, there are two tradable assets:
- Generation
- Movement of electricity

My proposals would encourage micro-generation (as lower transport costs would directly translate into lower prices for consumers), limit pollution, and incentivize low-carbon schemes. If micro-generation were not possible, Regional governments would invest in the national grid, profiting off of high-voltage power lines that run through their communities to transport electricity across great distances. They could simply install step-down transformers when they buy the power flowing across their lines in order to safely and cheaply bring it down to the level of household appliances.

In the model outlined in this book, pollution is measured and valued. If power generation produces any type of pollution, credits will have to be purchased from the pollution exchange. Green, low-carbon projects would create wealth in two different ways—through power generation and the savings of pollution credits.

Let us assume that a power generation company installs a thermal power unit near a coal mine. Once it has had its pollution level certified by the Emissions Standards Authority and bought the requisite pollution credits from the National Pollution exchange, it would be ready to generate power. In this case, only 10 per cent of the power generated is consumed by the immediate communities. The company then sells its surplus power to communities at some distance on the Power Trading Exchange for which it needs to buy the wheeling charges* on the same exchange to allow it to move its electricity from the point of generation to the point of consumption. It would have to do all of this at a price that is competitive with other sources of power available to the local community. Green power—like solar and wind—would suddenly become much more competitive, as communities would not require any 'pollution credits' and, if they were just providing power locally, they would not have to incorporate transportation costs (the wheeling charges) as well. However, if the power generated were large in relation to local needs—as the case with large hydroelectric, nuclear, or thermal projects—electricity could easily be transported (at a cost). Technological developments could have far-reaching implications on how power will be generated and transported in the future, and this model would accommodate such changes in a sustainable manner.

The Area

The Area government would mirror the Regional government's role in working out investment and revenue sharing for the development of infrastructure that affects several communities. The difference is one of scale. The Area administration would be looked after by the MP and 100 Community chairpersons, each

---

*The amount required for transmission of energy from generating plants to consumers or from generating plants to other purchasing/borrowing plants.

representing a Community comprising the Area. Its jurisdiction would extend over transport links, rivers, highways and inter-area links within its compass. While the Regional government administers the national water and power grids and major highways and rail tracks, the Area government would focus on localized infrastructure, coordinating the following activities between communities:

Development of transport infrastructure (ports, airports, railway stations and junctions)

In the instance of an airport, revenue could be generated from:
- Aircraft parking fees
- Slot fees (charge per aircraft movement)
- Retail, hospitality, general services
- Passenger-handling and cargo-handling fees

Building an airport requires land and money. Once communities possessing sufficient land agree in principle to build an airport, they could either cover the costs themselves or if they do not have sufficient funds, they could bring in an airport development company, and either share costs or sell the land to them. The same principles would apply to a port or a railway station.

Take the case of Delhi's airport in what would be the Area of Siri. As the asset is already in existence and the bulk of investment thereafter already made, it would be valued and converted to equity held by the National Asset Corporation. Any subsequent additions to this would be the prerogative of Siri's Area government, which will have to make the case for the investment to their relevant communities. In the meantime, other areas in the Region of Delhi that already possess airstrips such as Hindon and Safdarjung could decide to develop their airports.*

*The variance system would mean that noise pollution in inner-city airports will have to be kept to a minimum. London's City Airport is located in the heart of the city, five kilometres from Canary Wharf, the financial centre. Noise pollution is minimized by the airport only permitting smaller, quieter planes which are able to take a much steeper final approach path (thereby remaining higher and quieter for longer) and by a strict limit on the number of permitted flights.

This competition would ensure passengers get the best possible service.*

Development of Mass Transit Systems

In cities, this would take the form of initiatives such as the Delhi Metro that is currently under construction, while in rural areas it would be inter- and intra-Community transport networks. In Panchsheel, all of us who can afford to drive around Delhi because there is no reliable and comfortable mass transportation. The availability of metro service will mean that one of the key criteria for density has been met. The government of Siri Area can work with its communities to ensure that investments are made to meet all the other criteria for increasing density (see chapter 7). This would mean that an increase in density in the Panchsheel Community would allow a much higher Floor Area Ratio (FAR) for the construction of taller buildings. The increased FAR would result in higher property values that in turn would increase the property tax base of Panchsheel. In this way, the government of Siri Area would make it possible for all the communities within Siri to increase their density of population.

In Mussoorie, the Community could decide to ease the traffic gridlock that grips the city every summer, with a park-and-ride scheme, using a cable car. The government of Garhwal Area could broker a revenue-sharing deal between Mussoorie and the handful of communities in the nearby Doon Valley, which might not see increased revenue from Mussoorie's tourist traffic but will need to provide transportation links between the lower terminus of the cable car and its airport, freight terminals, and train station. In this instance, the communities of the valley would most likely benefit from a share of Mussoorie's additional revenue as well as from transit fees from passenger and freight traffic. By banning cars on its narrow hill roads, visiting Mussoorie would become a much more pleasant experience and the town would attract greater

*As is the case in London, which is served by six airports.

number of tourists of higher income levels which will translate into revenues for the town's businesses.

The management of Biodiversity and Forests zones

Under my proposals, every citizen would have an EPCQ for forest and biosphere. The Standards Authority would determine the criteria for what qualifies as forest and biodiversity zones. This would create a huge demand for these credits amongst the rapidly growing urban population. They will have to buy these credits from rural communities where there is a per capita surplus of forest or biodiversity. Godvar, for instance, which contains the Community of Sewari, straddles the Aravalli Range and contains recognized zones of biodiversity, with semi-arid forests, vegetation and wildlife. It is currently suffering terrible degradation, even though there are still exquisite natural environments in the interior of the Kumbhalgarh National Park. I remember the area eighteen years ago, before the land grabs and agriculture began. After the rain, the forest gullies would fill up with water creating natural *jheels* (waterbodies) teeming with birds, animals and different types of grasses. Today, local farmers are so desperately short of water that after the rain they rush to put portable diesel pumps into the jheels to irrigate their land.

In my model, it would pay to conserve forest and areas of biodiversity. The Area government of Godvar could help its communities profit enormously through selling of their surplus per capita forest and biodiversity credits. It would also encourage farmers in communities such as Sewari to convert their marginally productive, rainfall-dependent farms into forests.* This could not affect agricultural output because these lands generate hardly any surplus because of the type of soil and dependence on rainfall. But as I have discovered, they make good forest land as forests require a fraction of the water of the croplands. Remember the

---

*Most agriculture practised in semi-arid zones is single-crop, which is dependent on the annual monsoon between July and August.

parched earth on which little could grow that I converted into a jungle with hundreds of varieties of indigenous trees.

The Garhwal Area, also a zone of great biodiversity, is being destroyed at an alarming rate, particularly by mining.* With the advent of the per capita biodiversity credits, the local Community would have a much greater incentive to protect their biodiversity zones from mining, as the revenue earned from mining would have to be balanced with the foregone revenue from the sale of biodiversity credits. The Area and Community governments would be able to make informed decisions, and would be in a much better position than any centralized government to weigh the costs and benefits of the development and preservation issues.

The management of large waterbodies

The construction and maintenance of large fresh waterbodies is crucial to the nation's water security. Each of these bodies would be valued both in terms of its current and potential carrying capacity. Area governments will coordinate the investment- and revenue-sharing agreements between the communities that border the waterbody.

In Godvar Area, there is currently a massive sweet waterbody, the Jawai reservoir, which is bordered by three communities, one of which is Sewari. The water would belong to the residents of these three communities. It is currently being used to irrigate farmland, most of which belongs to the upper castes (Rajput Thakurs),† via an ancient canal system that was built for the benefit of the local rulers. Once sweet water becomes a tradable asset, all members of the Community will be able to benefit from it, instead of just a few. The Community and Area councils would also have considerable incentives to maintain the reservoir.

---

*The mining industry is a big employer of local thugs and goons, using them to 'silence' local protests. Hence their title as the 'mining mafia' and not the 'mining industry' as they prefer to be called.

†Traditional, hereditary feudal rulers and landowners.

Leasing of mineral, oil and gas exploration and development rights

This is a highly profitable and contentious area of development, because these activities can severely damage the environment of the communities in which they are situated. Activities such as strip mining and quarrying often destroy agricultural land and pollute groundwater. The Area and its communities would have to weigh the pros and cons of allowing such activities in their Area. Once it becomes profitable to preserve forests and biodiversity, the cost–benefit analysis of such projects would change. If they decided to go ahead, the Area government would have to ensure that citizens who were impacted by the project would get either:

a) Equity in the company developing the resources; or
b) Compensation; or
c) A share of the revenue from the resource extraction activities.

In India today, urban property owners benefit from local assets, whereas rural property owners are virtually penalized for theirs. In cities, if you own land and a metro station is built nearby, the value of your property increases dramatically. In rural areas, if you own land where there is potential for resource mining or development, this land will simply be acquired by the government. Once notified of the acquisition you are paid a pittance for your property.[8] Land acquired by the government under these draconian land acquisition laws is often transferred to powerful industrial lobbies for SEZs and other projects. This dualism is another example of how the rural poor are kept in poverty by the national government.

The Community

It is at the level of the Community where my proposals would have the most profound transformation. These changes would result in:

1. A revolution in participatory democracy where decentralized decision making combined with a well-resourced local administration (funded by property taxes) would empower Indians to take control of the issues that affect their daily lives.

2. Real costing that would mean many rural communities that are currently classified as 'poor' would have valuable assets, and consequently their wealth would increase dramatically.

3. A TC system that would incentivize the development of quality essential services, as the better the rating of a service, the more money they would receive from the Community government for TCs. Over time, this will lead to the existence of good schools, quality health care, clean water, proper sanitation. The service providers would become the norm for most Indians, even those in rural areas.

All the communities would have a local government that would focus on their needs, and would be run by members of their Community. Apart from the chairperson of the Community four members would also comprise the Community council. Community members would take control over the decisions that immediately affects their lives: how much forest to cut and how much to preserve? Whether to grant a local mining licence or not? Should reservoir water be used for agricultural irrigation or drinking?

I have attempted to provide communities with a set of tools that will allow them to deal with contentious issues and make collective decisions about the issues that concern the lives of their citizens.

Sewari is currently a desperately poor rural Community. Once real costing is introduced, they will find themselves sitting on huge assets: sweet water from the large local reservoir, forest, biodiversity and mineral resources. The Community would have to make decisions based on investment and perceived return. For example, they would need to decide whether it is worth spending a large amount on improving the local dam, dredging the reservoir and, foresting the catchments areas to improve collection, plugging the leaks, etc. Because the Standards Authority certifies water quality, the Community could check on the National Water Exchange to see how much their water is worth, allowing them to make a transparent cost–benefit analysis.

Sewari is also rich in biodiversity with the Kumbhalgarh National Park occupying a large area of land. This could be developed into a huge biosphere zone. However, it also has extensive marble reserves that are used in the construction industry. The council would have to weigh the costs of mining in terms of the loss of revenue from the biodiversity zone and the potential water loss to the reservoir from the conversion of the catchments into stone quarries. While the Community might gain a source of income from the marble mines, it would potentially lose revenue from the water (as a result of conversion of the catchment areas into stone quarries) and biodiversity quality and acreage (as a result of environmental degradation). The powerful mining lobby would have to contend with the Community council and its desire to maximize return for its members.

Now, imagine if the total amount of forest land in India was to decline. The increasing population combined with the fact that the amount of forest area per citizen is fixed by the Standards Authority means that the price per acre of forest would increase on the exchange. This would send a signal to communities such as Sewari, which has thousands of acres of land used for single-crop, rain-fed cultivation.* This type of agriculture has very low yields especially in arid areas (like Sewari) where rainfall is unpredictable. These farmers could now choose to convert their land into forest cover and trade it through their Community receiving a rental income from the lease of that land.

In Mussoorie, a similar debate would take place over forests: should they be cut down for valuable timber or preserved in order to generate annual revenue from the lease of forest credits? Once habitat rights are in place, the Community government would be forced to improve the living conditions in the town by providing access to sewage and, clean, drinking water and regulating development in accordance with the densification parameters.

---

*This is a form of subsistence agriculture since annual output of one crop leaves little or no surplus to be exchanged in the market. Further, dependence on rain means that crop productivity is determined by vagaries of weather. Since unstable irrigation does not allow for planning of crop output, no target could be set for yields, hence no surplus and no market exchange.

Mussoorie is very overcrowded and to meet the minimum habitat rights, the Community would have to make huge investments or develop alternative tracts of land so as to reduce overcrowding.* Unplanned development in the town has created a situation where most buildings are unsafe for human habitation.[9] The Community government would have to work on an urban plan that would decongest the town and meet the open space, access and sewage parameters guaranteed by the habitat rights. Remember, if habitat rights are violated, citizens can sue for compensation by bringing a class action suit against the government.

While Mussoorie, given its particular circumstances, might have to reduce its population density, Panchsheel's Community government would be greatly rewarded by an increase in density, as this equates to an increase in revenue from property tax. However, in order to increase the density, the Community would need to increase its FAR, which would be contingent on meeting the criteria of density rights specified in chapter 7.

The Panchsheel Community government would be compelled to work with the Area and Regional governments to clean Delhi's air as this is the habitat right that is currently most seriously violated.[10] In the short term, they may decide to impose congestion charges on private automobiles and use those funds to provide last-mile connectivity (linking the metro station to neighbourhoods with localized public transport, such as electric buses) to meet one of the key parameters for increased density. In the longer run, a number of changes resulting from the implementation of these proposals would inadvertently reduce traffic. With the removal of all planning distortions on land use, office and residential areas would exist in close proximity and basic services such as doctors, grocery stores, dairies, general stores, chemists and barbers would be easily accessible to most people.

The transport densification criterion would be met by the construction of a metro station in Panchsheel, combined with

*See, Jane Jacobs' distinction between density and overcrowding I have used in chapter 7.

incremental investments in 'last mile' public transport such as improved pavements, etc. Finally, the Community government would have to upgrade water supply, sewage systems and increase open space to meet the densification criteria.

In an effort to secure the property tax revenue that densification would generate, Community governments may encourage private real estate developers to take on the costs of the infrastructure investments necessary to meet the densification criteria.[11] The developers would do this in exchange for the right to develop and sell an agreed portion of the space created when the FAR is increased.*

The whole purpose of this book is to give citizens and policy makers the tools to make complex decisions on the basis of clearly understood principles to which a transparent logic can be applied. The success of my proposals is grounded in the fact that it is in almost everyone's interest to respect the law, which in turn gains legitimacy by virtue of its transparency, fairness and logic.

Once in place, this logic is largely self-regulating which removes the need for a large bureaucracy. If the Community councils make decisions that are in violation of these principles such as allowing mining when it is not in the economic interest of the Community, members of the Community can assess the violation on the basis of a simple cost–benefit calculation and then use the rights granted to them in associations. As Community members, they would enjoy all stakeholder rights given to members of an association (see chapter 6). They can either move for a notice or a referendum or block and overturn such a decision, provided they can muster the requisite majorities. If an issue-based referendum does succeed, it would be tantamount to a no confidence motion for the Community Council. The threat of a successful referendum would act as a tremendous

---

*This would be similar to the use of Transfer of Development Rights (TDR) in Mumbai slums. For each housing unit they construct for slum dwellers, the builders are given an incentive Floor Space Index (FSI) to construct houses for sale on the open market. The difference is that the FSI would be given in return for investment in Community infrastructure rather than for construction of dwellings.

deterrent to councillors who might be tempted to take bribes from special interests against the economic interests of their Community.

Meanwhile, the system of habitat planning and negotiable variances would mean that members of communities would have a much greater say in the issues that affect them on a daily basis. Noise pollution is a major problem in Mussoorie and Sewari. In both Mussoorie and Sewari the local temples and mosques have recently installed louder speakers, increasing the decibel level. My proposed system of habitat rights quantifies the acceptable level of noise, which means that these places of worship will have to bring their decibel levels down to the negotiable level, which is that amount exceeding the limit but below the inviolate threshold. They will then have to negotiate with residents who live in proximity to the noise to grant a citizens variance that would require a two-thirds approval to be granted.

Final Thoughts

While democracy and human rights exist on paper in India, only a small minority have the money, connections or luck to be able to exercise these rights. For the rest of India, the Constitution is simply a piece of paper. When the only way to achieve anything is to leverage a relationship of patronage, the nation has failed.

I am deeply worried about the future of India. It is being pulled apart by different forces. Amongst the rich, a new ideology is taking hold, 'the republic of one'. The elite have made themselves into tiny republics, with private security, health care, transport and a water borehole in each backyard. Neighbours are strangers. Expectations from the state are low. There is no sense of community.

Amongst India's poor, a different ideology threatens to tear the country apart. The Naxalites, armed left-wing extremists, now affect over 30 per cent of India's districts.[12] The issue is not one of politics, but of development. Under the present system, at least half a billion people will remain a long way from India's wealth for a long time to come. Hundreds of millions of Indians are so poor that, to quote Marx and Engels, they literally have, 'nothing to lose but their chains'.[13] If we do not rapidly give every Indian the opportunity to be a stakeholder, we face a bloody future.

I do not blame India's leaders for the current mess. They are locked into a system that makes it impossible for them to succeed. The new framework, a self-regulating system, proposed in this book would facilitate rapid, environmentally sustainable growth and put governance in the hands of the Indian people. I have sought to eliminate opportunities for the abuse of power at every level, through the creation of mechanisms that, to borrow from Madison, pit interest against interest and ambition against ambition.[14] I have outlined a way of ensuring that the constitutional rights of every Indian are not merely lofty ideals but translate into real, measurable benefits. Finally, I have shown that this is not some 'pie in the sky' utopia, but a feasible development path.

The management of India is one of the biggest challenges facing the world today. This book is a call to the people and the leaders of India. Such a mighty challenge requires vision. It requires ideology. It requires courage. It is time for India to discard its outdated policies and to lead the world in forging a new development pathway. The future of our country and our globe lies in the balance.

Jai Hind.

Notes

1. Population of Delhi Urban Agglomeration—comprising population of contiguous villages and towns—comes to 21.5 million. See Udit Misra, 'Delhi, not Mumbai, is India's Biggest City', *Mint*, 13 November 2007.
2. Somini Sengupta 'In Teeming India, Water Crisis Means Dry Pipes and Foul Sludge', *The New York Times*, 28 September 2006.
3. Andrew Buncombe, 'Unholy Water—Delhi's Rotting River', *The Independent*, 1 May 2008.

4. Ministry of Railways, Government of India, 'Railway Budget 2008–09'. Available at http://www.indianrailways.gov.in/budget-0809/budget-speech-eng-0809.pdf.

5. True, the recent financial 'turnaround' of Indian Railways is remarkable. But financial success alone does not account for overall efficiency. About 60 per cent of its earning goes into salary and pension accounts, leaving 40 per cent for all other expenses including innovative upgradation which is badly needed. On top of it, seven new zones were added to the existing nine in 2002–03 creating extra managerial and operational stress on a centralized set-up. This move—dubbed 'Hajipurization' of railways due to its populist nature—was questioned by several expert committees on railways and the Comptroller and Auditor General. See Kripal Singh, M.N. Berry, M.S. Gujral, M.N. Prasad and Y.P. Anand 'Hajipurisation of Indian Railways', Letters to the Editor, *The Hindu*, 22 July 2002. Railway is a public asset and I argue that right-scaling would improve its efficiency. For a critical assessment of Indian Railways' recent performance, see G. Raghuram, '"Turnaround" of Indian Railways: A Critical Appraisal of Strategies and Processes', Working Paper. No.2007–02–03, IIM, Ahmedabad, February 2007. Available at, http://www.iimahd.ernet.in/publications/data/2007–02–03graghuram.pdf.

6. Ministry of Tourism, Government of India, available at http://www.tourisminindia.com/indiainfo/states/uttarpradesh/accessibility.htm

7. According to the Indian Railways Fan Club (www.irfca.org), the Deccan Queen, running between Bombay and Pune, runs approximately a half-hour *slower* than it did when it first started running in 1930.

8. Take the example of the Special Economic Zones (SEZs) for which the government has been keen to acquire land. For one such proposed SEZ near Mumbai, the promoter is reported to be offering Rs 3–4 lakh per acre whereas the prevailing market price is said to be ten times that amount. Rajat Kumar Kujur, 'Special Economic Zone: The New Conflict Ground in India', Society for Study of Peace and Conflict, 7 February 2007, available at http://www.sspconline.org/article_details.asp?artid=art113. Importantly,

land acquisition for industrial projects and SEZs, considered unjust by locals, has been one of the reasons for violence in Singur and Nandigram areas of West Bengal.

9. See, Rajiv Rawat, 'Governance and Citizen Intervention in Urban Planning Processes of Dehradun, India', http://prayaga.org/documents/paper-upp.pdf.

10. Although the city has taken measures to control air pollution, threats remain. Nitrogen dioxide, ozone and other air toxics meant that in 2007 one of the busiest traffic intersections in the city, the ITO, registered clean air standards for particulates of less than 2.5 micron only on 36 per cent of the days and nitrogen dioxide only on 28 per cent of the days. Curbing this could arrest the premature death of 5,806 people annually. Anumita Roychowdhury, 'Air Quality in Delhi: The Leapfrog Agenda', *Mint*, 22 April 2008.

11. An example of such partnership is the agreement between the Delhi Metro Rail Corporation (DMRC) and India's biggest real estate developer DLF, synchronizing aspects of their respective metro rail services in Gurgaon, Delhi's satellite city. DLF is constructing metro rail to increase densification and values for its apartments. See, 'Gurgaon Metros touch a chord', *Express India*, 2 March 2008. Available at http://www.expressindia.com/latest-news/Gurgaon-Metros-touch-a-chord/279120/.

12. Figures as of August 2007. South Asia Terrorism Portal and Institute for Conflict Management (2007) *Datasheet: Maoist Conflict Map.* http://www.satp.org/satporgtp/countries/india/database/conflictmap.htm.

13. Karl Marx and Friedrich Engels, *The Communist Manifesto*, 1848, Chapter 4.

14. James Madison, 'The Federalist No. 51', *The Federalist Papers,* 1788.

Appendix 1

List of Ministries in the Indian Government

Ministry of Agro and Rural Industries

Ministry of Chemicals and Fertilizers

Ministry of Civil Aviation

Ministry of Coal

Ministry of Commerce and Industry

Ministry of Communications and Information Technology

Ministry of Company Affairs

Ministry of Consumer Affairs, Food and Public Distribution

Ministry of Culture

Ministry of Defence

Ministry of Development of North Eastern Region

Ministry of Earth Sciences

Ministry of Environment and Forests

Ministry of External Affairs

Ministry of Finance

Ministry of Food Processing Industries

Ministry of Health and Family Welfare

Ministry of Heavy Industries and Public Enterprises

Ministry of Home Affairs

Ministry of Housing and Urban Poverty Alleviation

Ministry of Human Resource Development

Ministry of Information and Broadcasting

Ministry of Labour and Employment

Ministry of Law and Justice

Ministry of Mines

Ministry of New and Renewable Energy

Ministry of Overseas Indian Affairs

Ministry of Panchayati Raj

Ministry of Parliamentary Affairs

Ministry of Personnel, Public Grievances and Pensions

Ministry of Petroleum and Natural Gas

Ministry of Planning

Ministry of Power

Ministry of Railways

Ministry of Rural Development

Ministry of Science and Technology

Ministry of Shipping, Road Transport and Highways

Ministry of Small Scale Industries

Ministry of Social Justice and Empowerment

Ministry of Statistics and Programme Implementation

Ministry of Steel

Ministry of Textiles

Ministry of Tourism

Ministry of Tribal Affairs

Ministry of Urban Development

Ministry of Water Resources

Ministry of Women and Child Development

Ministry of Youth Affairs and Sports

Department of Atomic Energy

Department of Space

States of India

Division	Area (sq.km.)	Population 2001 census
Andaman and Nicobar Islands (UT)	8,249	356,152
Andhra Pradesh	275,069	76,210,007
Arunachal Pradesh	83,743	1,097,968
Assam	78,438	26,655,528
Bihar	94,163	82,998,509
Chandigarh (UT)	114	900,635
Chhattisgarh	135,191	20,833,803
Dadra and Nagar Haveli (UT)	491	220,490
Daman and Diu (UT)	112	158,204
Delhi (UT)	1,483	13,850,507
Goa	3,702	1,347,668
Gujarat	196,022	50,671,017
Haryana	44,212	21,144,564
Himachal Pradesh	55,673	6,077,900
Jammu & Kashmir	101,387	10,143,700
Jharkhand	79,714	26,945,829
Karnataka	191,791	52,850,562
Kerala	38,863	31,841,374
Lakshadweep (UT)	32	60,650
Madhya Pradesh	308,245	60,348,023
Maharashtra	307,713	96,878,627
Manipur	22,327	2,166,788
Meghalaya	22,429	2,318,822
Mizoram	21,081	888,573
Nagaland	16,579	1,990,036
Orissa	155,707	36,804,660
Pondicherry (UT)	480	974,345
Punjab	50,362	24,358,999
Rajasthan	342,239	56,507,188
Sikkim	7,096	540,851
Tamil Nadu	130,058	62,405,679
Tripura	10,486	3,199,203
Uttaranchal	53,483	8,489,349
Uttar Pradesh	240,928	166,197,921
West Bengal	88,752	80,176,197
Total	3,166,414	1,028,610,328

Source: Census of India 2001
UT: Union Territory

Appendix 2

Map 1: India: Mineral Deposits and Forests

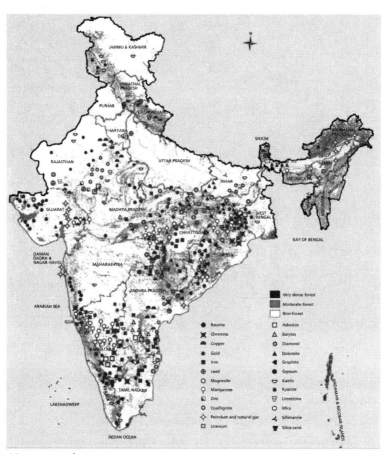

Map not to scale

Source: The Centre for Science and Environment, New Delhi

The international boundaries on the map of India are neither purported to be correct nor authentic by Survey of India directives.

Map 2: India: Poorest Areas and Natural Resources

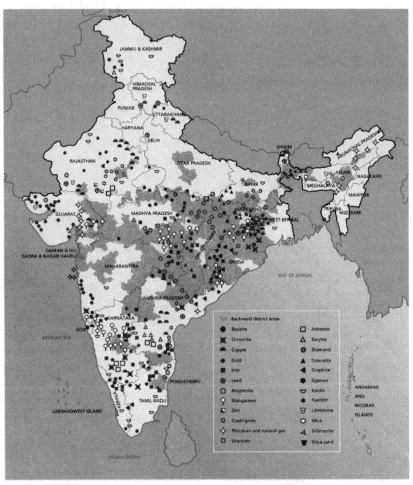

Map not to scale

Source: The Centre for Science and Environment, New Delhi

The international boundaries on the map of India are neither purported to be correct nor authentic by Survey of India directives.

Index